AF560759

# THE SOCIAL REALMS OF RELIGION

# The Social Realms of Religion

*New Researches on Religion and Society in Indian History*

*Edited by*

BIRENDRA NATH PRASAD

MANOHAR
2026

First published 2026
First eBook edition 2026



ISBN 978-93-6080-310-0 (hardbound)
ISBN 978-93-6080-815-0 (eBook)

*Published by*
Ajay Kumar Jain *for*
Manohar Publishers & Distributors
4753/23 Ansari Road, Daryaganj
New Delhi 110002

Typeset by Ravi Shanker, Delhi 110095

Cover design by Manoj Kumar

Printed and bound in India

# Contents

## PART III: NĀTHA SAMPRADĀYA IN ITS INTERACTIONS WITH SOCIO-ECONOMIC PROCESSES AND INSTITUTIONS

# List of Figures and Tables

## FIGURES

## TABLES

# Preface

Editing a book is essentially an exercise in academic collaboration. This book, too, is a product of collaboration with fellow scholars who kindly contributed their research articles. They were very prompt in responding to my requests. I thank all fellow scholars who contributed their research articles for publication in this book.

Thanks are also due to my wife (Mrs. Rashmi Prabha) and our three children—Pragati, Anurag, and Aditya—for their love, support, and care. I am indebted to them.

I put on record my thanks to Mr. Ajay Jain and Mr. Ananya Jain of Manohar Publishers & Distributors, Delhi, for their help and support in the publication of this book. It was always pleasing to work with their copy editors and other members of their production team.

An earlier version of the research article titled 'The Making of the "Self" and the "Other": The Representations of Hindus and Muslims in a Fifteenth Century Prākrit Text' was initially published in *Pāli Prākṛta Anuśīlanam* (journal of Kendrīya Sanskrit Viśwavidyālaya), Vol. 9, 2020, pp. 232-245. I thank the editors of this journal for kindly permitting the reprinting of this research article in this book.

All figures and tables in this book were provided by the respective contributors.

BIRENDRA NATH PRASAD
Centre for Historical Studies
Jawaharlal Nehru University
New Delhi

# Introduction

BIRENDRA NATH PRASAD

What do we mean by 'social realms of religion'? If we believe that religion, amidst a complex myriad of functions, also functions as an essential element of the organization of the social order of a society, then we may have to perceive religion not just as an abstruse philosophy that influences the complex relationship between the human world and the divine one, but also as a social phenomenon. Religion functions in a society by entering into a complex relationship with other social institutions and processes. It often has a very complex interface with the socio-economic and political processes of the society in which it operates. Both religion and society influence each other, and, as such, they cannot be studied in isolation from each other.[1]

In the context of a poly-religious culture like India, the patterns of interactions between religious processes and institutions with their social counterparts become more complex. In this poly-religious culture, different religions have to compete with one another for patronage from different sections of society. The patterns of evolution of the fate of major religions of India were, to a large extent, deeply intertwined with the kind of linkages different religions could establish with social processes and institutions. As most of these religions tried to mobilize patronage from the same society in which they operated in a given time and space, these competing religions (Hinduism, Buddhism, Jainism, and Ājīvika-dharma, in some instances) had to devise complex patterns of interactions with one another.[2] The pattern of interactions between these religions was never monochromic and ranged from coexistence, contest, subordinate integration, convergence, and occasional conflicts.[3] These processes functioned in the backdrop of the socio-economic and political developments in society with which these religious processes were deeply linked. The present book hopes to study some of these religious processes in the backdrop of the socio-economic and political processes of societies in which they functioned.

Broadly speaking, research articles in the present book explore three themes: (a) patterns of interactions between different ancient and early medieval Indian religions (Hinduism, Buddhism, Ājīvika-dharma) and their relationships with socio-economic institutions and processes, sixth century BCE onwards, (b) perceptions of Islam and Muslims in some Indic literary sources of medieval north India, and (c) Nātha Sampradāya and its interactions with social institutions and processes in Himachal Pradesh, Delhi and Maharashtra from the colonial to the contemporary periods. Covering the period from the sixth century BCE to the twenty-first century CE in a single book may be a bit strange, which we have attempted nevertheless, basically in view of the fact that there is a kind of civilizational continuity in India and the religious process of the past continue to exhibit their manifestations even today in some way, directly or indirectly.

## Buddhism in Interactions with other Religions and Socio-Economic and Political Processes

To understand this issue, one would like to have a very brief summary of the context in which Buddhism was born during the sixth century BCE. During the period of the Buddha, Upper and Middle Ganga Valley areas witnessed the birth of many philosophies, some of which later evolved into full-fledged institutional and social religions. The *dhamma* propagated by the Buddha had to carve out an autonomous space for itself in the midst of these competing philosophies. Unless a 'Buddhist' identity was delineated and defined, a significant section of society might not become convinced enough to extend material patronage to the Buddhist Bhikṣusaṅgha. The initiative in this process of reaching out to society was taken up by the Bhikṣusaṅgha. This process of reaching out to society unfolded through two or three interrelated processes. Some segments of society became convinced of the appeal of the new religion: some joined the Bhikṣusaṅgha by becoming Bhikṣus or Bhikṣuṇīs; some others, while remaining lay supporters, supported the Saṅgha materially. Gradually, having enough support in the ground, this new religion was forced to negotiate two more issues: (a) the issue of its relationship with the state, and (b) the issue of increasing competition with rival religions, which too were trying to expand in a similar manner. These two issues also impacted the trajectories of the relationship between Buddhism and the non-aristocratic segment of society. These processes often had regional and sub-regional variations.

The first two research articles in the present book deal with the theme of the social history of Buddhism in different parts of India in different periods of history from the above-mentioned perspective. The article by Ahmad Sohaib, titled '*Añña-Tithiya*s in the *Nikāya*s: Making Sense of Images, Convergences and Divergences', deals with the processes involved in the construction of a Buddhist 'self' identity through complex interactions with 'others' at the philosophical, doctrinal, institutional and ritual levels during the sixth century BCE period. Buddhism in this period was just one of the many Śramaṇa traditions of the Upper and Middle Ganga Valley areas, and it faced stiff competition from other Śramaṇa traditions: Jainism and Ājīvika-dharma, both of which had a significant presence in society.[4] Besides, the Brāhmaṇas commanded a significant place in society, not only in the ritual sphere but also in the political and socio-economic spheres. They acted as councillors and ministers to different kings. They also had a significant presence in the agrarian sector as *gahapati*. In the early Buddhist literary sources, Brāhmaṇas seems to have been perceived as the main competitor with whom early Buddhism developed a very complex relationship: they were the targets of determined criticism. Yet, as Uma Chakravarti has shown, they formed the single largest group in the early Buddhist Bhikṣusaṅgha.[5] How did early Buddhism negotiate the presence of Brāhmaṇas, Ājīvikas and Jainas and carved out an autonomous social space for itself? Ahmad Sohaib's interesting research article explores this issue. He argues that early Buddhists attempted to negotiate and engineer an identity for themselves by assiduously crafting a 'self-image' for themselves and strategically positing it against the image of the non-Buddhists, which also involved the highlighting the differences between the Buddhists and the non-Buddhists on certain issues of ritual, religious and ethical or moral significance.

It must be, though, admitted that despite these efforts, Buddhism could never create a fully autonomous space for itself in any part of India in any period of history: it almost always had to live in the shadow of the significant presence of other religions. Buddhism could never become 'The Great Tradition' in any part of India in any period. It could never become the only institutional repository for the legitimacy of the state in any part of India in any period, not even under Aśoka Maurya, the Kuṣāṇas, or the Pāla rulers of Bihar and Bengal.[6] Besides, Brāhmaṇas had greater integration with society because they had a kind of monopoly over *rites de passage*, a responsibility towards lay supporters which the Buddhist monks grossly overlooked.[7] Jaina monks were, of course, not as cavalier in officiating as specialists for *rites de passage* for the Jaina *Upāsaka*s/*Upāsikā*s.[8] It must be, though, admitted that the Jainas formed a very small minority in the religious demography of India, and, as such, there was no major challenge to Brahmanical monopoly over *rites de passage* in a major part of India.

So, sixth century BCE onwards, a complex interface developed between Buddhism, Brahmanism, the state and the common population, most of which did not have any rigid, impermeable religious identity. Both Buddhism and Brahmanism tried to spread their influence by finding favour with the kings and other segments of society. This resulted in conflicts in some areas.

The issue of Buddhist-Brahmanical encounters in the poly-religious landscape of India has also been probed in the next research article of the present book.

Umakant Mishra's article '*Cakrasaṁvara Tantra*, Subjugation of Maheśvara and Oḍra: Understanding Buddhist-Brahmanical Religious Equations in Early Medieval Odisha' looks into the issue of the evolution of cultic encounters between Buddhism and Brahmanism in early medieval Odisha through a combined analysis of literary, sculptural and epigraphic sources. This research article offers an interesting analysis of the methods through which Buddhism became an important element of the processes of tribal state formation and legitimation of polities that emerged from non-descript tribal backgrounds. The author argues that some of these polities often settled Brāhmaṇas in the tribal areas through *brahmadeya* land grants, which resulted in conflicts. So Odisha, as per Mishra, could witness the establishment of Brahmanical hegemony only after a protracted rivalry.

To sum up this part, while studying the trajectory of a particular religion—Buddhism for example—in a region, it is pertinent to consider the poly-religiousity of the social landscape, which entailed a complex interaction between different competing religions.

## Literary Perceptions of Encounters with Islam and Islamic Powers

Early eighth century CE onwards, Islam also became a factor in the religious matrix of north-western India. In CE 712, Sindh was conquered by the Arabs, who established their rule in that area. The establishment of the Arab rule in Sindh entailed the evolution of a very complex dialogue between Islam, Buddhism and Hinduism in the area.[9] Using Sindh as a springboard, the Arabs based in Sindh tried to expand to adjoining portions of the Indian subcontinent, a process in which they faced stiff resistance for many centuries. Gradually, some new Islamic powers emerged in Afghanistan and they, crossing the Khyber Pass, started raiding the areas to the east of the Hindu Kush Mountains. This culminated in the occupation of the Indo-Gangetic plains by the Ghurids in early thirteenth century CE.

Islamic expansion in the Indo-Gangetic plains was not a peaceful process. It also involved battles, wars, and atrocities imposed on the non-combatant population, who were often captured as war booty and sold into slavery in the slave markets of Central and Western Asia.[10] How did the Indian population perceive this process of the establishment and consolidation of a socio-religious order (Islam) that did not try to derive its legitimacy from any Indic religious system (Buddhism, Hinduism, Jainism)? How were the Ghurids perceived by their Indian adversaries? Were they perceived just as a political opponent? Or religious differences were also highlighted? This issue finds an interesting analysis in the next research article of the present book.

Jay Vardhan Singh's article, titled 'Representations of the Ghurids in a Twelfth Century Sanskrit Mahākāvya: A Contextual Analysis of the *Pṛthvīrāja Vijaya*' probes this question through an analysis of the *Pṛthvīrāja Vijaya*, a twelfth-century Sanskrit Mahākāvya that was composed in the court of Pṛthvīrāja Chauhāna, the Chauhāna king of Ajmer. *Pṛthvīrāja Vijaya* is one of the earliest Sanskrit literary sources, where the interaction with the Ghurids is mentioned. Singh's study of this text indicates that the Ghurids are often perceived to be inherently impure and beef-eaters who desecrate temples. This text, thus, clearly marks them as separate from the rest. It is this 'negative' perception of the Ghurids that becomes the basis on which a separate and distinct Muslim socio-religious identity emerges in later texts. By locating the *Pṛthvīrāja Vijaya* in its historical context, the author argues that the process of 'othering' had already begun in the twelfth century.

This process of 'othering' seems to have intensified in the subsequent centuries. The next article explores this issue with reference to fifteenth century CE Rajasthan. Birendra Nath Prasad and Jay Vardhan Singh's article, titled 'The Making of the "Self" and the "Other": The Representations of Hindus and Muslims in a Fifteenth Century *Prākrit* Text', looks into this issue through an analysis of a Prākrit text titled *Kānhaḍade Prabandha.* This text was written under the patronage of Kānhaḍade, the Chauhāna ruler of Jālor, Rajasthan. In *Kānhaḍade Prabandha*, the Hindu and Muslim religious identities appear starkly distinct, different and often in conflict with each other. The text not only uses terms like *Turaka* and *Hindū* for Muslims and Hindus, respectively, but it also shows a far greater understanding of the Islamic culture and religion.

## Nātha Sampradāya and its Interactions with Socio-economic Processes and Institutions in Colonial and Post-Colonial North India and Maharashtra

Next three chapters in the present book discuss the patterns of interactions between Nātha Sampradāya monasticism/asceticism and social institutions and processes in three different parts of India: Himachal Pradesh, Delhi and Maharashtra.[11] The chapter titled, 'The Construction of Monastic "Empire": Ascetics, State and Peasants in the Twetieth Century Himachal Himalayas', has been authored by Mahesh Sharma. The chapter titled 'Temple-ascetics and Community Formation: Three Case Studies from the Jāṭa Localities of Delhi' has been authored by Mihir Keshari. The main thrust of these two chapters is to study ascetic traditions in their societal contexts. Often, ascetic traditions within the Indian historical and cultural landscape have been idealized and understood as signifying an individual endeavour towards spiritual liberation or enlightenment of world-renouncing ascetics. However, academic studies concerning ascetic and monastic traditions have increasingly come to realize the necessity of locating ascetic traditions within the larger societal context, where monastic/ascetic community and non-ascetic community (i.e. the householder/ lay community) are studied in a relational sense. The patterns of relationship between these two communities often display multiple dimensions ranging from interdependence to a possible conflict. The understanding which emerges from such studies is bound to give us a fuller picture of historical realities which go into the making and unmaking of social entities and institutions.

The chapter by Mahesh Sharma aims to explore the social history of Nātha ascetic institutions in the state of Himachal Pradesh during the twentieth century. This chapter analyses the ways through which Nātha monasticism interacted with society. This interaction, however, was layered, in the sense that the interaction of Nātha monasticism with different layers of society differed, and it was largely based on the interests and power concerns of Nātha ascetics. Nātha ascetics established an alliance with the state, which facilitated a large-scale appropriation of agrarian lands belonging to peasants by different Nātha *maṭhas* in many parts of Himachal Pradesh. Sharma argues that the Nātha monasteries appropriated agrarian lands from peasants, and it was aided by the legal and land settlement regime of this area. Nātha monastics utilized the apparatus of the state in appropriating the agrarian lands of peasants, and in this process, they consolidated and enforced caste hierarchies.

An altogether different pattern emerges in the case of social roles of Nātha asceticism in Keshari's study of the temple ascetics of the Delhi area. He aims to explore Hindu temples as social spaces which facilitated the interaction of ascetic traditions with that of the lartger community. For this purpose, the chapter is divided into three sections. While the first section revisits the historiography of Hindu temples and builds an understanding where temples are not mainly seen through the prism of legitimization of royal power, be it in their creation or purposes. This chapter argues for a case of Hindu temples where they are understood as social institutions facilitating social cohesion, aiding and abetting the process of community formation. In this background, the institution of asceticism in Indian history is explored in the second section of the chapter, where the uniqueness of Hindu ascetic traditions is highlighted by establishing its linkages with that of temples. In this context, then in the third section, the individual case studies are discussed, where we see the phenomenon of community formation around the figure of wandering ascetics of Nātha Sampradāya, who, at some point in their course of life, settled in temples. In one instance, a temple was founded through the individual efforts of a non-aristocratic Jāṭa man who was influenced by the perceived charisma of Guru Gorakhnātha, but, after his (Jāṭa man's) death, the temple was institutionally taken over by Nātha Sampradāya ascetics and became part of the wide network of Nātha Sampradāya across northern India. This temple, though, survived solely on the patronage provided by the local community. In another pattern, a temple, established by another Jāṭa man, had a faint memory of a Nātha ascetic, whose *samādhi* still functions as the main cult spot within the temple premises, but does not have any active institutional affiliation with Nātha Sampradāya asceticism. This temple too depends totally on the patronage provided by the local community. Both temples aided and abetted the process of community formation. Keshari argues that patronage to these temples was perceived to be the mechanism through which an upward social mobility of the Jāṭas of this area was attempted. The pattern here is, thus, different from what Mahesh Sharma has inferred in the case of colonial Himachal Pradesh. Hence, it is important for us to undertake micro-studies. There was no uniform pattern in the social history of Nātha Sampradāya asceticism/monasticism as we move from one region to another. In Himachal Pradesh, some Nātha monasteries became centres for the exploitation of peasants. But, as the study by Keshari indicates, in some Jāṭa localities of Delhi, Nātha asceticism provided one of the institutional avenues for community formation and cohesion.

The next chapter too highlights the need to undertake the social history of the Nātha Sampradāya from a regional perspective. Many earlier studies on the Nātha Sampradāya have generally focused on north Indian Nātha ascetic traditions and have tended to generalize the patterns inferred from the study of north Indian Nātha ascetic traditions to the whole of India.

However, what is needed is to explore the peculiarities and diversities within Nātha traditions in different parts of India. In other words, we need to study Nātha Sampradāya in its regional context in different parts of India.

The chapter by Vijay Sarde, titled 'The Nātha Sampradāya in Maharashtra: An Ethnographic Exploration of a Living Tradition', offers an interesting perspective in this context. The aim of this chapter is to present an ethnographically vivid description of the living Nātha traditions of Maharashtra. This chapter provides an interesting analysis of Navanātha Jhuṇḍī Yātrā. This tradition of Navanātha Jhuṇḍī Yātrā involves a pilgrimage to sacred Nātha sites in the region by following the route connecting various sacred Nātha sites. This tradition of Navanātha Jhuṇḍī Yātrā, thus, creates a regional Nātha sacred geography, which contributes to the continuation of a lived Nātha tradition in the region. This lived Nātha ascetic tradition survives in this area totally through the patronage provided by the common devotees.

We will be amply rewarded if this book generates new researches in future.

## NOTES

1. Birendra Nath Prasad (ed.), *Monasteries, Shrines and Society: Buddhist and Brahmanical Religious Institutions in India in Their Socio-Economic Context*, Manak Publications, Delhi, 2011, pp. 2-5.
2. Among ancient Indian religions, Ājīvika-dharma seems to be the least studied one, mainly due to the fact that much of its own religious literature has vanished. In recent years (*c.* CE 2000 onwards), an assertive section of Dalit population of north India is trying to revive it as an endogenous religion of the Dalits. For a study of the attempts of this section for the revival of Ājīvika-dharma, see the chapter titled 'Buddhist Revival in Contemporary Uttar Pradesh, *c.* 2005 CE–2011 CE: Some Aspects of Ambedkarite and Ājīvika Discourses on Buddhism and Hinduism in Hindi Print Media' in Birendra Nath Prasad, *Religion in Society: Social Dimensions of Buddhism, Hinduism and Jainism in India*, Manohar, Delhi, 2023, pp. 151-95.

3. In recent years, some interesting studies have been attempted on the theme of patterns of interactions between different ancient and early Indian religions. Such studies explore this issue beyond the binaries of peaceful coexistence and assimilation. See, for example, Birendra Nath Prasad, 'Cultic Relationships Between Buddhism and Brahmanism in the "Last Stronghold" of Indian Buddhism: An Analysis with Particular Reference to Votive Inscriptions on the Early Medieval Magadha', *Buddhist Studies Review*, London, 30(2), 2013, pp. 181–99; idem, 'Evolution of the Patterns of Cultic Encounters between Buddhism and Brahmanism in the Religious Space of Some Excavated Buddhist Religious Centres of Early Medieval Bihar and Bengal: A Study Based on an Analysis of the Published Archaeological Data', *Religions of South Asia*, Sheffield/London, 12(3), 2018, pp. 314–50; idem, 'The Socio-Religious Dimensions of Dedicatory Inscriptions on Sculptures Donated to a Buddhist Establishment in Early Medieval Magadha: Kurkihar, *c.* 800 CE–1200 CE', *Journal of the Oxford Centre for Buddhist Studies*, vol. 7, 2014, p. 148; idem, 'Some Observations on the Inscribed Stone Sculptures of Aparājitā and Trailokyavijaya from Early Medieval Magadha', *Kalā: The Journal of Indian Art History Congress*, vol. XXV, 2019, pp. 77–82; idem, *Archaeology of Religion in South Asia: Buddhist, Brahmanical and Jaina Religious Centres in Bihar and Bengal, c. AD 600–1200*, Routledge, London and New York, 2021, pp. 543–68; A. Sohaib, 'The "Well-Taught" Ariyan Disciple and the "Untaught" Many Folk: Frames of "Inclusion" and "Exclusion" in the *Buddhadhamma* in the Pāli *Nikāyas*', in Birendra Nath Prasad (ed.), *Studies in the History and Culture of Ancient Indian Buddhism*, Research India Press, New Delhi, 2022, pp. 13–57; and Birendra Nath Prasad (ed.), *History, Economy and Religion: Mainland Southeast Asia, c. First Century CE—Fourteenth Century CE*, Manohar, Delhi, 2024, pp. 1–30.
4. That early Buddhism faced significant competitions from Jainism and Ājīvika-dharma even in the Śrāvastī area, which was one of the most important strongholds of Buddhism in the Gangetic plains, has been noted in a recent study by Rohit Kumar, 'Śrāvastī: Emergence, Structure and Cultural Profile of an Early Indian Political and Urban Centre (600 BCE to 600 CE)', unpublished PhD thesis, JNU, New Delhi, 2023, pp. 30–55.
5. Uma Chakravarti, *The Social Dimensions of Early Buddhism*, Munshiram Manoharlal, Delhi, 1996, pp. 122–49.

6. For an analysis of this issue during the Mauryan period, see Herman Tieken, 'Aśoka and the Buddhist *Saṅgha*: A Study of Aśoka's Schism Edicts and Minor Rock Edicts', *Bulletin of School of Oriental and African Studies,* London,2000, pp. 1-30. For the Kuṣāṇas, see Robert Bracey, 'Policy, Patronage, and the Shrinking Pantheon of the Kushans', in Vidula Jayaswal (ed.), *Glory of the Kushans: Recent Discoveries and Interpretations,* Aryan Books International, New Delhi, 2012, pp. 197-219. For the Pāla period, see Birendra Nath Prasad, *Archaeology of Religion in South Asia: Buddhist, Brahmanical and Jaina Religious Centres in Bihar and Bengal, c.* AD *600-1200*, Routledge, London & New York, 2021, *passim.*
7. P.S. Jaini, 'The Disappearance of Buddhism and the Survival of Jainism in India: A Study in Contrast', in his *Collected Papers on Buddhist Studies*, Motilal Banarsidass, Delhi, 2001, p. 142; Birendra Nath Prasad (ed.), *Social History of Indian Buddhism: New Researches*, Research India Press, Delhi, 2021, p. 1.
8. Jaini, op. cit.
9. For an interesting analysis of the social history of Buddhism in Sindh on the eve of the Arab conquest, see Warwick Ball, 'The Buddhists of Sind', *South Asian Studies*, 5(1), 1989, pp. 119-31. For the situation after CE 712, see D.N. MacLean, *Religion and Society in Arab Sindh,* Leiden: E.J. Brill, 1989.
10. For an analysis, see Scott C. Levi, 'Hindus beyond the Hindu Kush: Indians in the Central Asian Slave Trade', *Journal of the Royal Asiatic Society*, Third Series, 12( 3) (November 2002), pp. 277-88.
11. Hazari Prasad Dwivedi's *Nātha Sampradāya,* Allahabad, 1950, was one of the earliest academic studies of this Śaiva sect. His study was largely based on literary sources. Later studies have used a variety of sources in tracing the social history of Nātha Sampradāya in different parts of India and Nepal. See, for example, Veronique Bouillier, *Monastic Wanderers: Nāth Yogī Ascetics in Modern South Asia*, Manohar, Delhi, 2016; and Vijay Sarde, *The Archaeology of the Nāthasampradāya in Western India, 12th to 15th Century*, Routledge, Delhi, 2023.

## REFERENCES

Ball, Warwick. 1989. 'The Buddhists of Sind'. *South Asian Studies*, 5 (1): 119-31.

Bouillier, Veronique. 2016. *Monastic Wanderers: Nāth Yogī Ascetics in Modern South Asia.* New Delhi: Manohar.

Bracey, Robert. 2012. 'Policy, Patronage, and the Shrinking Pantheon of the Kushans', in Vidula Jayaswal (ed.), *Glory of the Kushans: Recent Discoveries and Interpretations*, 197-219. New Delhi: Aryan Books International.

Chakravarti, Uma. 1996. *The Social Dimensions of Early Buddhism.* New Delhi: Munshiram Manoharlal.

Dwivedi, Hazari Prasad. 1950. *Nātha Sampradāya.* Allahabad: Hindustani Academy.

Jaini, P.S. 2001. 'The Disappearance of Buddhism and the Survival of Jainism in India: A Study in Contrast', in his *Collected Papers on Buddhist Studies,* Delhi: Motilal Banarsidass. Originally published in *Studies in History of Buddhism,* ed. A. K. Narain, 81–91, New Delhi: B.R. Publisher, 1980.

Kumar, Rohit. 2023. 'Śrāvastī: Emergence, Structure and Cultural Profile of an Early Indian Political and Urban Centre (600 BCE to 600 CE)'. Unpublished PhD thesis, JNU, New Delhi.

Levi, Scott C. 2002. 'Hindus beyond the Hindu Kush: Indians in the Central Asian Slave Trade'. *Journal of the Royal Asiatic Society,* 12(3): 277–88.

Prasad, Birendra Nath (ed.). 2011. *Monasteries, Shrines and Society: Buddhist and Brahmanical Religious Institutions in India in their Socio-Economic Context.* New Delhi: Manak Publications.

_____ (ed.). 2023. *Maritime Southeast Asia: History, Culture and Religion.* New Delhi: Manohar. [International edition by ISEAS Publishing, Singapore.]

_____ (ed.). 2024. *History, Economy and Religion: Mainland Southeast Asia, c. First Century* CE*—Fourteenth Century* CE. New Delhi: Manohar. [International edition by ISEAS Publishing, Singapore.]

Prasad, Birendra Nath. 2008. 'Major Trends and Perspectives in Studies in the Functional Dimensions of Indian Monastic Buddhism in the Past One Hundred Years: A Historiographical Survey'. *Buddhist Studies Review (Journal of the UK Association for Buddhist Studies,* London), vol. 25(1): 54-89.

_____. 2013. 'Cultic Relationships between Buddhism and Brahmanism in the "Last Stronghold" of Indian Buddhism: An Analysis with Particular Reference to Votive Inscriptions on the Brahmanical

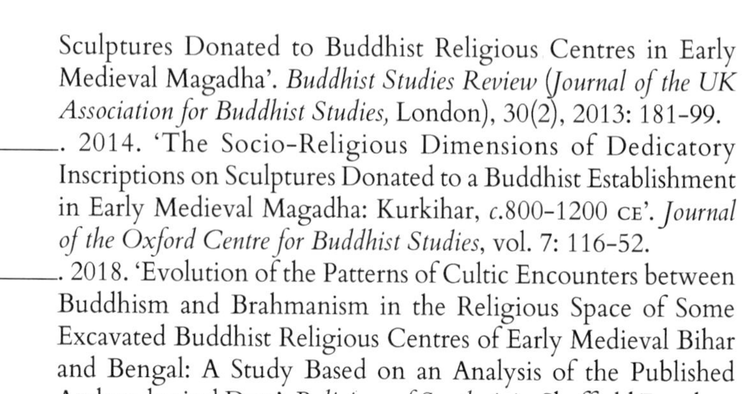

Sculptures Donated to Buddhist Religious Centres in Early Medieval Magadha'. *Buddhist Studies Review (Journal of the UK Association for Buddhist Studies,* London), 30(2), 2013: 181–99.

———. 2014. 'The Socio-Religious Dimensions of Dedicatory Inscriptions on Sculptures Donated to a Buddhist Establishment in Early Medieval Magadha: Kurkihar, *c.*800–1200 CE'. *Journal of the Oxford Centre for Buddhist Studies*, vol. 7: 116–52.

———. 2018. 'Evolution of the Patterns of Cultic Encounters between Buddhism and Brahmanism in the Religious Space of Some Excavated Buddhist Religious Centres of Early Medieval Bihar and Bengal: A Study Based on an Analysis of the Published Archaeological Data'. *Religions of South Asia*, Sheffield/London, 12(3): 314–50.

———. 2019. 'Some Observations on the Inscribed Stone Sculptures of Aparājitā and Trailokyavijaya from Early Medieval Magadha'. *Kalā (Journal of Indian Art History Congress)*, vol. XXV: 77–82.

———. 2021. *Archaeology of Religion in South Asia: Buddhist, Brahmanical and Jaina Religious Centres in Bihar and Bengal, c.* AD *600–1200.* London and New York: Routledge. [South Asian edition by Manohar, Delhi.]

———. 2021b. 'Introduction', in Birendra Nath Prasad (ed.), *Social History of Indian Buddhism: New Researches*: 1–18. New Delhi: Research India Press.

———. 2022. 'Introduction', in Birendra Nath Prasad (ed.), *Studies in the History and Culture of Ancient Indian Buddhism:* 1–12. New Delhi: Research India Press.

———. 2023. *Religion in Society: Explorations in the Social Dimensions of Buddhism, Hinduism and Jainism in India.* New Delhi: Manohar.

Sarde, Vijay. 2023. *The Archaeology of the Nāthasampradāya in Western India, 12th to 15th Century*. Delhi: Routledge.

Sohaib, A. 2022. 'The "Well-Taught" Ariyan Disciple and the "Untaught" Many Folk: Frames of "Inclusion" and "Exclusion" in the *Buddhadhamma* in the Pāli *Nikāyas*', in Birendra Nath Prasad (ed.), *Studies in the History and Culture of Ancient Indian Buddhism*: 13–57. New Delhi: Research India Press.

Tieken, Herman, 2000. 'Aśoka and the Buddhist Saṅgha: A Study of Aśoka's Schism Edicts and Minor Rock Edicts'. *Bulletin of School of Oriental and African Studies* 63(1): 1–30.

# PART I

# BUDDHISM IN INTERACTIONS WITH OTHER RELIGIONS AND SOCIO-ECONOMIC AND POLITICAL PROCESSES

CHAPTER 1

# *Añña-Tithiyas* in the *Nikāyas*

## Making Sense of Images, Convergences and Divergences

AHMAD SOHAIB

Unravelling the assemblage and negotiation of religious identities is admittedly a more complex and vexatious task than mere reporting and recounting of doctrines, philosophies, religious phenomena, events, activities, etc. This is more so in the case of any ancient religious community, viz., that of the Early Buddhists, where it is more an attempt to comprehend and make sense of the imperativeness of articulating acutely, divergences and distinctions of the 'self' (Buddhists) vis-à-vis the 'others' (non-Buddhists). For often shared bonds are underplayed to highlight the dissimilarities (with 'others') and it is these elements of differentiations that come to constitute our 'self-identity' and the 'otherness' of the 'other'. However, it is easier said than done, as it is amply clear that the theme of the 'Early Buddhist identity' is both a highly knotty and contentious issue. The problematics of untangling the stratagem employed for the construction and negotiation of the Early Buddhist identity is further entangled and complicated due to the seemingly formidable and peculiar nature and constraints of our sources. Notwithstanding the limitations, we can still disentangle the nature of the Early Buddhist identity and the related issues.

A perusal of Early Buddhist texts makes it evident that the Early Buddhist identity was located within the existing socio-religious realities of the age. As a religious group/community sensitive to unstable social and religious conditions—as they contested and competed with other adversarial religions—they strived to carve out a categorically unambiguous identity in inter-personal religious encounters. More often this is done as a measure of 'self-assertion' of distinctiveness from 'others'. Noticeably thus, at a rudimentary level, the Early Buddhists attempted to negotiate and engineer an identity for themselves by assiduously crafting a 'self-image' for themselves and strategically positing it against the image of the non-Buddhists. Such an identity was constructed both at the religious and social level and was often tied up with their religious, philosophical and spiritual superiority or/and the highness of moral-ethical norms, etc.

It has been argued that religious communities are often imagined and, such an imagining is achieved largely through a sacred language and a written script. The two criteria are evidently inadequate to invent an imagination for the Early Buddhists. Nonetheless, the Early Buddhist community and their identity were constructed in certain concrete ways. The religious affiliation to the Buddha's *Dhamma* along with significant definitional categories employed for either the 'inclusion' or exclusion' of claimants to (be part of the) *Buddhadhmma*, served as one of the bases of such an 'imagining' of the Early Buddhist identity. However, in itself the usage of terms of self-description and perception arising out of such an identity, are not sufficient. The sharedness of such an identity at a collective state is imperative to impart a consciousness of constituting a community in the religious sense. In this regard we observe that the basic tenets and doctrinal standpoints of Early Buddhism were sufficiently cohesive and divergent from those of the 'other' religious philosophies to warrant being identified by the 'others' as a separate (Buddhist) religious community.

Thus, what comes across is that the amalgamation of a patent Early Buddhist identity was negotiated at various levels and through adopting diverse tools, techniques and strategies. One such strategy that we shall explore in this paper is the strategy of underscoring contestation and differentiation by playing up elements of distinction and non-equivalence of the Buddha's *Dhamma* vis-à-vis 'other' *dhammas* and vehement criticism of the latter (non-Buddhist) *dhammas* and their various practices.

Let's first get a glimpse of some passages, as cited below, to underline the above strategy, before we proceed to discuss the theme at length.

Foremost in virtue were the men of old, those brahmins who remembered ancient rules. But these backsliders with their 'let us recite', drunk with the pride of birth, walk wrongfully. Such ways as fasting, couching on ground, bathing at dawn, recitings of the Three, wearing rough hides, and matted hair and filth, chantings and empty rites and penances, hypocrisy and cheating and the rod, washing, ablutions, rinsing of the mouth, these are caste marks of the brahmin folk. Things done and practised for some trifling gain.[1]

Now at that time several Jainas on the Black Rock on the slopes of (Mt.) Isigili came to be standing erect and refusing a seat; they were experiencing feelings that were acute, painful sharp and severe.... Your reverence Nāṭaputta, the Jaina ... speaks thus: 'If there is Jains, an evil deed that was formerly done by you, wear it away by this austerity.'[2]

Now at that time the wanderer Sandaka was sitting down with a great company of wanderers shouting out with a loud noise, a great noise, talking various kinds of inferior talk, that is to say talk on kings, thieves, great ministers, armies, fears, battles, food, drink, clothes, beds, garlands, scents, relations, vehicles, villages, market town, towns, the country, women, heroes ... talk about becoming or not becoming thus or thus.[3]

The passages cited above provide a panoramic view of the recurrent images of some of the conspicuous non-Buddhist categories as found in the *Nikāyas* and contemporaneous to the times of the Buddha. The first of these concerns the Brāhmaṇas; from whom incidentally Early Buddhism drew the bulk of its recruits. It presents a varied picture of the Brāhmaṇas and their characteristics. The second portrays the Jain renouncers (*nigaṇṭhas*) who indulged in certain excruciating ascetic practices, which they beheld as leading to the annulment of evil *kamma* (deeds). Finally, we have the Wanderers of the other sects (*añña-tithiyas*) who are seen indulgent in low, inferior, frivolous and loose talk, both about the mundane and the super mundane. It is these varied images of a few of the multitude[4] of non-Buddhist categories that we propose to explore in this paper. However, before that we would like to make clear the import of the three key terms used in the title of this paper, namely, 'Images', 'Convergences' and 'Divergences'.

By 'Images' we mean the representation or the reflection of the non-Buddhists, i.e. their perceived image as gleaned from our sources, the *Nikāyas*. While we talk about 'Convergences and Divergences', we shall be primarily dwelling upon delineating the cross currents of early Buddhism, which often ran counter to those of the non-Buddhists on certain issues. To put it simply, we shall be concerned to show how far the Early Buddhist ideas and perspectives were similar or different from their contemporary non-Buddhist perspectives on certain ethical, ritual and religious points. It is common knowledge that the Buddha while preaching took over some of the terminologies and idioms from the pre-existing religious and philosophical systems and gave it a new Buddhist sense to invest it with a moral and ethical sense. He also at times redefined and reinterpreted certain existing issues of religious and moral value, thus differing from the prevalent ones. It is in these senses that we talk about the 'Convergences and Divergences'. These have also a bearing upon the construction of an Early Buddhist identity; for often shared bonds are underplayed and differences highlighted to constitute 'we' and 'they'. However, we must caution that the exercise undertaken in the following pages is not to give an 'insiders' *versus* 'outsiders' account; it is beyond the purview of this work. We are basically concerned with unravelling and presenting the multitude of images of the non-Buddhist categories as mentioned in *Nikāyas*, and to highlight the differences between the Buddhists and the non-Buddhists on certain issues of ritual, religious and ethical or moral significance. This, in our consideration, has crucial implications in the articulation of Early Buddhist identity.

In a religious setting, at a collective level, not infrequently the perception of a shared identity (collective) is often sharpened vis-à-vis religious adversaries and challengers by underplaying those elements and strands of religious beliefs, tenets, and practices, etc., that seemingly betray a sense of convergence with the 'others'. Determined attempts are made not merely to highlight the religious, doctrinal, and theological divergences from 'others' but also to disassociate at multiple levels from the 'debased'/False religions of 'others'. As a strategy, such an endeavour is aimed at constituting a community in the religious sense, where some core tenets, doctrines, philosophical standpoints, and practices are underscored to be conclusively divergent from those of the 'other' religious philosophies, so as to merit being identified by the 'others' as an autonomous and distinct religious community. Around a spectrum of religio-philosophical standpoints, divergences from 'others' on similar themes are played up and sharpened to articulate a strong sense of a distinct religious identity and community. This we believe, was a strategy that the Early Buddhists adopted to articulate the divergence(s) of the *Buddhadhamma* from the welter of religious sects/groups (*añña-tithiya*s).

More than the commonality of ideas (religious, philosophical, etc.) between the 'self' and the 'other', significant differences, distinctions and contestations—in the realm of religious beliefs and practices—are played out to create and highlight the consciousness of 'self-identity' and the 'otherness' of the 'other'. In our case we notice that in a particular cultural milieu of the sixth century BC onwards, a multitude of religious philosophies are competing and contesting against each other; perhaps both for winning over followers to their fold and cornering material support. Apparently, this was on account of the commonality of religious ideas, concepts, practices, etc., between one another. Buddhism, being a product of this age and facing similar challenges, did well to differentiate itself from close rivals, viz.,

Brahmanism and Jainism. This they strategically achieved by investing 'new' meaning into the several contested and common religious ideas, doctrines, and practices, thereby creating a distinction between 'themselves' and the 'others'. We are thus persuaded to argue that the Early Buddhists did constitute a community in a religious sense. Notwithstanding the early sectarian divergences within Buddhism, the overall basic religious tenets of Buddhism sufficiently differed from the surrounding welter of religions and philosophies contemporaneous to Buddhism.

In the following pages, we shall be dwelling upon the description of the different non-Buddhist categories in the following order: (a) Brāhmaṇas, (b) the Nigaṇṭhas (Jainas), (c) the Ājīvikas, and finally (d) the Pabbājakas (Wanderers) and 'other' ascetic groups. We shall take up the category of Brāhmaṇas as the starting point of our discussion on account of the fact that they are the most conspicuous category that finds reflection and portrayal in the *Nikāyas*. References to them in the *Nikāyas* are not merely preponderant but the Brāhmaṇas are also quite frequently the butt of scathing attacks and ridicule by the Buddha and his followers. Before progressing further, as a word of caution we may say that if the following deliberations sound a trifle narrative, then we must say, that given the theme of the paper it is but both inevitable and unavoidable.

## I. THE BRĀHMAṆAS

Regarding the Brāhmaṇa-Buddhist relation, B.G. Gokhale opines that initially there was a 'gradual accommodation if not partial synthesis'.[5] Mrs. Rhys-Davids had echoed a similar opinion much earlier, when she saw no open hostility between them, though she accepted a certain degree of discontent on either side.[6] Notwithstanding these, throughout the *Nikāyas* we notice that the Brāhmaṇas are segregated for a special scathing attack, which is both perplexing and intriguing. We shall see what the image of the Brāhmaṇas was, to deserve such a treatment at the hands of their opponents, i.e. the Early Buddhists.

For convenience's sake, we have divided this section into various sub-sections, which also purport to make the image of the Brāhmaṇas clearer.

### (i) *Brāhmaṇas and their Superior Social Position*

Much has gone down in writing since some of the early scholars on Buddhism emphatically declared that Buddhism was a revolt and a protest movement against Vedic Brahmanism, which particularly challenged and rejected the caste system in general and the social superiority of the Brāhmaṇas in particular. While agreeing partly,[7] we shall restrict ourselves to essential points and arguments, though the theme itself has the potential to consume an entire volume of writing.

The Brāhmaṇas claimed a superior caste and social position for themselves, and the foundation for this is laid in several discourses of the *Nikāyas*, as we recurrently come across such stock phrases as:

> Only Brāhmaṇas form the best caste, all other castes are low; only Brāhmaṇas form a fair caste, all other castes are dark; only Brāhmaṇas are pure, not non-Brāhmaṇas; Brāhmaṇas are the own sons of Brahma, born of his mouth.[8]

The analysis of this passage reveals that: (a) the *Puruṣasūkta* hymn was being reinforced in the period of the Buddha, and (b) the Brāhmaṇas had become conscious of their class interest.[9] Perhaps this may also mean that with the consolidation of monarchies in the Middle and Upper Ganga Valley, the Brāhmaṇa priestly class had acquired control and status, which they sought to reinforce by claiming caste superiority.

The Early Buddhists reacted against such claims of priestly Brāhmaṇas in a variety of ways. For instance, in a passage of the *Aggañña Sūtta*,[10] the Buddha counters their superior position by theorizing that the four *vaṇṇas* (Sanskrit, *varṇa*) grew out of an undifferentiated stock by virtue of the division of labour. P. Chandra remarks that by this the Buddha served a dual purpose: (a) he made caste functional, and (b) he downgraded the assumed superior position of the Brāhmaṇas.[11]

On an empirical ground also, the Buddha questions the Brahmanical superiority of being born of Brahma's mouth when he says:

> Brāhmaṇa wives of Brāhmaṇas are known to have their seasons, and to conceive and give birth and to give suck. Yet these Brāhmaṇas born of woman like everyone else speak thus ... only Brāhmaṇas form the best caste....[12]

What is inherent in this statement of 'fact' given by the Buddha, is that it rejects the divine origin theory propounded by Brāhmaṇas and substitutes it by a biological theory.

In the *Ambaṭṭha Sūtta*, the Buddha reacted once more against such claims of the Brāhmaṇas, when the Brāhmaṇa Ambaṭṭha is forced to admit that the latter's lineage can be traced to a black baby born of a slave girl of the Śākyas.[13] What is most significant here is that the Buddha stresses on the 'black' and thus the indigenous origins of Ambaṭṭha, in contrast to the Brāhmaṇas' sole claim of being of white *vaṇṇa*. This *sūtta* also shows that in matters of purity of descent, Brāhmaṇas were far more lax than the Khattiyas (Kṣatriyas), for the former would accept as their own and accord full Brāhmaṇas status to the offspring of a Khattiya-Brāhmaṇa alliance, whereas the Khattiyas would never do so, due to impurity of descent on the Brāhmaṇas' side.[14]

The Brāhmaṇas' pride in the purity of their caste-blood or descent and their wisdom of the three Vedas *(tevijja)* is alluded to in the *Nikāyas*. The *Sonadanda Sūtta* (*Dīgha Nikāya*, *Sūtta,* no. 4) defines the Brāhmaṇa as well—born on both sides of the mother and father through seven generations back, unchallenged and without a slur or reproach in point of birth, studious, knowing the *mantras* by heart, and one who has mastered the Vedas.[15] Even before the Buddha could counter such a pretension, in the *Vasettha Sūtta* we find the Brāhmaṇa Vasettha arguing with his compatriot Canki that 'if one is of moral habits and right practice then one is a Brāhmaṇa'.[16] If we accept Vasettha's explanation then anyone could become a Brāhmaṇa or loose their status upon behaving immorally.

The Buddhists again reacted to such a definition of a Brāhmaṇa based on purity of their blood and their unparalleled knowledge of the Vedas. We have already seen that in the *Ambaṭṭha Sūtta* the Buddha counters such a claim by showing that the Brāhmaṇa Ambaṭṭha had a mixed and debased ancestry. Here in the *Sonadanda Sūtta,* the Buddha begins his criticism by asking Sonadanda to list out the prerequisites which, according to the Brāhmaṇas, make a person Brāhmaṇa in the true sense. The latter promptly enumerates them as: purity of *varṇa,* mastery of the Vedas, a fair complexion, virtue (*śīla*), and learning or wisdom (*pāṇḍitya*). However, upon strict scrutiny and cross-examination by the Buddha, Sonadanda is forced to accept that of these five, only the last two, i.e. virtue and wisdom, are extremely essential to make a person Brāhmaṇa.[17] We notice that these two are not specific to any class or group, and hence anyone could become a Brāhmaṇa, by the admission of Sonadanda himself.

At another level, the Buddha countered Brahmanical superiority by: (a) redefining a 'true' Brāhmaṇa,[18] (b) reinterpreting *tevijja,* and (c) contrasting them with the ancient Brāhmaṇas, i.e. those of past ages. In the *Vasettha Sūtta,* the Buddha puts forward the ideal philosophical definition of a Brāhmaṇa. According to it, one does not become a Brāhmaṇa merely by parentage, but a Brāhmaṇa is one who has high morals, is free from desiresand attachments to mundane things, is non-covetous, is self-restrained, and knows the Truth.[19] This remained the standard Buddhist answer to 'Who is a "true" Brāhmaṇa?' It disputed the idea of Brāhmaṇas' superiority based on birth and gave a moral and spiritual meaning to brahmanhood. K.R. Norman, commenting upon the revised version of the theory of a 'true' Brāhmaṇa, states:

in Brahmanical Hinduism a Brahman *(brm* – 'to be strong') was a Brāhman by birth, and was a kinsman of Brahmā ... but by adopting a different etymology (*brmh*—'to destroy'), he was able to justify his view that a Brāhman was one who destroyed evil.[20]

Speaking in a similar vein, Uma Chakravarti opines that the 'Buddha did not reject the Brāhmaṇas as a conceptual category, but he used it in the sense of an ideal value to represent acquired spiritual merit that was open to all.'[21] To put it short, he is described as a role model of the 'best' man in society. This definition by implication also negated the mythological origin of Brāhmaṇas and downgraded their pretensions of *varṇa* superiority based on it.

The *Tikaṇṇa* and *Jānussoni Sūtta*s of the *Aṅguttara Nikāya* make a distinction between the threefold knowledge (*tevijja*) of Brāhmaṇas and its import in the Buddha's *Dhamma*. The former employed it to mean knowledge of the three Vedas. However, according to the Buddhists the true *tevijja* was not one steeped in sensual pleasures and luxury, and vacuously reciting the Veda *sans* comprehending their true meaning. But he was an *arahant,* who possessed the three knowledge of: (a) his former lives, (b) the rebirths of others through witnessing their rise and fall in Heaven or Hell, and (c) the way to *nibbāna*.[22] It was precisely these three qualities that the (so-called) Brāhmaṇa contemporaries of the Buddha lacked due to having renounced those states that make one Brāhmaṇa and adopting instead those that make one a non-Brāhmaṇa.[23] Commenting upon this redefinition of *tevijja* by the Buddha, Peter Masefield states:

> Just as the Brahmin's claim was intended to remove him from the purely mundane sphere and accord him a divine origin, so too was the true Brahmin, as *savaka,* no longer of the world but one with his being rooted in the Deathless.[24]

In several passages of the Pāli *Nikāya*s, the Buddha is very critical of the present lot of Brāhmaṇas on the ground that they did not care to live up to the social and religious ideal[25] of their predecessors. In a passage of the *Dīgha Nikāya,*[26] the narrative traces the degradation of the present lot of the Brāhmaṇas and draws the contrast between the spiritually inclined Brāhmaṇas of the ancient time and the materialist Brāhmaṇas of the Buddha's age. In this criticism of the priestly Brāhmaṇas, the Buddha, far from being critical of the early ideal of the Brāhmaṇa as possessor of Brāhmaṇa, instead uses this against his contemporary counterparts who are found lacking in several respects, viz. (a) they merely repeat the words of former sages, (b) they live a life of great luxury, (c) live in fortified towns, (d) are addicted to sensual pleasures, and have become greedy for money and women.[27] In contrast to them stood the 'sages of yore', who made *mantras*, practised chastity for forty-eight years, did not marry outside their caste, practised celibacy, rectitude, mildfulness, austerity, compassion, patience, etc., and while sacrificing did not slaughter animates but collected ghee, rice, butter, honey, etc., i.e. to say that they offered sacrifices righteously. The entire narrative suggests 'the incapacity of the Brāhmaṇas to resist the materialist orientation of the society',[28] and advocacy to return to the ancient true Brahmanism and ideals, which the Buddhists claimed they were preserving. It was a fervent plea to return to the conservatism of the past, and to uphold the ideals of the Vedic society.

In another significant passage, more disparaging remarks are made: the Buddha says that indeed five qualities of ancient Brāhmaṇas are to be found today, but more often in dogs than in Brāhmaṇas.[29] Here the Brāhmaṇas are censured for their sexual promiscuity, excessive indulgence in sensual desires and material possessions and also for their lack of concern for the purity of their caste or descent, which seems to be the foremost concern among the Khattiyas.

However, the Buddha was not content with merely refuting the supposed higher position of the Brāhmaṇas. He simultaneously elevated the Khattiyas to the highest social grade in the *varṇa* hierarchy. The Buddha primarily laid the foundation for constructing the social superiority of Khattiyas on the basis of their purity of descent, as noticed earlier in the *Ambaṭṭha Sūtta*, where he says that while the Brāhmaṇas accord full Brāhmaṇa status to a child born of a Brāhmaṇa-Khattiya alliance *(pratiloma)*, the Khattiyas themselves do not admit such an issue/offspring born out of an *anuloma* or *pratiloma* alliance, into their caste, even if either parent might be a Khattiya or a Brāhmaṇa. Once again in the *Assalāyana Sūtta,* the Buddha maintains that all castes are of equal purity.[30] But he attacks the claims of caste-conscious Brāhmaṇas to social superiority on the ground that their purity of blood might be suspect, as he says:

> Do you, sirs, know whether their mothers, their mothers' mother back through seven generations, consorted only with Brāhmaṇas, and not with non-Brāhmaṇas? [He goes on to repeat the same for the father's side.][31]

On the basis of these references, the Buddha concluded that the Khattiyas were superior to the Brāhmaṇas, who are lower.[32] It is interesting to note that the Buddha avers that even when a Khattiya has fallen to the deepest degradation, he is still superior to Brāhmaṇas.[33] We think that it is a curious assertion and goes counter to the Buddha's stress on *kamma* (deed), which was supposed to determine the status of a person.

The *Esukāri Sūtta* (*Majjhima Nikāya*, no. 96) indicates that occupations were linked to castes. It presents the Brahmanical arrangement of *varṇa* stratification based on the hierarchy of services, with the lower classes. In this *sūtta,* the Brāhmaṇa Esukāri tells the Buddha that the Brāhmaṇas ordain four types of services: (i) where a Brāhmaṇa may be served by a Brāhmaṇa, Khattiya, Vessa or Sudda, (ii) where a Khattiya may be served by a Khattiya, Vessa or Sudda, (iii) where a Vessa may be served by a Vessa or a Sudda, and (iv) where a Sudda may may be served by a Sudda.[34] Scholars like Uma Chakravarti are of the view that the Buddha rejected the Brahmanical division of society based on higher classes being served by lower ones.

However, we would argue that this Brahmanical arrangement of social hierarchy was not rejected by the Buddha. Instead, either he or the redactors of the sacred texts (of the Buddhists) utilized it to claim a superior position for the Khattiyas.[35] Throughout the *Nikāyas* we notice the Brāhmaṇas serving the Khattiyas in different capacities, and at least in our sources nowhere do we have a reference pointing to the other way. Our view is confirmed by a list of professions followed by the Brāhmaṇas as given in the *Brahmajāla Sūtta*, where they are said to act as a 'go-between, as wit on kings, ministers of state, Khattiyas, Brāhmaṇa or young men'.[36] Elsewhere, they are seen functioning as *dūtas* and *amaccas*. They also worked in capacities like *mahāmattas*, treasury accountants, and superintendents.[37]

Hence we notice that Early Buddhists turned the Brahmanical bases for their caste/class superiority on its head to claim a superior position for the Khattiyas. First, they showed the Brāhmaṇas to be lax in matters of purity of bloodand descent, contrary to the Khattiyas, who were more strict in these matters. Besides, they showed the Brāhmaṇas serving the Khattiyas, thus falsifying their theory of caste-hierarchy based on a gradation of services.

We may, thus, ask: why were the Early Buddhists staunchly uncharitable to the Brāhmaṇas? Related to it is the issue: did the Buddha reject a *varṇa*-based society?' Regarding the first, some scholars have propounded a tenuous link between the Brāhmaṇas and the hostile attitude of the Buddhists (as well as the Jainas) with the fact that their religious leader(s) had an affiliation with the Khattiyas. We cannot altogether rule out such a bias creeping into their sacred texts at a later stage. Regarding the second question, we shall not be dwelling much, save a few comments, as it is not the aim of this paper to explore in detail 'whether the Buddhists repudiated in entirety the *varṇa*-based society?' It is a complex theme and requires too long a discussion than is otherwise permissible. Suffice to say that several scholars have unanimously vouched for the view the Buddha did not aim to reject the *varṇa*-based classification of the society. We would like to cap his issue with remarks from a couple of eminent scholars. In this connection, Y. Krishan remarks: 'the Buddha by his teaching unwittingly strengthened the caste system by explaining it in terms of the doctrine of *karma*'.[38] Thus, the Buddhists did not reject the institution of *varṇa,* but restored the Aryan society to its earlier purity and conservatism; it was in danger of losing, as Celestian Bougle puts: 'if they worked at replacing the roof, they never gave a thought to changing the foundation'.[39]

### (ii) *Vedic Yajñas: A New Interpretation*

One of the most striking features of the *Nikāya*s is their general impatience with ritual observances of the Brāhmaṇas, in particular, the Buddha's abhorrence of animal sacrifice. Several passages in the *Nikāya*s mention such sacrifices. It seems that the Brāhmaṇas were obsessed with *yajñas,* as a reference is made in the *Bālapaṇḍita Sūtta*[40] that 'certain people are seen running like Brāhmaṇas at the smell of sacrifice'. A description of such a sacrifice is given in the *Kūṭadanta Sūtta* and some other similar passages. Here, we find the Brāhmaṇa Kūṭadanta preparing for a great sacrifice.[41] Before initiating it, he questioned the Buddha regarding the best way of offering sacrifice, and the latter tells him the story of the King Mahāvijita, who in ancient days offered sacrifices, but no living beings were killed. The Buddha tells him of the sixteen requisites of a sacrifice, each one higher and greater in value than the earlier ones. In the *Kosala-Saṁyutta* of the *Saṁyutta Nikāya,*[42] a similar description of a great sacrifice ordered by the King Pasenadi occurs.

Apart from direct references, we have in the *Nikāya*s many other allusions to sacrifices. In a passage of the *Majjhima Nikāya,* we find priests being referred to as those who lived on milk, offerings to fire and who advised the kings to perform sacrifices.[43] Similarly, in the *Aṅguttara Nikāya*, we find the Brāhmaṇa Sangārava stating to the Buddha that, 'we brahmins, let me tell you, offer sacrifices and cause others to do so',[44] which brings merit to both 'who offers sacrifice or causes others to do so'. Once again, in another passage of the same text, it is stated that those who practice animal sacrifice in the pathetic faith that it shall lead to Heaven are doomed to punishment.[45] An indirect reference to sacrificesisalso found in the *Tevijja Sūtta* (*Dīgha Nikāya*, *Sūtta*, no. 13) which speaks of four kinds of chief priests: (a) the *hotṛ*, i.e. the caller, who recited hymns, inviting gods to sacrifice, (b) the *udgāytar* (singer), who prepared and presented the sacrifices, (c) the *adhyaryu* (executor), and (d) the Brāhmaṇa or the high priest, who protected the sacrifices from evil influences.

In all the references cited earlier (where mention is made of a great sacrifice), what is most notable is the fact that the Buddha—quite curiously—did not altogether abrogate the idea of sacrifice *per se*. In fact, he accepted it as the way to avoid, what John Dewey calls the 'world of hazards',[46] albeit with a major shift in emphasis on 'what was to be offered'. He gave it an ethical meaning while retaining at the same time its spiritual fervour, by de-emphasizing the sanguinary nature and concept of a sacrifice, and substituting it with one, where inanimate material things could be offered. This is borne out by several references but one, which unequivocally echoes such a sentiment, occurs in a passage of the *Aṅguttara Nikāya*, where the Brāhmaṇa Ujjaya inquiries the Buddha whether he praised all sacrifices. The Buddha replies that neither does he censure all sacrifices, nor praise it all.[47] He specifically tells him that he reproaches or disapproves of all those sacrifices where living beings are slaughtered.[48] In the succeeding *sūtta*, in reply to a similar question from another Brāhmaṇa called Udayin, the Buddha declares that sacrifices which are free from cruelty are meritorious.[49] In the *Kūṭadanta Sūtta* also, in reply to a question, the Buddha states that performances of *yajñas* with ghee, oil, butter, curd, honey, sugar, etc., leads to rebirth in Heaven.[50] Elsewhere, he states that those indulging in animal sacrifices are doomed for Hell.[51] To cut the matter short, the Buddha tried to invest the *yajñas* with a new interpretation, eliminating on the one hand the aspect of animal slaughter and adding on the other hand, ethical principles. At times (as in the *Kūṭadanta Sūtta),* he completely dematerialized the nature of *yajñas* when he stated that there were even better forms of *yajñas,* which could be formed by making regular gifts to virtuous persons, by constructing *vihāra*s, by taking the *triśaraṇa,* by adopting *śikṣāpadas*, by absorbing into the four forms of meditation, etc.[52]

In a study[53] of the Buddhist adaptation of sacrifice, Roy

Clayton Amore has shown that Buddhists consciously substituted Vedic sacrifice with the practice of merit-making. Masefield explains it to say that just as earlier, the Brāhmaṇas, with their possession of divine power, meditated in order to ensure the efficacy of the sacrifice, so now it was the *sāvaka,* who through his participation on the supermundane plane could mediate this power in the practice of alms-giving into which that sacrifice had been transformed.

(iii) *Rites and Rituals*

Throughout the *Nikāya*s, the image that we get of the Brāhmaṇas is one of a worldling engrossed in numerous rites and rituals, which were invariably criticized by the Buddha to show and demonstrate the superiority of his ethics. However, the references to them in the *Nikāya*s, are not only rare and isolated but are also abbreviated. Hence, we shall restrict ourselves to only a few of them. We shall examine here these rites and rituals under three sub-heads, viz., (a) rites of purification, (b) *śrāddha* or *peta* rites, and (c) household rites.

(a) *Household rites*: We begin by taking up the last one. In the *Sigālovāda Sūtta,*[54] the Buddha encounters a young householder Sigāla, who intent on obeying his father's last wishes, has set out to worship the six quarters (i.e. the four major directions, the nadir and the zenith). The Buddha immediately gives this an ethical connotation as opposed to merely geographical content. The six quarters, east, south, west, north, the nadir and the zenith, should be taken as representing parents, teachers, wife and children, friends and companions, servants and work people, and religious teachers and Brāhmaṇas respectively.[55] Turning to each direction one should think of them in their order. Thus, the Buddha transformed an otherwise mechanical ritual bereft of ethical value, into a device for recalling and revering all those whose lives impinge on the performer.

A passage of the *Aṅguttara Nikāya* echoes a similar opinion of the Buddha when he instructs the Brāhmaṇa Uggatasarīra—

who had prepared a great sacrifice—on the three fires that should be abandoned, and the three that should be honoured and worshipped. It also indirectly refers to the fact that the Brāhmaṇas of the day were engaged in performing fire rites, as in the case of the Brāhmaṇa Sundarikāyan.[56] The three fires that are to be abandoned are the fires of passion, delusion and hatred.[57] The three fires to be worshipped are: (i) the fire fit for oblations; which is regarded as referring to parents, (ii) the fire of the householder; which alludes to wives, children, slaves, workers, etc., and (iii) the fire worthy of religious offerings; which included the ascetics and Brāhmaṇas, who are morally and spiritually perfect; and thus should be honoured and tended.[58]

(b) *Purification rites:* The Brāhmaṇas of the Buddha's age had made it a practice of going down to the river to bathe, hoping thereby to wash their evil deeds. We have a good number of such direct and indirect references to the Brahmanical belief in purification by water. In the *Vatthūpama Sūtta,* the Brāhmaṇas Sundarikā Bhāradvāja asks the Buddha, whether he too 'goes down to wash in the Bāhuka' River,[59] which he says is considered by the many as a means of purification and merit, whereby evil deeds are washed away. The Buddha rejects such ritual bathing as a means to wash one's sins and instead stresses on 'inner-washing', which he says could be obtained from freeing the mind from all attachments, sensual pleasures, evil deeds, and ignorance. He says that a man cleansed of mind does not need to go to the river to purify the body. Another reference points to the Brāhmaṇa Sangarava indulging in such water purification,[60] twice a day: morning and evening.[61] Here the Buddha clarifies from him, the veracity of his belief in purification by water, to which the Brāhmaṇa Sangarava replies in the affirmative.[62] And upon asking the advantage of such a rite, the Brāhmaṇa replies to the Buddha that it cleanses the evil deeds.[63] In all these references the Buddha rejected the efficacy of such purification by water rites, and substituted these with a set of ethical rules and regulations as manifest in his 'inner-washing' method. This is reiterated at a sermon delivered to Cunda; a lay disciple of the

Buddha who expresses his faith in the purification rituals expounded by the Brāhmaṇas. The Buddha passing strictures against it, explains to Cunda that these defilements or impurities are the products of the body, speech and mind, and in the discipline of the *Ariyan*, purification depends upon purging oneself of these defilements.[64] This he calls the *Ariyan* method of purification. In the same passage cited earlier, Cunda, describes the Brāhmaṇas as those 'who carry water-pots, wear lily garlands ... touch green grass ... worship fire....'[65] Thus the Brāhmaṇas are seen here as believers in purification by soil, cow dung, or green grass and tending to fires.[66]

(c) *Śrāddha (After-death) rites:* References to after-death rites are not only infrequent and isolated in the *Nikāya*s, but they also lack a description of any recognized mode of performing these rites. One such brief reference occurs in a passage of the *Saṁyutta Nikāya.* Here, the son of the Gahapati Asibandhaka calls on the Buddha and narrates to him certain curious practices of the Brāhmaṇas of the West, who 'when a man has died and made an end, they lift him up and carry him out, call on him by name and speed him heavenwards'.[67] This description is very short and abrupt, and according to Wagle, it resembles the 'three stages of cremation rites mentioned in the *Sūtra* literature'.[68] The *Aṅguttara Nikāya* refers to a fire from the funeral pyre blazing at both ends and in the middle smeared with cow dung.[69] The translator F.L. Woodward thinks that it refers to the smearing of torches with dung at the cremation.

Explicit reference to *Śrāddha* (Pāli: *Sāddha*) occur at a couple of places in the *Aṅguttara.* The Brāhmaṇa Jānussoni explaining its significance in the lives of the Brāhmaṇas says: 'We Brāhmaṇas give charitable gifts: we make the (*śrāddha*) offerings to the dead saying: 'may this gift to our kinsmen ... who are dead and gone be of profit. May our kinsmen ... enjoy this offering'.[70] Thereafter, Jānussoni is inquisitive about the efficacy of such a rite. The Buddha replies that only if the departed person arises in the realm of *peta,* can such offerings to the dead profit him. If he is reborn in the realms of animal world, Purgatory, among human beings, or in the company of *devas*, then such offerings do not have the capacity to profit them; for in that case, they have to subsist on the food proper for the inhabitants of that world.[71] It is noteworthy that while accepting their efficacy in a particular case, the Buddha denies it the power to bring post-mortem merit to the departed soul, so as to decrease or abolish his/her woes. He only invests it with a subsistence function.

Finally, we would like to point out that the Brāhmaṇas considered feeding of the Brāhmaṇas (upon the death of a person) as the most important function. Herein, they restricted its enjoyment to only good Brāhmaṇas, viz., the *tevijja* Brāhmaṇas, as only they could be invited;[72] Brāhmaṇas ostracized by their community for social offence were not to be invited.[73] Rejecting the Brahmanical death rites, the Buddha said that only people with good conduct could attain Heaven. The aspirations, offerings, etc., of others and kinsmen, are in vain to bring happiness after death for those who have been debauched and of bad conduct.

The entire discussion on these *śrāddha* rites leads to the theme of making merit and its potentiality of being transferred to others. It is not our intention to go into any deeper investigation or analysis of merit transfer in Buddhism. However, we hasten to add that there is an almost unquestioned and overwhelming acceptance of merit transfer in Early Buddhism, despite its doctrinal differences, and it is quite clear from the *Nikāyas*; albeit its potentiality is accepted provided gifts were made to virtuous person.

### (iv) *Customs, Habits and Vocations*

The Brāhmaṇas did not always follow rigid rules of endogamy. This, as we have already seen, is clear from the *Ambaṭṭha Sūtta,* where the Brāhmaṇa Ambaṭṭha himself accepts that they indulged in *pratiloma* marriages. This reference has been cited earlier and is too well known to be repeated here.

In a significant passage of the *Aṅguttara*,[74] we find mention of the five types of Brāhmaṇas: (i) the *Brahma*-like, (2) the *deva*-like, (3) *mariyādā* Brāhmaṇas (i.e. those who followed traditions), (4) those who broke traditions, and (5) the Brāhmaṇa outcastes.[75] What is significant here is that it not only indicates their social and spiritual positions but also points to their marital choices and practices. The first type was the one who studied the Vedas and begged for their livelihood. They renounced the worldly life and remained celibate. The second lived as a *grahapati,* later renounced the household life and practised the four meditations. While the third was also a householder, who did not renounce and lived in accordance with old traditions. The second and the third types, married only a Brāhmaṇa girl of pure caste, with a ritual in which water was poured on the bride.[76] We believe it points to another of those purificatory rites of the Brāhmaṇas. The fourth not only lived as householders but broke tradition and married girls from other *varṇa*s and *jāti*s. The fifth also took up girls from other lower castes and even followed debased occupations. Among these, only the first three types of Brāhmaṇas are approved by the Buddha. The last two, though disapproved, do not seem to lose their caste affiliation. That the Brāhmaṇas chanted *mantras*[77] and accepted *gurū-dakṣiṇā*[78] (fee) for teaching or reciting the Vedas, is clear from some of the passages in the *Nikāya*s. These *mantra*s were considered to be effective means of purifying oneself of the strains of past deeds.

In the *Nikāyas,* the bulk of the references to the Brāhmaṇa occur in two contexts: (a) Brāhmaṇa-Gahapatis, and (b) Brāhmaṇa-mahāsālas. The references are too many and too frequent to need citing. We have restricted ourselves to a few of them only.

The Brāhmaṇa-mahāsālas were the landed magnates, often seen living in a Brāhmaṇa-gāma, enjoying the fruits of a land grant by the kings. A stock description[79] of such a Brāhmaṇa is found in the third *sūtta* of the *Dīgha,* which is the first of the *Nikāya*s. Some such Brāhmaṇa-mahāsālas mentioned are: Caṅkī, Tarukka, Pokkharasadi, Jānussoni, Todeyya and Sonadanda. We believe that they belonged to the priestly class as they are often described as 'learned' in the Vedic texts and experts in the performance of Vedic rituals.

Hence, Gokhale is of the opinion that even in the wake of the popularity of Buddhism, the Brāhmaṇas retained their popularity and that they hardly suffered in any major way in their vocational reward. The upshot of his argument is that whatever little the Brāhmaṇas lost in the sphere of social and religious prestige was more than adequately compensated by their new gain in the economic sphere as manifested in the land grants.[80] He states the Vedic cult 'created its own economic base in the *brahmadeya* lands'.[81] We do not think that the Brāhmaṇas at any time—with their entrenched position—lost their social or religious prestige, except in the eyes of the Buddhists. However, the compound term Brāhmaṇa-gahapatis in the *Nikāya*s[82] reinforces our image of them as landed gentry based on agriculture. However, these Brāhmaṇas, as Uma Chakravarti rightly points out, 'continued to be identified with priestly functions rather than the economic function'.[83] In her opinion, it is a 'descriptive term'.

The *Nikāya*s present the picture of the Brāhmaṇas as an occupationally diverse and heterogeneous category following both priestly and a multitude of un-Brahmanical functions, which were often considered *hīnakamma/sippa*s, by the Buddhists. The *Brahmajāla Sūtta*[84] gives the most comprehensive list of such low professions followed by them. Some of them were as follows: gleaning medicinal herbs, charioteers, bards, begging alms, trading, animal husbandry, hair-dressing, shampooing, etc. Elsewhere, we have the reference of a Brāhmaṇa following the profession of scrap-hunters.[85] Gokhale thinks that it reflects a deliberate attempt on the part of the Buddhists to ridicule their opponents.[86] Though we concede that often the Brāhmaṇas and the Buddhists did not see eye-to-eye with one other, we still do not think that Gokhale's supposition is valid.[87] However, we may again concede that the list cited at this *sūtta,* may be an exaggerated[88] version of the actual practice and thus may reflect a bias of the compilers of the canon.

A number of passages in the *Nikāyas* mention the Brāhmaṇas as royal functionaries mostly working in the capacity of *purohits*. Gokhale points out that probably their function was not circumscribed by Brahmanical ritual but in fact, went beyond that.[89] We find an element of truth in his statement, as we find the Brāhmaṇa Vassakāra[90] and Sumidha involved in erecting fortifications for the city of Pāṭaliputra.[91] Also, references to them as *dūtas* and *amaccas*, show that they functioned in political capacities too. We have references to *mahāmattas*, treasurers, accountants and superintendents. An isolated reference is found of probably a carpenter in Bhāradvāja Brāhmaṇa.[92]

The Brāhmaṇas of the period are also seen engaged in popular religious practices, and involved in certain occult rites and cults like appeasing the evil spirit, interpreting dreams,[93] foretelling,[94] fortune-telling, determining lucky numbers, sites, dates and time, performing magic spells, exorcism, palmistry, prognostication, etc.

### (v) Jaṭila, *Ascetic Brāhmaṇas*

In addition to worldly Brāhmaṇas, there were *samaṅa*-Brāhmaṇa; some of whom were shaven-headed. The most prominent of these were the *Jaṭilas*, who were ascetics with matted hair. We can guess about the dress of these *Jaṭilas* from a description of Māra in disguise, as given in *Saṁyutta Nikāya*, where he is described as one 'with a great matted topknot, clad in a whole antelope skin...holding a staff of *uḍumbara* wood'.[95] They were also called *tāpasas* or *pabbājakas*[96] (wanderers) who returned to forests or riverbanks and performed rites of fireworship[97] and occasionally entered into philosophical debates.[98] An obvious reference to the *Jaṭilas* is found in the *Majjhima,* where while the matted hair ascetic Keniya, the fire worshipper *Jaṭila* and his other *Jaṭila*-followers were busy preparing a meal for the Buddha and his disciples, the Brāhmaṇa Sela is seen restless, inquisitive and curious, wondering whether it was a preparation for a great sacrifice or a feast.[99]

Another strange reference to *Jaṭilas* occurs in the *Kosala*-

*Saṁyutta* of the *Saṁyutta Nikāya.* Here, mention is made of 'seven ascetics of those who wore the hair matted'.[100] Besides, we also have references to other non-Buddhist renouncers, viz., *Nigaṇṭhas*, other wanderers, etc. They all are described as 'with hairy bodies and long nails, carrying a friar's kit'.[101] It appears that the Buddhist attitude toward these *Jaṭilas* was favourably disposed, as they were exempted from the probationary period of four months, to receive ordination in the *Saṅgha.* This was probably because they were believers in *kamma.* However, it appears to run counter to their criticism by the Buddhists, if we consider the Brāhmaṇas, who performed fire-rites and purification by water, to be *Jaṭilas*. The evidence thus appears to be incongruous and doubtful.

### (vi) *Brāhmaṇa-Buddhist Interaction and Relation*

Finally, we would like to round off the discussion on the Brāhmaṇas at the point we began, i.e. the Brāhmaṇas-Buddhist relation. That the Brāhmaṇas were unfriendly to the Buddha is clear from a couple of derogatory terms like *samaṇa-muṇḍaka*,[102] etc. used by them. In the opinion of some scholars, the 'Brāhmaṇas feared an attack on their special privileges',[103] by the Buddhists and hence their hostility towards them. We do not concur with the proposition that the term *samaṇa-muṇḍaka* reflects reviling by the Brāhmaṇas and demonstrates hostility between the two. Our objection is based on the fact that it is only in some stray cases that out of anger such an utterance is made, and these are deviations rather than the norm. Also, we do not find any obvious reference where such a term is used deliberately for sneering. However, the behaviour of Ambaṭṭha[104] and Mānathadda,[105] as well as of the certain Bhāradvāja Brāhmaṇas[106] does indicate that at times they refused to pay respect to the Buddha and reviled him.

The bulk of the *sūttas* in the *Nikāyas*, give us an entirely different picture, where we have references of Brāhmaṇas approaching or inviting the Buddha for a talk on *dhamma*,[107] at the end of which almost invariably the concerned Brāhmaṇa undergoes a change of heart and mind, and convinced of the Truthfulness of *Buddha Dhamma,* embraces it. Interestingly, these meetings are marked by courtesy[108] on both sides. In cases of rich Brāhmaṇas, the Buddha is treated with respect and his views are often accepted. In contrast to this, in the *Tevijja Sūtta* we find an incongruous reference to a contemptuous and sneering attitude of the Buddha, who condemned the Brāhmaṇas as men of mere faith and not true knowledge.[109] Weighing the two types of attitudes, Mrs. Rhys-Davids concludes that the sneering and lowered esteem of the Brāhmaṇas is a later feature.[110] However, we think that one cannot say this with any degree of certitude as the evidence is imponderable. Moreover, in our opinion, both these attitudes existed side by side. The Buddha was critical of the priestly class of Brāhmaṇas who indulged in frivolous rites and rituals, while he held no grudge toward the householder Brāhmaṇas who sought him for a piece of *dhamma*-talk. Gokhale, on the basis of the above friendly relation between these Brāhmaṇas and the Buddha, and by also considering the fact that most of the converts and recruits to the *Saṅgha* were Brāhmaṇas, concludes that the 'accommodation between the Brāhmaṇas and the Early Buddhists far outweighed, rivalry, antipathy and hostility between the two'.[111]

Tracing the relation between the two, Uma Chakravarti perceives a tension between the Brāhmaṇas and the Buddhist ideals of a householder and renouncer.[112] According to the Buddhist ideals, he was neither of the two. He was not a renouncer like a Buddhist monk; neither was he a householder analogous to the *gahapati*, who pursued productive obligation. In her words, the Brāhmaṇas in the Buddhist literature occupy a 'negative mediating position, in that he was neither a renouncer nor a true householder.'[113]

N. Wagle,[114] through the distinctive employment of 'formalisations', i.e. forms of address between individuals, discerns the social relationship between the Brāhmaṇas and the Buddhists. He says that this relationship is characterized by four stages: (i) farthest are hostile Brāhmaṇas who addressed the Buddha as *samaṇa,* (ii) next were those favourably inclined, and addressed him as *bho*, (iii) *upāsaka*s, and (iv) nearest were the *arahant*s and monks.[115] We think that the last two categories are unnecessary, as they are Buddhist and thus in anyway were liable to be favourably disposed towards the Buddha. According to Wagle, the Brāhmaṇas maintained an uncompromising and 'hostile equality'[116] with the Buddha, who acknowledged their special position by addressing them as Brāhmaṇa or by *gotta* name.[117] In our view, it is a very tenuous argument as Wagle has missed the socio-linguistic attitudes[118] and issues involved in such interpersonal relations.

## II. THE NIGAṆṬHAS

The Pāli *Nikāya*s refer to Nigaṇṭha Nāṭaputta as the leader of a group of religious sects whose followers are referred to as Nigaṇṭhas. Throughout the *Nikāya*s, we come across many allusions—both direct and indirect—to them. However, most of them do not help us in bringing out their picture, primarily because they are philosophical in nature. Nevertheless, there are several references which can be used to project their image. We see that they are practitioners of extreme penance, believers in a 'distinctive' theory of *kamma* (Sanskrit, *karma),* observed *uposatha* (like the Buddhists), preservers of certain vows, and indulged in debates, etc. It is along these lines that we shall be exploring their portrayal in the *Nikāya*s.

### *(i) Ascetic Practices of the Nigaṇṭhas*

A conversation recorded in the *Cūladukkhakkhandha Sūtta* (*Majjhima Nikāya*, no. 14), between the Śākya Mahānāmā and the Buddha gives a lucid picture of one of the Jain (Nigaṇṭhas) ascetic practices. The latter informs Mahānāmā that once he had seen the Nigaṇṭhas on the Vulture peak, standing erect, refusing to squat down and enduring acutely excruciating pain, etc.[119] This is an allusion to the *Kāyotsarga* of the Jaina ascetics.[120] The Nigaṇṭhas, who were engaged in such severe penance, told the Buddha that according to their preceptor, the Nāṭaputta, past deeds could be destroyed through such ascetic practices, for it is by preserving proper control over body, mind and speech, that one can reduce the effects of past *kammas.* To put it briefly, Nāṭaputta the Jain taught the annihilation of old *kammas* by severe austerities and the prevention and accumulation of any new (evil) *kamma* by resorting to inaction.[121]

The Buddha who was highly critical of any sort of self-mortificatory exercises, was quick to point out the illogicality of the Jain doctrine and derided them for the fact that even though they were not sure whether they had actually performed an evil *kamma* or not, they were practising such austerities. The Buddha also rejected self-mortification as the *modus operandi* for acquiring good *kamma* and burning away the evil ones that would eventually lead to *nibbāṇa.* In his opinion these austerities are only hindrances rather than aid. He favoured a Middle Path[122] that avoided devotion to sensual pleasure and self-torture.

### (ii) *Nigaṇṭhas' Belief in* Kamma

The above discussion leads to the doctrine of *kamma* (*karma*) in the classical Indian tradition. The Nigaṇṭhas, like the Buddhists, were the upholders of *kiriyāvāda*[123] philosophy and seem to have been preoccupied with the problem of *kamma* (as evident in the *Nikāyas*). Notwithstanding the fact that the Buddhist themselves believed in *kiriyāvāda,* we find numerous references in the *Nikāyas*, where they confront the Jain viewpoint on *kamma* and try to discredit them, which as Jaini points out, 'were fundamental to the overall Jaina Worldview'.[124]

Below we shall first present the Jain views and belief in *kamma* and thereafter we shall demonstrate their divergence with the Buddhist view, to bring out the 'fundamental' difference between the two religious systems.

The *Nikāyas* contain significant references to the Jaina doctrine of *karma.* The *Upāli Sūtta* (*Majjhima Nikāya, Sūtta* no. 56) not only refers to the Jaina theory of *kamma* but also distinguishes it from the Buddhist viewpoint on the same. Here, in reply to a question by the Buddha ['How many (kinds of) wrongs, Tapassin, does Nāṭaputta, the Jain, lay down for the effecting of an evil deed?'[125]...], the Nigaṇṭha Dīghatapassin replies that Nāṭaputta lays down three such wrongs, namely, wrongs of body, speech and thought:[126] the *tridaṇḍa kamma.* Upon being further probed regarding the relative gravity of the three,[127] Dīghatapassin declares that according to his preceptor Nāṭaputta, the *Kāyadaṇḍa*, i.e. the 'wrong of body is more blameable',[128] for effecting an evil deed, and is the most heinous of the three. The Buddha on the other hand, upon being similarly questioned by Dīghatapassin—pertaining to the laying down of deeds for effecting evil deeds—contends that of the three deeds of body, speech and mind, the last one, i.e. *manokamma* (deed of mind) is the most serious one.[129] What is obvious here is that unlike the Jainas, who considered *Kāyadaṇḍa* as the most abominable of the 'three wrongs', the Buddha envisaged the *manodaṇḍa* as the most execrable and grave.[130]

Thus, it is clear that in the Jaina scheme of *kamma,* the deed itself rather than the intention behind it, was the most instrumental and significant factor for the operation of *kamma*, whereas in the Buddhist understanding of *kamma*, the centrality of stress was on what is usually translated as intention/volition, i.e. *cetanā*; and *kamma* is virtually defined as *cetanā.* Second, we notice that the difference between the two essentially relates to the 'relative ethical significance' of deeds, words and thoughts. Since deliberate intention to do a deed is essential to the ethical quality of the deed(s); it is categorized as essentially evil or good.

We might pose a question at this juncture: 'Why do the Buddhists emphasize on intentional stimulus to be the prime factor in determining the ethical content and fruit of the concerned act?' The passage where such an emphasis on intentionality in the Buddhist scheme of *kamma* and ethics occurs does not provide any clue to the Buddhist motive(s) behind the said stress. Hence, we are forced to speculate the reason(s) for it. In our opinion, the Buddha's scheme to elevate 'wrong or evil intention' as the most heinous one, was a deliberate and calculated strategic move that was essentially in line with his few basic societal concerns. These were: (a) his sustained de-emphasis on gory *yajñas* (sacrifices), and (b) his endeavour to provide a boost to the sagging moral and ethical standards of the age. We think that by declaring unequivocally, that the 'intention of a deed' was the instrumental operational factor in *kamma*, the Buddha attempted to curb and put a ceiling on all premeditated acts of violence and immorality, even before they could be translated into actions or perpetrated. He simultaneously, thus, encouraged people to think good and act good. In short, it was a *regulative device for social control.*

Richard Gombrich, in a perceptive paper,[131] cogently argues for and perceives social control as 'built into the Buddhist philosophy of *Karma* doctrine.'[132] He makes a distinction between the psychological and philosophical aspects of the *kamma* doctrine. On the philosophical level, by declaring intention as the sole powerful determinant of the moral/immoral quality of action, the Buddha dissuaded the populace to withdraw from or shun immoral thoughts. Thus the focus swiftly shifts from man's actions to his moral character and qualities. Richard Gombrich, in this connection, significantly remarks:

> When the Buddhist philosophy declares that good *kamma* = good intentions = purification of mind = spiritual progress *(nirvāna),* terms are being equated which have different emotional implications and moral overtones.[133]

To put it straight, the Buddhist doctrine of *kamma*, intrinsic to which was a system of rewards and retributions, was inculcated as above to restore and advance moral values and to a correct view of the world.[134]

The views of Nigaṇṭha Nāṭaputta on *kamma* are further delineated in a passage of the *Aṅguttara Nikāya*, which is identical to the one in *Majjhima.* Here the Licchavi Abhaya informs Ānanda that Nāṭaputta proclaims that through ascetic practices and penances, one can clean the slate or wipe off one's own past's dirty *kamma* and simultaneously bridge the gulf between rebirths and liberation through inaction.[135] In two similar passages recorded in the *Majjhima*,[136] the Buddha contests the Jaina's claim to their knowledge of the past and its deeds and makes them acknowledge their lack of such knowledge. Hence, he mocks the Jainas that if they are so ignorant of such past deeds then how they could be sure of its ethical and moral value and quality? Hence their doctrine here is proved fatuous. The Buddha also negates the possibility of altering the effects of previous evil or bad *kamma*s by the practice of senseless austerities.

Similar traditional doctrines of inaction are found in several passages of the *Nikāya*s. In one such passage in the *Aṅguttara*, we find three different views on *kamma*, namely: (i) the view that held all miseries and happiness as products of earlier actions, (ii) the view that held them to be machinations of a Supreme Deity and (iii) the view that held them to be uncaused or unconditional.[137] We notice that out of these three theories, the first definitely belongs to the *Nigaṇṭhas*.[138] Criticizing the above, the Buddha points out that, owing to earlier actions, eventually men will become murderers, criminals, stealers, liars, etc.[139] He considers it a completely fallacious viewpoint.

As opposed to the Jainas, the Buddhist view of *kamma* is explained in *Cūlakammavibhaṅga Sūtta*[140] and *Mahākammavibhaṅga Sūtta*.[141] We shall not go into the details of it. Suffice to say that in the former, the Buddha explains the disparities in human fortunes in terms of one's deeds alone, as he says: 'deeds divide beings, that is to say, by lowness and highness'.[142] Thus here '*Kamma* retains its interest mainly in relation to past lives rather than as a predictor of the results of present conduct'.[143] The *Mahākammavibhaṅga* provides the Buddhist perception of the working mechanism of *kamma*. The thrust of the *sūtta* is that the effect of a comparatively weak deed may be superseded and offset by the effect of a comparatively strong deed, or by the accumulated effect of a series of weak but good deeds. This is not the place to go into any deeper analysis of the working of the *kamma* according to the Buddhists.[144] Suffice to say that according to this *sūtta*, deeds done or ideas seized at the moment of death are particularly significant. This is, however, not to suggest that the final thoughts of a dying man 'are able fundamentally to alter the value of the *karma* heaped up during his whole life'.[145]

We conclude this section on *kamma* in the words of the two eminent Buddhalogists. One of them—James McDermott—comments: 'Gotama [turned] Nāṭaputta's own position back against the Jainas in such a way that his own stance remained uncompromised.'[146] Speaking in a similar vein, Richard Gombrich contends: The Buddha turned the doctrine of *Kamma* on its head. He ethicized it completely and made morality intrinsic to it and so denied all soteriological value to ritual.'[147] For the Early Buddhists, it was axiomatic that moral values were the foundation of good and moral behaviour.

(iii) *The* Uposatha *of the Nigaṇṭhas*

It is common knowledge that the *śramaṇaṇa* tradition and its followers, to whom the Buddhists, the Nigaṇṭhas, and a host of other sects belonged, observed *uposatha* (Sabbath) on certain lunar days of the months. These were basically occasions when the Buddhist monks and householders assembled, recited the *sūttas*, reviewed them, and confessed breaches of conduct.

In the *Aṅguttara Nikāya,* a passage records three kinds of *uposatha* (Sabbath). The Buddha, here, enumerates them as (i) Gopālaka *uposatha* (herdsman Sabbath), (ii) Nigaṇṭha *uposatha* (Sabbath of the naked ascetics) and (iii) the Ariyan *uposatha*[148] (those of the Buddhists). The Buddha criticizing the *uposatha* of the *Nigaṇṭhas* states: 'Then again on the Sabbath day, they exhort a disciple thus: "I have no part in anything anywhere, and herein for me there is no attachment to anything".'[149]

Furthermore, he continues: 'As soon as that night has passed, he resumes the use of his belongings.'[150] He considers it to be stealing and declares such a Sabbath to be unprofitable. Thereafter, he points to his own attitude towards Sabbath, i.e. the Ariyan Sabbath, which constitutes the 'purification of a soiled mind'[151] by a method proper to each individual, depending on the person concerned.[152]

Scholars are of the opinion that while the second and the third refer to the Jainas and Buddhists, there is a doubt over the identification of the first one, i.e. the Sabbath of the herdsman. B.J. Bhaskar tentatively hints that it refer to those of the Brāhmaṇas, or the Ājīvikas, or was a part and parcel of the Nigaṇṭhas. We think that it definitely does not refer to the last category, as they have already been ascribed the second type of Sabbath. In our opinion it probably refers to the Cārvākas, who are known to be addicted to hedonist philosophy. The description given shows him to be engrossed in pleasurable and in materialistic thoughts,[153] which was characteristic of them. We think that here the Buddha is employing puns. We discount the possibility of it for belonging to the *Ājīvikas*, because they are nowhere mentioned as observing any sort of Sabbath.

### (iv) *Ethics of the Nigaṇṭhas*

The *Nikāya*s contain stray and abbreviated references to such particular vows and abstentions that could be said to constitute the ethics of the Nigaṇṭhas. They are seen to advocate abstinence from five faults, namely: injury, falsehood, stealing, unchastity, and worldly attachment (*parigraha*). And the Jain vows can be classified under two heads: (a) *anūvrata*s (partial vows), and (b) *mahāvrata*s (complete vows), i.e. limited or total abstinence from the five faults mentioned earlier. The former is prescribed for the Jain householders and the latter for renouncers.

The *Sāmaññaphala Sūtta*[154] (*Dīgha Nikāya*, *Sūtta* no. 2) records the *cātuyamsaṃvara (*fourfold self-restraint) as belonging to Nigaṇṭha Nāṭaputta. However, scholars have pointed out that this appears to be an inaccurate and spurious record, for it refers to only fourfold restraints which belonged to an earlier tradition of Pārśvanātha and not to the doctrine of Nāṭaputta.[155] In yet another passage, we find that only four restraints or vows have been ascribed to Nigaṇṭha Nāṭaputta. Here Asibandhaka's son, a follower of Nāṭaputta informs the Buddha that the former teaches a *dhamma,* according to which a liar, a stealer, a slayer and a fornicator are doomed to the woeful state of Purgatory.[156] We notice that the vows referred to are only four, instead of the five supposed to have been laid by the teacher of the Nigaṇṭhas. Besides, abstinence from sexual misconduct is recorded here separately from 'attachment to worldly pleasures'.

It is our submission that in the two passages, the fourfold restraints or vows need not necessarily belong exclusively to the older tradition of Pārśvanātha and may have very well been part and parcel of Nāṭaputta's *dhamma.* We believe that the people reporting them may have missed the importance that Nāṭaputta was trying to emphasize upon 'abstinence from sexual passions' when he separated it, from 'passionate attachment to things mundane/worldly'. We notice that there is a very delicate and subtle difference between the two, which the average worldling may not have been able to discern. Besides, we cannot altogether rule out the possibility that those ascribing to these doctrines or the teachings of Nāṭaputta may have been guilty of mis-representing his actual injunctions. The evidences in the *Nikāya*s show that the different sections of people were inquisitive to know from the Buddha if what they had heard from others about the *Buddha Dhamma* was true and whether they were report-ing it correctly. In light of this, we cannot altogether cancel or nullify the possibility of a loss of actual doctrine or a slight misrepresentation of it: effected either consciously or sub-consciously.

Our view is more or less confirmed by the fact that a passage of the *Aṅguttara Nikāya*[157] actually does mention the five ways of falling into sin as taught by Nāṭaputta, viz., (i) destruction of animates, (ii) taking what is not given voluntarily, (iii) speaking lies, (iv) passionate addiction to evil desires, and (v) taking liquor and intoxicants. However, here there is a certain degree of incongruity. The fifth one should have been a passionate attachment to worldly matters (*parigraha*). But we think that addiction to liquor and intoxicants is subsumed within the *parigraha.*

The Buddhists were also familiar with the *Dīghavrata*s[158] of the Nigaṇṭhas. An allusion to it is made in yet another passage in the *Aṅguttara.* Here the Buddha tells Visākha that the Nigaṇṭhas took a vow not to go beyond the four directions—east, west, north and south—which they thought saved them from violence at least in the prescribed limitation. The Buddha is, however, critical of their vows[159] on the ground that in this they exhort 'kindness and compassion towards some creatures only, but not towards others'.[160]

The Pāli *Nikāyas* also mention certain disciplinary vows of the Jain renunciants. We have already referred to the *Kāyotsarga* of the Jain ascetic (see section {i} on Nigaṇṭhas' Ascetic Practices), thus we shall not be deliberating upon it. Another Jain practice we have referred to earlier is their *uposatha* (*prosadhopavāsa*). Reference for other Jain ascetic practices and vows is extremely scrappy and scanty, and we find very few of them in the *Nikāyas*. Hence, we suspend this section at this juncture.

### (v) *Jaina Epistemology*

The *Nikāyas* contain very few and scattered references to Jain epistemological points. Basic to the Jain philosophy was *anekāntavāda*, i.e. reality has infinite characters, which cannot be perceived or known all at once. Different people present different pictures of the same reality, and hence they are partially true. Consequently, they indulge in debates claiming their truth as absolute. The Jains or the Nigaṇṭhas, however, tried to reveal the truth by trying to establish the theory of non-absolutism (*anekāntavāda*),[161] with its two components: (a) *nayavāda* and (b) *syādvāda*.

The Pāli literature indicates some of the characteristics of *nayavāda*. In a passage,[162] the Buddha mentions ten possible ways of claiming knowledge while addressing the *Kālāmas*; out of which the eighth, i.e. *nayahetu,* has been taken by scholars to indicate that it reveals Jain influence on Buddhism. Scholars have gone to the length of suggesting that the *nayavāda*, integral to which was the acceptance of partial truth, directly influenced the Buddhist philosophy[163] as manifested in their acknowledgement of *paccekasaccas* (individual and partial truths). We, however, do not concur with such a relative viewpoint. It is common knowledge that the Jain canonical texts were compiled later than the Pāli *Nikāyas*. Hence, we cannot ascertain with any degree of certainty the flow of the current of influence in either direction. Second, the mere fact that a belief, assertion, statement or doctrine, found in a stratum 'B' that incidentally also finds mention in an earlier stratum 'A', does not necessarily always point to the fact that the former (i.e. 'B') was influenced by and is a remnant of the later stratum (i.e. 'A').[164]

However, rudiments of *syādvāda* are most prominent in the *Nikāyas*. In its classical form, it delineated seven possible judgements, which could be predicated on an entity, involving both positive and negative attributes—an acknowledgement of its possible inexpressible nature, where an entity was thought to exist, not to exist, and was inexpressible. Though similar to Scepticism, it was not a form of Scepticism,[165] as it was 'merely an acknowledgement that linguistic expressions relating to the world ought to be structured with appropriate awareness of the nature of reality being described.'[166] To put it simply, it pleaded for representing or expressing the realities of the world once they are thoroughly understood, with the use of effective and appropriate language, so as not to distort them.

Notwithstanding the lack of direct reference, the *Nikāyas* seem to be aware of some features of *syādvāda*, as is evident from the way the Buddha confronts Saccaka, the *Nigaṇṭha*. Pointing out the incongruity, the Buddha states: 'Your last speech does not agree with your first, nor your first with your last.'[167] Here attention is drawn to the self-contradictory statements of Saccaka. We are a bit sceptical about the assertions of certain scholars that self-contradiction is a repeated criticism made against *syādvāda* by their opponents.[168] A more direct reference to *syādvāda* is found in the *Dīghanakha Sūtta* (*Majjhima Nikaya*, *Sūtta* no. 74), where *Dīghanakha*[169] mentions the three kinds of theory upheld by him, viz., (a) I agree with all views, (b) I agree with none (view), and (iii) I agree with a few.[170] His views are taken as the predication of *syādvāda*. The *Majjhima* also refers to logical discussions and debates in which the Nigaṇṭhas indulged with the Buddhists with a premeditated desire to defeat the latter.[171] Here the Nigaṇṭhas are described as '*vitaṇḍāvādins*', i.e. those who were primarily interested in displaying their dialectical skills and defeating their opponents. Saccaka is described in the *Majjhima* as 'a controversialist, giving himself out as learned, much honoured by many folks',[172] eager to take up his stand against the Buddha and defeat him.[173] Upāli is another Nigaṇṭha mentioned who takes leave of Nāṭaputta to refute the Buddha.[174]

To conclude, we can say that the Jain attitude towards these debates was probably both to investigate the defects in 'other' philosophies and more so to defeat their followers and demonstrate their superiority.

## III. THE ĀJĪVIKAS

A.L. Basham,[175] has done a great service to all those interested in the study of ancient Indian religious history, by producing the only full-fledged study on the *Ajīvikas*,[176] a vanished Indian religious sect. The term 'Ājīvika' according to Basham, is used in dual senses: (a) primarily for the followers of Makkhali Gosāla, and (b) in a loose sense for the wider class of mendicants.[177] He bases his arguments on the *Sandaka Sūtta.* But this *sūtta,* as Jayatilleke points out, criticizes only the four types of unsatisfactory and false religions. Nowhere are these views associated with specific names of individuals. It is Basham who identifies the teachings with one or the other teacher on the basis of the words.[178] Thus, such identification is erroneous. Similarly, some ascetic and begging practices mentioned in the *Nikāyas*, are linked or identified with those of the *Ājīvikas*, which as we shall see later, is again an erroneous conclusion.

Basham's full-length study, based on a variety of literary and epigraphical sources, touches upon almost all conceivable spheres of *Ajīvika*s activity, viz., ascetic practices, begging and dietary habits, ordination into the Order, penance, *Ajīvika sabhā*, initiation ceremony, etc. However, since our study is based on the *Nikāya*s (the first four only), we shall not be able to construct a similar complete image of the *Ājīvika*s as the references are lacking.[179]

## (i) *Ascetics' Begging and Dietary Practices*

In the *Kassapasīhanada Sūtta*[180] (*Dīgha Nikāya*, *Sūtta* no. 8), a set of ascetic practices are given, which are accounted in the opinion of some recluses as characteristic features of samaṇaship (recluseship). Rhys-Davids ascribes these practices to the *Ājīvika* recluses. However, this appears to be neither very sound nor appealing. As clear mention is not made to it and with the sacred texts of the *Ājīvika*s not preserved for us, it is not possible to crosscheck the 'supposed' ascetic practices of the *Ājīvika*s. What is even more significant is that it clearly declares them (i.e. the practices) to be characteristic of recluseship and does not distinguish this from the recluseship of the *Ājīvika*s. Hence in our opinion, it is a more general reference rather than a more specific one to the *Ājīvika*s.

The *Mahāsaccaka Sūtta* presents an interesting picture of the begging and dietary practices of Makkhali Gosāla and at least two of his predecessors: Nanda Vaccha, and Kisa Sankicca. In reply to the Buddha's question to Saccaka (the Nigaṇṭha): 'How certain recluses maintain themselves with respect to the development of the body?' the latter answers with reference to the three, i.e. Gosāla, Nanda and Kisa, that they are men of loose habits. The whole passage merits reproduction below:

But what have your Aggivessana, heard about the development of body? For example, Nanda Vaccha, Kisa Sankicca, Makkahli of the Cowpen—these, good Gotama, are unclothed, flouting life's decencies, licking (their hands after meals), not those to come when asked to do so, not those to stand still when asked to do so. They do not consent (to accept food) offered to (them) or specially prepared for (them), nor to (accept) an invitation (to a meal). They do not accept food straight from the cooking pot or pan, nor within the threshold, nor among faggots, nor among rice pounders, nor when two are people eating, nor from a pregnant woman, nor from a woman giving suck, nor from one co-habiting with a man, nor from gleanings, nor near where a dog is standing, nor where flies are swarming, nor fish, nor meat. They drink neither fermented liquor nor spirits nor rice-gruel. They are one-house-men, one-piece-men, two house-men, two-piece-men.... They take food once a day, and they take food once in two days, and they take food once in seven days. They live intent on the practice of eating rice at regular fortnightly intervals.[181]

Basham, in a restrained tone, puts forward the premise that some of these practices were followed by the *Ājīvika*s, though he is quick to add that the description applies to a wider class of ascetics. Scholars have expressed disagreements with these practices being followed by the *Ājīvika*s.[182] We also think that instead of specifically referring to *Ājīvika* practices it points to certain general practices followed by ascetics of all traditions. Our objection and reservation premised on the fact that: (a) in this passage Saccaka only draws an analogy between the practices of Nanda, Kisa and Makkhali Gosāla, with those of some unidentified recluses and Brāhmaṇas, (b) of the three mentioned, the first two: Nanda and Kisa Sankicca, have no definite historical connection to be considered as the founders of the *Ājīvika* sect, preceding Makkhali Gosāla, (c) In a passage of the *Mahāsīhanāda Sūtta,* the Buddha recounts similar ascetic practices to which he was addicted much before his Enlightenment.[183] Thus, its reliability as applying exclusively to the *Ājīvikas* is questionable, for we notice here that the Buddha in his pre-Enlightenment phase indulged in such abominable practices, supposed to be those of *Ājīvikas* also; a sect whose leader, Makkhali Gosāla, the Buddha severally detested later on. Hence these practices are those followed in general by the ascetics of the age.

Scholars[184] have drawn parallels between certain begging practices of the *Ājīvikas* as supposed to be presented in the above passage and the one quoted in *Aupāpatika Sūtra* (which contains a list of the seven types of *Ājīvikas*). For instance, the one, two or seven house men of the *Majjhima* have been equated with the latter's one who begged at every alternate, second, third or seventh house. Basham points out the falsity of such identification, for these categories are not the same as appearing in the *Majjhima.* When correctly interpreted and as confirmed by Buddhaghoṣa, in the case of *Majjhima,* it meant those who confined their begging to one, two, three or seven houses or patrons and not as one who skipped one, two, three, etc., houses while begging.

It would be apt to enquire into the Buddhist stance on the

development of the body as opposed to the one told by Saccaka. According to the Buddha, a body cannot be developed without proper development of the mind.

(ii) *Feigned Austerity and Non-spirituality*

If we accept that the practices listed in the *Mahāsaccaka Sūtta* refer to the *Ājīvika*s, who fall within the broader category of ascetics, then we notice that the *Ājīvika*s are guilty of feigning austerity. Here, the Buddha questions Saccaka whether these recluses, namely, Nanda, Sankicca or Makkhali Gosāla, 'keep going on so little?'[185] The answer given by him is interesting, where Saccaka accuses them of eating good spicy food, drinking excellent beverages, and thus increasing their physical strength.[186]

The Pali texts generally describe the *Ājīvikas* as foolish, repulsive and hypocrites. In the *Majjhima Nikāya,* an allusion pertaining to the non-spirituality of the *Ājīvika*s is adduced. Here the wanderer Vacchagotta enquires from the Buddha: 'Now, good Gotama, is there any Naked Ascetic, who at the breaking up of the body is an end-maker of ill?'[187] The Buddha's answer is negative. Vacchagotta repeats his question, by enquiring about their possibility of having at least attained Heaven.[188] In this case, the Buddha concedes that ages back he remembers one such ascetic having reached Heaven.[189] An analysis of this passage reveals a few interesting facts, viz., (a) no specific mention to *Ājīvika*s is made; it only mentions the class of naked ascetics—they could have been both the *Nigaṇṭha*s and the *Ājīvika*s; as the latter professed nudity, (b) once again Basham identifies them with the *Ājīvika*s, (c) the ascetic who aeons back are reported to have been successful in reaching Heaven is held to be a believer in *kamma* and one who professed *operative kamma.*[190] It is on this basis that Basham says that perhaps he was 'not an orthodox follower of Makkhali Gosāla'.[191]

What is most significant here is that the Buddha acknowledges this particular ascetic's success in reaching Heaven, primarily owing to his belief in operative *kamma*, i.e. intrinsic to this is the fact that since he believed and upheld certain moral values he reached Heaven. We wonder what would have been his reaction had he not been a believer in *kamma*. Again, we have objections to Basham's assertion that he was not an orthodox follower of Gosāla. Basham has completely overlooked the fact that Gosāla was a contemporary of the Buddha, while the ascetic mentioned here lived ages before in one of the previous births of the Buddha. Also, the mere fact that he was one who professed *kamma*, does not disqualify him from being a follower of the *Ājīvika*s of ancient times. We think that the boot is on the other foot, i.e. to say the present lot of *Ājīvika*s are a degraded bunch of the more righteous ancient predecessors. We cannot rule out this possibility altogether since we notice that in the case of Brāhmaṇas, the Buddha actually lavished praises on the Brāhmaṇas of the past ages and bemoaned the degradation of their present lot. Thus, 'can we rule out such a probability in the case of the *Ājīvika*s? May be not.

A more direct disparaging and denigrating remark to Gosāla is found in the two passages of the *Aṅguttara Nikāya*, where the Buddha declares him to be to the loss of mankind and his views to be the most perverted and the meanest one.[192] The Buddha's criticism is basically against Makkhali's theory of *akiriyāvāda* (non-causation), which denied moral values and responsibility.

As a digression, we would like to ask 'Why are the Buddhists so vehemently opposed and critical of the *Ājīvika* Makkhali Gosāla and his followers?' Basham thinks that Gosāla and not Mahāvīra was the chief opponent of the Buddha.[193] However, we do not agree with him, for the simple logic that they are not as frequently and as vigorously attacked in the *Nikāya*s, as is the case with the Brāhmaṇas or the Nigaṇṭhas. They also find far fewer references than the other two categories. In our opinion, the Brāhmaṇas were the dreaded opponents of Buddhists. Uma Chakravarti advocates this hostility to the fact that while the Buddhists were proponents of the doctrine of causality and the power of human effort in determining futures, the *Ājīvika*s were just opposed to it. Hence, they were singled out for attack. While Uma Chakravarti is right in her analysis, we hypothesize and take cognisance of certain additional factors for this hostility between the Buddhists and the *Ājīvika*s. One of the reasons for such an antipathy could be the Buddha's dissenting attitude towards self-mortification and disapproval of extreme asceticism. We can understand the motive(s) behind it in light of the competitive tension between different sects at two levels: (a) for the numerical growth of their sect, and (b) for cornering material benefits from the laity. With each sect engaged in such a competition the sanctity of the (Buddhist) Order and the austerity of their practices was an important aspect not to be ignored,[194] but to be most boldly underlined. As I.B. Horner comments:

> For until Gotama began to teach the doctrine of the Middle Way, in which he [denounced] austerities public opinion had been much swayed and influenced by the exhibition of self-inflicted torture done in the name of holiness.[195]

In this regard the *Ājīvika*s far outweighed the Nigaṇṭhas and the Buddhists in the rigidity of monastic and ascetic rules, etc., and may have perhaps appropriated more alms. We may also view this in the light of the Buddha having practised austerities like that of the *Ājīvika*s prior to his Enlightenment had seen their utter futility and hence detested those who refused to give it up for better moralities and practices.

## IV. PABBĀJAKAS AND 'OTHER' ASCETICS

The Pāli term for all shades of itinerant wanderers[196] is *pabbājaka*s (Sanskrit, *parivrājaka*s). They are frequently referred to in the *Nikāya*s. This is understandable given the fact that out of the sixty-two heretical sects mentioned in the Pāli canon, only six are distinctly two heretical sects, and only six are distinctly mentioned. The rest are classified under blanket terms like the 'wanderers of other sects' or 'certain ascetics'. However, in spite of the umpteen references to them—perhaps only second to the Brāhmaṇas and the monks—these references are not very helpful in constructing their image. This is due to the fact that most of these references are almost exclusively philosophical in content and nature. And our intention is not to delve into any philosophical analyses.

### (i) *Wanderers Seeking* Dhamma-*talk or Holding Discussions with the Buddhists*

The *pabbājaka*s are seen as one who often sought a *dhamma* talk from the Buddha upon meeting him and never shied away from taking on the Buddhists in metaphysical and doctrinal debates. The references are too numerous to be quoted, and neither it is our intention to discuss the topic from a philosophical perspective. Suffice it to say that they discussed and debated with the Buddhists on a very broad range of themes, namely on the eternity of the body and soul,[197] relative truth of other *dhammas*,[198] omniscience of certain teachers and the Buddha,[199] faith in the preceptor,[200] suffering and its causes,[201] knowledge of cause and effect,[202] wrong views,[203] *kamma* and rebirth,[204] *nibbāṇa*,[205] *arhantship*,[206] asceticism,[207] *brahma-vihāras*,[208] etc. What is significant is that in all these discussions, the position of the Early Buddhists vis-à-vis these themes, diverged from those tenaciously held by these *pabbājaka*s of alien views. A discussion on these would require too arduous an effort than is possible here. Hence, we adjourn it.

### (ii) *Wanderers Claim Equality with* Buddha Dhamma

In several *sūtta*s,[209] the *pabbājaka*s (wanderers) are seen fervently claiming a religious or doctrinal status at par with the Buddha and his *dhamma*, which the Early Buddhists, in turn denied them with equal fervour. They are seen as not willing to acquiesce to the wanderer's claim to equality with the *Buddha Dhamma.* The Buddhists systematically and repeatedly refuted such a claim.

What is significant here is that we notice a tension between the Wanderers and the Buddhists on certain doctrinal points. While the former are ardently staking equality, the latter are reluctant to admit the same and even go to the extent of negating it. We are not sure of the motive(s) for such behaviour on either side. Perhaps the Buddha's behaviour can be construed by the fact that in a welter of views, the Buddha was trying to claim a distinctiveness for his *dhamma,* and hence a separate and distinct identity of the Buddhists, as opposed to the non-Buddhists. He was also simultaneously claiming a superiority of his *dhamma.* The competition between different sects cannot be altogether ignored.

### (iii) *Attire, Diet and Residence*

A significant passage in the *Aṅguttara Nikāya* gives us a clear picture of the attire, dietary habits and dwelling places of these wanderers. Here the Buddha himself informs the assembly of monks that the 'Wanderers holding other views enjoin these three forms of aloofness: aloofness from robes, from alms-food, from lodging.'[210] The succeeding passages detail this aloofness. This aloofness when carefully studied, reveals their ways of dressing, dietary preferences and dwelling or resting places.

Regarding the dress they were enjoined for wearing, mention is made of coarse, hemp clothes, clothes of different fibres, discarded corpse's clothes, rags from a rubbish heap, tree barks, antelope skins, clothes made of *kuśa*-grass, blankets made of the hair of men, horse or owl's wing, etc.[211]

In matters of diet, they were enjoined to feed on vegetables, millet, raw rice, wild rice, water plants, flour of oil seeds, grass and cow dung. They kept themselves alive by eating forest fruits and roots, etc.[212] These wanderers also enjoined aloofness from lodging and instead laid injunctions to dwell in a forest, at the root of a tree, in a cemetery, in the open air, on a heap of straw, in a thatched shelter, etc.[213] The Buddha goes on to show how his views on aloofness diverged from those of wanderers. He says that in his *dhamma,* the three aloofness mean quite another thing. They stand for aloofness from a (i) immoral acts, speeches and thoughts, (ii) wrong views, and (iii) defilements.[214] Only one who remains aloof from these three has reached perfection.

### (iv) *Social Position of the Pabbājakas*

An unusual but significant allusion in the *Saṁyutta Nikāya* gives us a fair idea of the social position of the wanderers as opposed to the Buddhist renouncers (monks). It presents a picture of the Buddha and his monks and the wanderer Susīma and his retinue staying at Rājagaha, at about the same time. The Buddha and his company were the cynosure of the laity, as they were 'honoured, revered, beloved, ministered unto and reverently welcomed; ... obtaining supplies of the requisites for clothing, sustenance, lodging',[215] etc. But on the other hand, the heretical wanderers were neither honoured, welcomed, revered, nor obtained supplies from the laity for their clothing, food, lodging etc.[216] Realizing the stark difference and reality, the followers of the wanderer Susīma egged him on to cross-over to the fold of the Buddha's *dhamma,* so that they could as well become worthy of such a reception from the laity. Cajoled thus, Susīma actually visits the Buddha and his company and after requesting ordination, he actually converts and joins the *Saṅgha.*[217]

### (v) *Frivolous Talk and Reviling*

The *Nikāya*s contain copious allusions to the wanderers' habit of indulging in low and inferior talks, which they mouthed loudly. Stock descriptions of this appear at the beginning of this paper. B.G. Gokhale thinks that it throws interesting light on the wanderers' attitude towards what is traditionally called 'history'. In his opinion, certain 'low talk' of the wanderers, viz., tales of kings, ministers, armies, battles, stories of communities, villages trading towns, heroes, and adventures on sea, etc., are precisely 'the stuff out of which the chronicles of history are made.'[218]

Should we, then, conclude that while the *pabbājaka*s had a sense of history, the Early Buddhists failed to evolve and inculcate it? We, however, refrain from making such bold assertions. The passage cited above is merely a pointer to the fact that the Buddha detested such indulgence in frivolous talks, which he called 'low' and 'inferior'. It is not difficult to unearth the Buddha's motive behind such denigration. The Buddha, in our view, being concerned with the release of many folk from the cycles of *saṃsāra* (i.e. rebirths), considered these debased talks as impediments in the way of striving for the 'final release' (*nibbāṇa*). Being primarily a soteriology, the attitude of early Buddhism towards these talks, has to be construed in this perspective.

Finally, these *pabbājaka*s are also seen indulging in abusing and reviling the Buddha. The *Māgandiya Sūtta* (*Majjhima Nikāya*, *Sūtta* no. 75) has a passage, wherein the wanderer Māgandiya seeing the sleeping place being made ready by a Brāhmaṇa for Gotama, comments that it was a poor sleeping place for Gotama, who was a destroyer of growth.[219] I.B. Horner explains iwith the help of commentary, to conclude that while Māgandiya held that there should be an overall development of all the six spheres, the Buddha, in contrast, called for a restraint or rather destructionand control or curbing of these senses.[220]

## (vi) *Other Ascetics*

Apart from the references we have already cited in different contexts, we have in the *Nikāya*s, allusions to two ascetic practices. In a *sūtta* of the *Majjhima,* we have reference to two ascetics, namely, Punna, the bovine ascetic and Seniya, who was an unclothed canine ascetic.[221] The former had undertaken the 'cow-practice', putting on a horn and a tail and grazing with cows.[222] The latter, who had similarly undertaken a 'dog-practice', remained naked, acted and behaved like a dog in all manner. Similar reference to an ascetic who behaved like a dog occurs in the *Dīgha Nikūya.*[223] (*Pātika Sūtta*, no. 24). In all these cases, the Buddha predicts that since they hold wrong views, after death they shall arise either in Hell or in the animal world. In our opinion, the Buddha's denial for them to be born in a higher realm of Heaven or at least in the world of human beings, stems from the fact that he recognized them to be practitioners of immoral acts and practices which were not conducive to *nibbāṇa.* His objection was based on their lack of possessing *sammādithi* (Right View).

## CONCLUSION

To recapitulate, we notice that the Brāhmaṇas—who among all the non-Buddhist categories are most copiously represented—are earmarked and attacked in the most earnest fashion. Perhaps the Buddha's tirade was especially against the priestly class of Brāhmaṇas. Besides, the pretension of the Brāhmaṇas regarding the social superiority of their *varṇa,* was vigorously contested by the Buddha, both on empirical and logical grounds. Redefining a true-Brāhmaṇa, the Buddha equated him with the *ariyasāvaka.* Besides, we repeatedly notice in the early Buddhist texts that the Buddha persistently and roundly condemns the animal sacrifices and loses no opportunity to criticize meaningless Brahmanical rituals. While doing so, the Buddha denied them the power to alter one's destiny and *karma,* and hence negated their moral and soteriological value. In most cases, he re-interpreted them, substituting the ritual with moral and ethical principles. This subversion of sacrifices and rituals may have slightly undermined the priestly position of the Brāhmaṇas, though we think that it may not have greatly affected their socio-religious position.

The Niganṭhas find far fewer references compared to the Brāhmaṇas. Their asceticism is censured and declared as futile for the destruction of bad *kamma.* The Buddhists fundamentally differed from the Niganṭhas on *kamma* and its working, as they made 'intention' central to determining the moral quality of an act. The ethics of intention was invented by the Buddha with definite social and moral ends in view.

The Ājīvikas rarely find explicit references, and it is almost impossible to reconstruct their comprehensive or even a partially satisfactory image from the *Nikāyas* alone. The dietary and begging practices often ascribed to them refer to a more general category of ascetics than to the Ājīvikas alone, who are shown as feigning austerity but generally lacking moral and spiritual character.

In the Buddhist perception, the real threat to their 'existence' was from the Brāhmaṇas and the Nigaṇṭhas. This, we presume, was because: (a) the former were too numerous and too entrenched to be overwhelmed and checkmated, and (b) the latter had a striking likeness with the Buddhists, who were intent on constructing a distinct identity for themselves, as opposed to other sects. Throughout the Pāli *Nikāya*s, the Buddha laboriously articulates the doctrinal, theoretical, and philosophical differences and divergences between his *Dhamma* and the *dhammas* of 'other' religious sects (*añña-tithiya*s). If the Buddha is seen articulating such differences recurrently, it was not without reasons. Our submission is that such endeavours differentiate between his *Dhamma* and the *dhammas* of the *añña-tithiya*s were geared towards articulation of Early Buddhist identity, for often it is *our* differences that constitute our identity vis-à-vis the *others*.

## NOTES

1. *The Book of Kindred Sayings*, IV, pp. 74-5.
2. *Cūladukkhakkhandha Sūtta* (*Majjhima Nikāya*, *Sūtta* no. 14); *Middle Length Sayings*, I, pp. 121-2.
3. *Middle Length Sayings*, II, p. 192. A similar abbreviated description occurs in *Middle Length Sayings*, II, p. 203.
4. Among the non-Buddhists during the age of the Buddha, the *Nikāya*s mention sixty-two such groups. However, only very few of them find supportive evidence in the *Nikāya*s. Hence we shall restrict ourselves to these few categories, to study them.
5. B.G. Gokhale, 'Early Buddhism and the Brahmanas', in A.K Narian (ed.), *Studies in History of Buddhism*, Delhi: B.R. Publishing Co., 1980, p. 68.
6. See: C.A.F. Rhys-Davids, 'The Relation Between Early Buddhism and Brahmanism', *Indian Historical Quarterly*, vol. X, 1934, p. 275.
7. We agree that the Buddha rejected the social superiority of the Brāhmaṇas. But he never rejected *varṇa* divisions *per se*. Even while redefining a Brāhmaṇa, he never rejected them as a conceptual category and only downgraded their status to that of the Khattiyas.

8. *Middle Length Sayings*, II. pp. 273, 341; *Dialogues of the Buddha*, III, p. 78, etc.
9. P. Chandra, 'Buddhism as an Instrument of Social Change', in Madhu Sen (ed.), *Studies in Religion and Change*, Delhi: Books & Books, 1983, p. 94.
10. *Dialogues of the Buddha*, III, pp. 82-91.
11. Chandra, op. cit., pp. 96-7.
12. *Middle Length Sayings*, II, p. 341. Also see: *Dialogues of the Buddha*, III, p. 78.
13. *Dialogues of the Buddha*, I, p. 115.
14. Ibid., pp. 119-20.
15. *Dialogues of the Buddha*, I, p. 146; *Middle Length Sayings*, II, pp. 355, 379; *The Book of Gradual Sayings*, III, pp. 146, etc.
16. *Dialogues of the Buddha*, I, pp. 152-3.
17. Ibid.
18. For a Buddhist definition of a Brāhmaṇa, see *Dialogues of the Buddha*, I, p. 317; *The Book of Kindred Sayings*, I, pp. 206-7; *The Book of Kindred Sayings*, V, pp. 82-4, 170-2; *The Book of Gradual Sayings*, II, pp. 62-4; *The Book of Gradual Sayings*, IV, p. 117, etc.
19. For details see *Middle Length Sayings*, II, pp. 382-5.
20. K.R. Norman., 'Theravāda Buddhism and Brahmanical Hinduism: Brahmanical Terms in Hindu Guise', in T. Skorupski (ed.), *Buddhist Forum*, vol. II (Seminar Papers, 1988-90, School of Oriental and African Studies, University of London), Delhi: Heritage Publishers, 1991, p. 196.
21. Uma Chakravarti, *Social Dimensions of Early Buddhism*, New Delhi: Oxford University Press, 1987, p. 44.
22. 'To know his former birth, see heaven and hell, to have attained destruction of rebirth,—If any brahmin hath this threefold lore, that is the one I call "*Tevijja-brahmin*"' (*The Book of Gradual Sayings*, I, pp. 149, 150). Also see, *The Book of Kindred Sayings*, I, p. 208.
23. *Dialogues of the Buddha*, I, pp. 245f.
24. Peter Masefield, *Divine Revelation in Pali Buddhism*, London: George Allen & Unwin, 1986, p. 156.
25. These ideals are now to be found in the *ariyasāvakas*, i.e. those in possession of the Right View, who are now said to be true Brāhmaṇas.
26. *Dialogues of the Buddha*, I, pp. 129f. Also see: *The Book of Kindred Sayings*, IV, pp. 74-5).
27. *Dīgha Nikāya*, II, p. 245.

28. Ckakravarti, *Social Dimensions*, p. 43.
29. *The Book of Gradual Sayings*, III, pp. 162-3.
30. *Middle Length Sayings*, II, p. 347.
31. Ibid., pp. 348-9.
32. 'Whether one compares women with women or men with men, the *Kshatriyas* are higher and the Brahmans inferior' (*Dialogues of the Buddha*, I. p. 210).
33. Ibid., p. 121.
34. *Middle Length Sayings*, II, p. 366.
35. True, the Buddha did not explicitly claim the superior position of the Khattiyas on such a premise, but the evidence in the *Nikāyas* is such that we can construe such a claim. Probably the Buddha eschewed from making such a claim because that would have run contrary to the Buddhist doctrine of *kamma*.
36. *Dialogues of the Buddha*, I, p. 15.
37. For details see: *Dīgha Nikāya*, II, pp. 71-2.
38. Y. Krishan, 'Buddhism and the Caste System', *Journal of the International Association of Buddhist Studies*, 9(1), 1986, p. 71.
39. C. Bougle, *Essays on the Caste System* (translated by D.F. Pocock, Cambridge: Cambridge University Press, 1971), p. 73.
40. *Middle Length Sayings*, III, pp. 209ff.
41. 'And just then a great sacrifice was being got ready on behalf of Kūṭadanta, the Brahman. And a hundred bulls, and a hundred heifers and a hundred goats, and rams had been bought to the post for sacrifice.'
42. *The Book of Kindred Sayings*, I, p. 102. For a similar reference, see: *The Book of Gradual Sayings*, IV, p. 24. In both these references the numerical strength of animals increases.
43. *Middle Length Sayings*, II, pp. 8-9.
44. *The Book of Gradual Saying*, I, p. 151.
45. *The Book of Gradual Sayings*, III, pp. 216f.
46. John Dewey, *The Quest for Certainty* (Gifford Lectures, 1929), Fourth impression, Capricorn Books, New York, 1960. Cited in David J. Kalupahana, *Buddhist Philosophy*, Honolulu: University of Hawaii Press, 1976, p. 56.
47. *The Book of Gradual Sayings*, II, p. 49.
48. Ibid.
49. Ibid., p. 51.
50. An almost similar reference occurs at *Pāyasi Sūtta* (*Dīgha Nikāya*, II, pp. 354f).

51. *The Book of Gradual Sayings*, III, pp. 216f.
52. *Dialogues of the* Buddha, I, pp. 182f.
53. R. Clayton Amore, *The Concept and Practice of Doing Merit in Early Theravāda Buddhism*, Columbia, 1970. Cited in Masefield, op. cit., p. 156.
54. *Dialogues of the Buddha*, III, pp. 173-4.
55. Ibid., p. 180.
56. This particular Brāhmaṇa after performing a fire-rite offers the remainder of the oblations to water (*The Book of Kindred Sayings*, I, pp. 209-13).
57. *The Book of Gradual Sayings*, V, p. 25.
58. *The Book of Gradual Sayings*, V, pp. 26-7.
59. *Middle Length Sayings*, I, p. 49.
60. In the *Nikāyas* several abbreviated references mention such purificatory rites. See: *The Book of Kindred Sayings*, IV, p. 218; *The Book of Gradual Sayings*, V, pp. 152, 176, etc.
61. The Book of Kindred Sayings, I. p. 231.
62. 'Is it indeed true, *brāhmin*, that thou art a water-purifier...thou make it a religious practice to go down into water, both evening and morning? That is so, Master Gotama' (ibid., p. 232).
63. 'In this way Master Gotama, the evil deed that I do during the day, these by my bathing I cause to be borne away the same evening; the evil deeds that I do at night...borne away the next morning', ibid.
64. *The Book of Gradual Sayings*, V, pp. 176-80.
65. Ibid., pp. 175-6.
66. Narendra Wagle, 'Minor Rites and Rituals Attributed to the *Brāhmaṇas* in the *Nikāya* Texts of the Pali Canon', *Journal of the Oriental Institute of Baroda*, 17(,4), 1968, pp. 63-72. has explained these rites and rituals in the light of the *Gṛhya* and *Dharmasūtras*, which enjoins water on earth to be used for purification, till the bad smell of excreta is removed. Similarly, ground is to be purified by wet cow dung, whereas mutterings of holy texts are to be performed by holding *kuśa* grass in hand. While tending to fire in the Pāli *Nikāyas* probably refers to *homa* rite of morning and evening oblation to domestic fire.
67. *The Book of Kindred Sayings*, I, p. 218.
68. Wagle, 'Minor Rites and Rituals', p. 367. However, Wagle fails to elaborate the three stages he is referring to, and we are unsure as to what they are.

69. *The Book of Gradual Sayings*, II, p. 104.
70. *The Book of Gradual Sayings*, V, p. 180.
71. For details, see ibid., pp. 181-2.
72. *The Book of Gradual Sayings* I, p. 150. ('Master Gotama, he who has a sacrifice to make, or an offering to the dead ... should give it to the Brāhmaṇas who are possessors of the threefold love.')
73. *Dialogues of the Buddha*, I, p. 120.
74. *The Book of Gradual Sayings*, III, pp. 163-8.
75. Ibid., p. 164.
76. Ibid., p. 165.
77. *The Book of Kindred Sayings*, V, p. 102.
78. 'We *brahmins*, Master Gotama, select a teacher's fee for our teacher' (*The Book of Kindred Sayings*, I. p. 244).
79. 'Now at that time, the Brāhmaṇa Pokkharasadi was dwelling at Ukkatha, a spot teeming with life, with grassland, with woodland and corn on royal domain, granted to him by the king Pasenadi of Kosala, as a royal gift with power over it as if he were the king.' (*Dialogues of the Buddha*, I, p. 103). Similar references occur at: *Dialogues of the Buddha*, I, p. 144; *Dīgha Nikāya*, I, pp. 87, 127, 235; *Middle Length Sayings*, I, p. 343; *Majjhima Nikāya*, II, pp. 164, 400; *Middle Length Sayings*, II, pp. 400. etc.
80. For details see: B.G. Gokhale, 'Brahmanas in the Early Buddhist Literature', *Journal of Indian History*, vol. 48, no. 4, 1970, pp. 53-4.
81. Ibid., p. 53.
82. See: *Dialogues of the Buddha,* I, pp. 133, 136; *Middle Length Sayings*, II, p. 209; *Majjhima Nikāya*, II, p. 450, etc.
83. Chakravarti, *Social Dimensions*, p. 72.
84. *Dialogues of the Buddha,* I, pp. 16-25.
85. *The Book of Kindred Sayings*, V, pp. 199f.
86. Gokhale, 'The Brahmans', p. 54.
87. We disagree with Gokhale for the simple reason that the practice of the Brāhmaṇas carrying out un-Brahmanical professions was not uncommon.
88. A close scrutiny of the list reveals that many similar professions are repeated under different heads, thus making the list voluminous.
89. Gokhale, 'The Brahmans', p. 71.
90. He is mentioned as a 'great official' of Magadha. See *The Book of Gradual Sayings*, II, pp. 49, 179.
91. We think that with the Buddhist de-emphasis on yajñas and rituals

and their ethicization, the Brāhmaṇas would have been virtually forced to diversify their vocations.

92. He is described as carrying wood from jungle for making gables, roof-terraces, etc. (*The Book of Kindred Sayings*, I, p. 227, n. 2).
93. In the *Kosala-Saṁyutta*, we are told (as per the commentary) that the King Pasenadi of Kosala prepared for the celebration of sacrifice, on the advice of his *purohit*, in order to prevent a threatened and unseen future danger, foreseen by the Kosalan king in dream (*The Book of Kindred Sayings*, I, p. 102, n.1).
94. In a passage of the *Aṅguttara Nikāya*, where there occurs a list of certain chief disciples, the name of Vangisa also finds place. This Vangisa was a Brāhmaṇa (before conversion) and foretold people's future by tapping skull. He was a 'skull-tapper or psychometizer of dead men's skull' (see *The Book of Gradual Sayings*, I, p. 18, n.10).
95. *The Book of Kindred Sayings*, I, p. 147.
96. In a passage of the *Saṁyutta*, we have a reference to the Wanderer Sivaka, who is described as one with 'Top-knot' (*The Book of Kindred Sayings*, IV, p. 154). We wonder whether this itinerant ascetic was also a *Jaṭila*.
97. Perhaps, the Brāhmaṇas mentioned in the *Nikāyas*, as fire-worshippers and making fire-oblations, were *Jaṭilas*: though not all of them were so.
98. See *Dīgha Nikāya*, I, p. 151; *Saṁyutta Nikāya*, I, 182; *Aṅguttara Nikāya*, I, 145.
99. *Middle Length Sayings*, II. p. 334 (*Majjhima Nikāya*, II, p. 105).
100. *The Book of Kindred Sayings*, I. p. 104.
101. Ibid.
102. See *Dialogues of the Buddha*, I, pp. 109, 110, 117, etc.
103. Gokhale, 'The Brahmanas', p. 58.
104. *Dialogues of the Buddha*, I, p. 112.
105. *The Book of Kindred Sayings*, I, 224.
106. Ibid., pp. 201, 204.
107. *Dialogues of the Buddha*, I, pp. 267ff; *Majjhima Nikāya*, *Sūtta* nos. 60, 94, 100; *The Book of Kindred Sayings*, I, pp. 220-1, 224-6; *The Book of Kindred Sayings*, V, pp. 307-11; *The Book of Gradual Sayings*, I, pp. 138-9; *GS*. III. pp. 237-8, 258-9, etc.
108. *The Book of Kindred Sayings*, I, p. 220; *The Book of Kindred Sayings*, II, p. 51; *The Book of Gradual Sayings*, III, p. 237.

109. *Dialogues of the Buddha*, I, p. 305.
110. Mrs. Rhys-Davids, 'Early Buddhism and Brahmanism' See, pp. 281-2.
111. B.G. Gokhale, 'Early Buddhist Elite', *JIH*, vol. 43, 1965, p. 75.
112. For a Brāhmaṇa and Buddhist viewpoint of householder and renouncer see: *The Book of Kindred Sayings*, I, pp. 27-9.
113. Uma Chakravarti, 'Renouncer and the Householder in Early Buddhism', *Social Analysis*, No.13, May 1987, p. 78.
114. N. Wagle, *Society at the Time of Buddha*, Bombay: Popular Prakashan, 1966.
115. Ibid., p. 48.
116. Ibid., p. 77.
117. Ibid., p. 69.
118. Madhav M. Deshpande, stressing upon socio-linguistic attitudes contends that there were linguistic tensions between the Brāhmaṇa and the non-Brāhmaṇa monks during the Buddha's time, and it is not un-natural to notice these converts to Buddhism carrying their Brahmanical socio-linguistic attitudes to Buddhism. (Madhav M. Deshpande, *Socio-linguistic Attitudes in India: An Historical Reconstruction*, Ann Arbor: Karoma Publications, 1979, p. 42). In another work too, Deshpande has stressed the same, when he thinks that the early Buddhists carried their socio-linguistic attitude to the language they employed in social interaction (see Madhav M. Deshpande, *Sanskrit and Prakrit: Sociolinguistic Issue*, Delhi: Motilal Banarsidass, 1993, p. 7).
119. *Middle Length Sayings*, I, p. 121. (We have quoted the full reference earlier. See the second passage cited at the beginning of the paper.)
120. The Jaina ascetic remained nude; the Jaina householder perhaps wore a red loincloth (see; *The Book of Gradual Sayings*, III, p. 273).
121. 'Your reverence Nāṭaputta ... speak thus: 'If there is Jains an evil deed that was formerly done by you, wear it away by severe austerity. That which is the non-doing of evil-deed in the future is from control of body, from control of speech, from control of thought here and now...' (*Middle Length Sayings*, I, pp. 121-2). Also cf. the Jaina view of *kamma* present at *Devadaha Sūtta* (*Majjhima Nikāya*, *Sūtta* no. 101; *Middle Length Sayings*, III, p. 6). Similar view also occurs at *Aṅguttara Nikāya*, I, p. 220 (*The Book of Gradual Sayings*, I. p. 200).

122. It is our premise that the middle way adopted by the Buddha was a strategic device to win recruits to his fold, as it had the potentiality to attract both, those who detested and found it onerous to practice extreme self-mortification and those who frowned upon sensual addictions and hedonism.
123. As opposed to the *Kiriyavādins* were the *Akiriyavādins* like Purana Kassapa, Makkhali Gosāla, Pakuddha Kaccayana et. al.
124. P.S Jaini, 'Karma and the Problem of Rebirth in Jainism', in Wendy D. O'Flaherty (ed.), *Karma and Rebirth in Classical Indian Tradition*, Delhi: Motilal Banarsidass, 1983 (1st pub, California: University of California Press, 1980), p. 218.
125. *Middle Length Sayings*, II, pp. 36-7 (*Majjhima Nikāya*, I, p. 372).
126. 'Friend Gotama, Nāṭaputta the Jain lays down three (kinds of) wrongs for effect and evil deed ... that is to say, wrong of body, wrong of speech, wrong of mind' (ibid., p. 37).
127. 'But Tapassin, of three wrongs ... which is the wrong that Nāṭaputta the Jain lays down as more blameable in effecting an evil deed' (ibid.).
128. 'Friend Gotama, of these three ... Nāṭaputta the Jain lays down that wrong of body is the more blameable in effecting an evil deed ... wrong of speech is not like it, wrong of mind is not like it' (ibid.).
129. 'Tapassin of these three deeds thus divided, thus particularised, I lay down that deeds of mind is more blameable in effecting an evil deed ... deed of body is not like it, deed of speech is not like it' (ibid., p. 38).
130. Thus, it appears that, as opposed to the Buddhists, the Jainas either plainly underestimated or did not realize or totally negated the significance of the mind (*citta*). However, B. Jain Bhaskar cogently argues otherwise. In his view, Nāṭaputta did not at any stage envisage bodily action which is devoid of intention and volition and the 'true significance of Nigaṇṭha Nāṭaputta's attitude to threefold action can be conveyed only when *kāyadaṇḍa* is understood and translated not merely as bodily action but as thought converted into action' (B. Jain Bhaskar, *Jainism in Buddhist Literature*, Nagpur: Aloka Prakashan, 1972, p. 74). He concludes that the Buddha indicated the same idea but articulated its characteristics in a different manner. Supporting his contention, he cites reference found in the *Aṅguttara*, where Nāṭaputta is designated as a *kiriyavādin* (believers in the doctrine

of action/*karma*) while the Buddha is said to be both a *kiriyavādin* and *akiriyavādin* (*The Book of Gradual Sayings*, IV, pp. 125-6). He is *kiriyavādin* as he teaches the performance of good deeds (ibid., p. 125) and he is *akiriyavādin* since he teaches abstention from evil deeds (ibid., p. 126).

131 Richard F. Gomnbrich, 'Buddhist Karma and Social Control', *Comparative Studies in Society and History*, vol.17, 1975, pp. 212-20.

132. Ibid., p. 216.

133. Ibid.

134. For details see: ibid., pp. 216-19.

135. 'Sir, Nāṭa's [*sic*] Son, the Unclothed ... proclaims the making an end of former deeds by ascetic practice, and the breaking down of power of fresh deeds by inaction' (*The Book of Gradual Sayings*, I, p. 200; *Middle Length Sayings*, I, pp. 121-2; *Middle Length Sayings*, III, p. 6).

136. *Middle Length Sayings*, I, pp. 122; *Middle Length Sayings*, III, pp. 4f.

137. *The Book of Gradual Sayings*, I, p. 157. For similar reference, also see, *The Book of Kindred Sayings*, II. p 28; *The Book of Gradual Sayings*, IV, p. 154.

138. Cf. *Middle Length Sayings*, I, p. 121; *Middle Length Sayings*, III, p. 3.

139. *The Book of Gradual Sayings*, I, p. 158.

140. *Middle Length Sayings*, III, pp. 248-53.

141. Ibid., pp. 254-63.

142. Ibid., pp. 249.

143. Gombrich, 'Karma and Social Control', p. 217.

144. For a detailed analysis of this *sūtta* see: James P. McDermott, *Development in Early Buddhist Concept of Kamma/Karma*, Delhi: Munshiram Manoharlal, 1984, pp. 18-20; idem, 'Karma and Rebirth in Early Buddhism', in W. D. O'Flaherty (ed.), op. cit., pp. 173-9.

145. H. von Glasenapp, *Immortality and Salvation in Indian Religions*, (trans. E.F.J. Payne), Calcutta: Sushil Gupta Pvt., Ltd., 1963, p. 50.

146. McDermott, *Buddhist Concept of Kamma*, p. 69.

147. Richard F. Gombrich, *Theravada Buddhism: A Social History from Ancient Benaras to Modern Colombo*, London: Routledge and Kegan Paul, 1988, p. 66.

148. *The Book of Gradual Sayings*, I, p. 185.
149. Ibid., p. 186.
150. Ibid.
151. Ibid., p. 187.
152. For details of this method see: ibid., pp. 187ff.
153. 'Some sabbath-keeper here thus reflects: tomorrow I shall eat such and such food, both hard and soft. And he spends the day engrossed in covetous desire. Such Visākha is the herdsman's sabbath' (ibid., p. 186).
154. See *Dialogues of the Buddha*, I, p. 74.
155. According to scholars like B.J. Bhaskar and others, the four vows of Pārśvanātha were revised by Nāṭaputta, who found it imperative to delink 'abstention from sexual conduct' as a vow separate from *parigraha (*abstinence from worldly attachment). Probably Nāṭaputta was compelled to specify it as a separate vow in order to underline its significance in view of the moral laxity he may have observed among laity. It has been thus argued that the Buddhists were unaware of such modifications (see, Bhaskar, op. cit., pp. 94-5).
156. 'Thus, Lord, does the Unclothed Nāṭa's Son, teach doctrine to his followers: "Whosoever slayeth living creature...taketh what is not given, whosoever acts wrongly in respect of sensual passion, whosoever tell lies—all such go to the Woeful Lot, to Purgatory."' (*The Book of Kindred Sayings*, IV, pp. 223-4).
157. *The Book of Gradual Sayings*, III. p. 199.
158. It was a lifelong vow to restrict one's mundane activities in all directions from well-known objects.
159. Another indirect reference to such a vow is found in the *Pātika Sūtta* (*Dīgha Nikāya* no. 24), which mentions that the Buddha met at Vaiśālī a certain ascetic named Kandaramasuka, who maintained seven life-long vows, namely: (i) nudity, (ii) chastity, (iii) maintaining by spirituous drink and flesh-eating, (iv) never going beyond certain directions, etc. We notice that all these, except the third one represent Jaina vows (see *Dialogues of the Buddha*, III, p. 14).
160. *The Book of Gradual Sayings*, I, p. 186.
161. In the commentary on the *Brahmajāla Sūtta* (*Dīgha Nikāya, Sūtta* no. I), Buddhaghoṣa quite dubiously ascribes the philosophies like Annihilationism and Eternalism to Nāṭaputta. According to him they were taught by Nāṭaputta to his two pupils prior to his

death (commentary on *Dīgha Nikāya*, II, pp. 906-7, cited in Bhaskar, op. cit., p. 173). However, this account of Buddhaghoṣa cannot be accepted as true, as pointed out by Bhaskar (ibid.). Rudiments of *anekāntavāda* can nevertheless be traced to the Buddhist approach to answer a question in Pali literature, which describes four ways: (a) categorical reply, (b) analytical reply, (c) reply by counter question, and (d) evading a question (for details see *The Book of Gradual Sayings*, I, pp. 178-9).

162. *The Book of Gradual Sayings*, I, pp. 171-2.
163. See Hajime Nakamura, *Comparative History of Ideas*, Delhi: Motilal Banarsidass, 1992 (1st pub., London: Kegan Paul International, 1975), p. 232; K.N. Jayatilleke, *Early Buddhist Theory of Knowledge*, Delhi: Motilal Banarsidass, 1980 (rpt., 1st pub., London: George Allen and Unwin, 1975), p. 356.
164. Similar view as the second one has been expressed by Jayatilleke (op. cit.), albeit in a different context and we have a taken a cue from him.
165. 'The Jaina *syādvāda* appear to be the opposite to the Sceptics', when faced with similar epistemological problem. The Sceptics doubted all logical possibilities, whereas the Jainas asserted their partial truthfulness in some way or the other.
166. Paul Dundas, *The Jainas*, London: Routledge and Kegan Paul, 1992, p. 199.
167. *Middle Length Sayings*, I, p. 285 (a similar reference occur at *Middle Length Sayings*, II, p. 41).
168. Bhaskar, op. cit., p. 202. In our opinion it merely points to self-contradiction in a person's statement. And self-contradiction was probably not a feature of *syādvāda*. It does not point to the ambivalent attitude, which was a prominent feature of *syādvāda*. Moreover, whatever apparent self-contradiction appear in it, can be explained by taking cognisance of the fact that it sought to express the nature of entities and worldly realities, as they were. The variations in nature of such different realities interpreted differently often made them appear contradictory. It should not be forgotten that *syādvāda* asserted that all theories are true in some respect or the other. Hence such acknowledgement of partial truth made certain possibilities appear running parallel to each other, which were construed as contradictions.
169. Initially he was an upholder of *ucchedavāda*, and probably

belonged to Sanjaya's school of thought. Later he converted to the fold of *Nigaṇṭhas* before joining the Buddha's Order.

170. *Majjhima Nikāya*, I, p. 498.
171. See *Middle Length Sayings*, I, pp. 39, 61-2, 281.
172. *Middle Length Sayings*, I, p. 280.
173. Ibid., p. 281.
174. 'I will refute the words of the recluse Gotama on this point of controversy ... will I, speech by speech, tug the recluse Gotama forward, tug him backwards...' (*Middle Length Sayings*, II, p. 39).
175. A.L Basham, *History and Doctrine of the Ājīvika: A Vanished Indian Religion*, Delhi: Motilal Banarsidass, 1980 (1st pub. London: Luzac & Co., 1951).
176. The Ājīvikas have left no written Scripture of theirs. Hence their image could be constructed by piecing together their references found in other religious texts. Since our study is confined to the *Nikāyas* it is difficult to construct their wholesome image.
177. Basham, op. cit., pp. 96-7.
178. Jayatilleke, *Theory of Knowledge*, p. 140.
179. It is noteworthy that had we taken the last, i.e. the *Khuddaka Nikāya* into consideration then perhaps we could have got a better and more comprehensive picture; in the *Jātakas* we have references to their penance, immorality, their *sabhās*, etc.
180. *Dialogues of the Buddha*, I, pp. 223ff.
181. *Middle Length Sayings*, II, pp. 292-3. (*Majjhima Nikāya*, I, p. 238).
182. Kamta P. Jain in a paper ('The Jaina References in the Buddhist Literature', *Indian Historical Quarterly*, vol. II, 1926, pp. 698-702) cogently argues that these practices refer to the Jaina ascetics. His basic objection is to the fact that the word *acelakas* was used for a general category of ascetics and not exclusively for the Ājīvikas, and more importantly nudity and vegetarianism were characteristics of the Nigaṇṭhas. The Ājīvikas at this juncture were not at all strict vegetarians. For details see ibid., pp. 698-700.
183. *Middle Length Sayings*, I, pp. 103-4 (*Majjhima Nikāya*, I, p. 77).
184. B.M. Barua, 'The *Ājīvikas*', *Journal of the Department of Letters* (Calcutta University), vol. 2, 1920, pp. 1-80. Cited in Basham, op. cit., p. 111.
185. *Middle Length Sayings*, I, p. 293.
186. 'Now and then they eat very good solid food, partake very good

soft food, savour very good savourings, drink very good drinks. They build up their bodily strength with these, make their bodies grow and become fat' (ibid.).

187. *Middle Length Sayings*, II, p. 161.
188. Ibid.
189. 'Although I, Vaccha, recollect ninety-one eons, I do not know of any Naked Ascetic who attained Heaven, except one; and he professed *Kamma*, he professed operative *Kamma*' (ibid.).
190. Operative *kamma* is described in the *Majjhima Nikāya* (*Sūtta* no. 136) as a deed of strong ethical force that bears its fruit as expected.
191. Basham, op. cit, p. 135.
192. *The Book of Kindred Sayings*, I, pp. 29, 265.)
193. Basham, op. cit., p. 55.
194. Several passages in the *Nikāya*s show that the populace held those who practised austerities and self-mortification as worthy of respect, honour and gifts (*dāna*)
195. I.B. Horner, *The Early Buddhist Theory of Man Perfected*, Delhi: Oriental Books Reprint, 1979 (1st pub. London: Routledge and Kegan Paul, 1936), pp. 87-8.
196. They were called 'Wanderers' because except during the monsoon they spent their time wandering in different regions and directions. They probably never settled down into an organized monastic order. Expounding their religio-philosophical viewpoints they entered into debates and discussions upon meeting learned men and religious teachers.
197. *Dialogues of the Buddha* I, pp. 244 ff; *Middle Length Sayings*, II, pp. 162 ff; *The Book of Gradual Sayings*, V. pp. 133-7, etc.
198. *Dialogues of the Buddha*, II, pp. 162 ff.
199. *Middle Length Sayings*, II, pp. 159 ff, etc.
200. Ibid., pp. 203 ff.
201. *The Book of Kindred Sayings*, II, pp. 14-19.
202. Ibid., pp. 84-92; *The Book of Kindred Sayings*, IV, pp. 276 ff, etc.
203. *The Book of Kindred Sayings*, III, pp. 202 ff.
204. *The Book of Kindred Sayings*, IV, pp. 154 ff, 170 ff, 279 ff; *The Book of Gradual Sayings*, V. pp. 252 ff, etc.
205. *The Book of Kindred Sayings*, IV, pp. 170 ff; *The Book of Kindred Sayings*, V, pp. 10-11, 22-3, 60-3. etc.
206. *The Book of Gradual Sayings*, IV, pp. 245-7, etc.

207. *Dialogues of the Buddha*, I, pp. 223 ff; *The Book of Gradual Sayings*, I, pp. 271-5; *The Book of Gradual Sayings*, V, pp. 130-2, etc.
208. *The Book of Gradual Sayings*, II, pp. 182-4, etc.
209. *Cūlasihanāda Sūtta* (*Middle Length Sayings*, I, pp. 85-90), *Mahādukkhakkhanda Sūtta* (*Middle Length Sayings*, I, pp. 110 ff), etc.
210. *The Book of Gradual Sayings*, I, p. 220.
211. Ibid.
212. Ibid.
213. Ibid., pp. 220-1.
214. 'Here in a monk is moral, he has abandoned immorality, from that he is aloof. He has right view, he has abandoned wrong view, from that he is aloof. He has destroyed the *asavas* ... from that he is aloof. Now in these three sorts of aloofness, this monk is called 'one who has reached perfection' (ibid.).
215. *The Book of Kindred Sayings*, II, p. 84
216. Ibid.
217. Ibid., p. 85.
218. B.G. Gokhale, *New Light on Early Buddhism*, Bombay: Popular Prakashan, 1994, p. 1. He primarily sees an attitude of disinterest among the Early Buddhists towards history and alludes it to the Buddhist philosophy of impermanence, *dukkha* and *anatta*. However, he subsequently sees a paradox as reflected in their pronounced historical outlook connected with the Buddha's life (ibid., p. 2).
219. *Middle Length Sayings*, II, p. 181. For the wanderers reviling the Buddhists, also see: *The Book of Kindred Sayings*, III. p. 93; *The Book of Kindred Sayings*, IV. pp. 269 f).
220. Ibid., n. 2.
221. *Middle Length Sayings*, II, p. 54.
222. Ibid.
223. *Dialogues of the Buddha,* III, pp. 11-12.

## REFERENCES

*Primary Sources*

*Anguttara Nikaya*, ed. R. Morris & E Hardy., 5 vols., London: PTS, 1885-1900. Trans. F.L. Woodward & E.M. Hare., *The Book of Gradual Sayings,* 5 vols., PTS translation series, vols., 22, 24-7,

London: Luzac & Co., 1951-5 (1st pub., OUP for PTS, London, 1932-6.)

*Digha Nikaya*, ed. T.W. Rhys-Davids and J.E. Carpenter, 3 vols., London: PTS, 1890-1911. Trans. T.W. Rhys-Davids & C.A.F. Rhys-Davids., *Dialogues of the Buddha*, 3 vols. SBB, vols. 2-4, PTS, Oxford UniversityPress, London, 1899-1921 (rpt. London: Luzac & Co., 1971-3).

*Majjhima Nikaya*, ed. V. Trenckner and R. Chalmers, 3 vols., London: PTS, 1888-99 (rpt. 1948-51). Trans. R. Chalmers, *Further Dialogues of the Buddha*, 2 vols., London: PTS, 1888 (rpt. 1926-7); I.B. Horner, *The Middle Length Sayings,* 3 vols., PTS, Translation series nos. 29-31, London: PTS, Luzac & Co., 1954-9.

*Samyutta Nikaya,* ed. L. Feer, 6 vols., London: PTS, 1884-1904. Trans. C.A.F. Rhys-Davids & F.L. Woodward., *The Book of Kindred Sayings or Grouped Suttas.,* 5 vols. PTS, Translation series, nos. 7, 10, 13, 14, 16, London: Oxford UniversityPress, 1917-30 (rpt. London: Luzac & Co., 1950-6).

*Vinaya Pitaka,* ed. H. Oldenberg, 5 vols., London: PTS, 1879-83. Trans. T.W. Rhys-Davids and H. Oldenberg, *The Vinaya Texts,* 3 vols., SBE, vols. 13, 17, 20, Oxford, 1881-5 (rpt. Delhi: Motilal Banarsidass, 1975); I.B. Horner, *The Book of Discipline,* 6 vols, SBB, nos. 10-14, 20 and 25, London: Luzac & Co., 1938-66.

## *Secondary Works*

Amore, R. Clayton. 1970. 'The Concept and Practice of Doing Merit in Early Theravāda Buddhism', Ph.D. thesis, Columbia: University of Columbia.

Barua, B.M. 1920. 'The *Ājīvikas*'. *Journal of the Department of Letters* (Calcutta University), vol. 2: 1-80.

Basham, A.L 1980. *History and Doctrine of the Ājīvika: A Vanished Indian Religion*, Delhi: Motilal Banarsidass (1st pub. London: Luzac & Co., 1951).

Bhaskar, B. Jain. 1972. *Jainism in Buddhist Literature*, Nagpur: Aloka Prakashan.

Bollee, W.B. 1974. 'Buddhists and Buddhism in the Earlier Literature of the Svetambara Jains', in L.S. Cousins et al. (eds.), *Buddhist Studies in Honour of Ms. I.B. Horner*: 27-39, Reidel: Dordrecht.

Bougle, C. 1971. *Essays on the Caste System* (trans. D.F. Pocock), Cambridge: Cambridge University Press.

Chakravarti, Uma. 1983. 'Renouncer and Householder in Early Buddhism'. *Social Analysis: The International Journal of Anthropology*, no. 13: 70–83.

_____. 1987. *Social Dimensions of Early Buddhism*, New Delhi: Oxford University Press.

Chandra, P. 1983. 'Buddhism as an Instrument of Social Change', in Madhu Sen (ed.), *Studies in Religion and Change*, Delhi: Books & Books.

Deshpande, Madhav M. 1979. *Sociolinguistic Attitudes in India: An Historical Reconstruction*, Ann Arbor: Karoma Publications.

_____. 1993. *Sanskrit and Prakrit: Sociolinguistic Issue*, Delhi: Motilal Banarsidass.

Dewey, John. 1960. *The Quest for Certainty* (Gifford Lectures, 1929), 4th impression, New York: Capricorn Books.

Dundas, Paul. 1992. *The Jainas*, London: Routledge and Kegan Paul.

Glasenapp, H. von. 1963. *Immortality and Salvation in Indian Religions*, (trans. E.F.J. Payne), Calcutta: Sushil Gupta Pvt., Ltd.

Gokhale, B.G. 1965. 'Early Buddhist Elite'. *Journal of Indian History*, vol. 43: 391-402.

_____. 1970. 'Brahmanas in the Early Buddhist Literature', *Journal of Indian History*, vol. 48 (4): 51-61.

_____. 1980. 'Early Buddhism and the Brahmanas', in A.K. Narain (ed.), *Studies in History of Buddhism*: 67–80, Delhi: B.R. Publishing. Co.

_____. 1994. *New Light on Early Buddhism*, Bombay: Popular Prakashan.

Gombrich, Richard F. 1975. 'Buddhist Karma and Social Control'. *Comparative Studies in Society and History*, vol. 17: 212–20.

_____. 1988. *Theravada Buddhism: A Social History from Ancient Benaras to Modern Colombo*, London: Routledge and Kegan Paul.

Hirakawa, A. 1993. *A History of Indian Buddhism- from Sakyamumi to Early Mahayana* (trans. & ed. Paul Groner) Delhi: Motilal Banarsidass (1st pub. Hawaii: Univ. of Hawaii Press, 1990, Buddhist Tradition series, no. 19).

Horner, I.B. 1979. *The Early Buddhist Theory of Man Perfected*, Delhi: Oriental Books Reprint, 1979 (1st pub. London: Routledge and Kegan Paul).

Jain, Kamta P. 1926. 'The Jaina References in the Buddhist Literature'. *Indian Historical Quarterly*, vol. II: 698–702.

Jaini, Padmanabh S. 1974. 'On the *Sarvajñatva* (Omniscience) of Mahavira and the Buddha', in L. Cousins et al. (eds.), *Buddhist Studies in Honour of I.B. Horner*: 71-90. Dordrecht: Reidel & Co.

———. 1983. 'Karma and the Problem of Rebirth in Jainism', in Wendy D. O' Flaherty (ed.), *Karma and Rebirth in Classical Indian Tradition*: 219-38. Delhi: Motilal Banarsidass (1st pub., California: University of California Press, 1980).

Jayatilleke, K.N. 1980. *Early Buddhist Theory of Knowledge*, Delhi: Motilal Banarsidass. (rpt., 1st pub., London: George Allen and Unwin, 1975).

Kalupahana, David J. 1976. *Buddhist Philosophy*, Honolulu: University of Hawaii Press.

Krishan, Y. 1986. 'Buddhism and the Caste System'. *Journal of the International Association of Buddhist Studies*, vol. 9(1): 71-83.

Masefield, Peter. 1986. *Divine Revelation in Pali Buddhism*, London: George Allen & Unwin.

McDermott, James P. 1983. 'Karma and Rebirth in Early Buddhism', in Wendy D. O' Flaherty (ed.), *Karma and Rebirth in Classical Indian Tradition*: 173-9. Delhi: Motilal Banarsidass. (1st pub., California: University of California Press, 1980).

———. 1984. *Development in Early Buddhist Concept of Kamma/Karma*, Delhi: Munshiram Manoharlal.

Nakamura, Hajime. 1992. *Comparative History of Ideas*, Delhi: Motilal Banarsidass (1st pub., London: Kegan Paul International, 1975).

Norman, K.R. 1991. 'Theravāda Buddhism and Brahmanical Hinduism: Brahmanical Terms in Hindu Guise', in T. Skorupski (ed.), *Buddhist Forum*, vol. II: 193-200. (Seminar Papers, 1988-90, School of Oriental and African Studies, University of London), Delhi: Heritage Publishers.

Rhys-Davids, C.A.F. 1934. 'The Relation Between Early Buddhism and Brahmanism'. *Indian Historical Quarterly*, vol. X, 1934: 274-87.

Wagle, Narendra. 1966. *Society at the Time of Buddha*, Bombay: Popular Prakashan.

———. 1968. 'Minor Rites and Rituals Attributed to the *Brāhmaṇas* in the *Nikāya* Texts of the Pali Canon'. *Journal of the Oriental Institute of Baroda*, vol. 17(4): 63-72.

CHAPTER 2

# *Cakrasaṃvara Tantra*, Subjugation of Maheśvara and Oḍra

## Understanding Buddhist-Brahmanical Religious Equations in Early Medieval Odisha

UMAKANTA MISHRA

This article attempts to understand the interreligious equations between the Brahmanical religions and Buddhism in the early medieval period by analysing the myth of the taming of Maheśvara in the two Vajrayāna texts, namely the *Sarvatathāgata-tattvasaṃgraha* and *Cakrasaṃvara Tantra.* The latter text, while describing the theme of the surrender of Maheśvara to the Buddhist deity Cakrasaṃvara/Heruka, describes the origin of 64 *Bhairava*s created by Maheśvara in his fight with Cakrasaṃvara. Three of the 24 Bhairavas created by Lord Śiva were located in Odisha. Juxtaposing this theme with the religious landscape of early medieval Odisha and literary traditions on interreligious equations, the present paper explores the hostile interdependency between Buddhism and Śaiva-Śākta religion in Odisha from the seventh century to the fourteenth century CE.

### Subjugation of Maheśvara in *Yoga Tantra* of *Tattvasaṃgraha*

Myths perform various functions in religious traditions. The most commonly employed Mantrayāna myth, however, is developed from various sections of the *Sarvatathāgata-tattvasaṃgraha*, *The Summary of All Tathāgatas Reality* (abr. *Tattvasaṃgraha*), codified in the early eighth century. Traditionally, the text is understood as the complex interweaving of myths and rituals, all under the directorship of the cosmic Buddha, Vairocana. Of particular interest are Chapters 1, 6, and the epilogue of this text. Chapter 1 deals with the culmination of the career of the Bodhisattva Sarvārthasiddhi. He had reached the zenith of his spiritual quest to attain supreme awakening and had proceeded to the tree of awakening. All the Buddhas then appeared to him and broke the news that he cannot achieve his goal through his current level of *samādhi* (concentration); he needed the consecrations (*abhiśeka*) obtained by the contemplations transforming his body, speech, and mind into adamant (*vajra*). He then attained the adamantine status and, accordingly, became the Buddha Vajradhātu, with all the rights and privileges pertaining thereto. Subsequently, he followed all the *Tathāgata*s back to the Adamantine Jeweled Palace (*vajramaṇiratnakūṭāgāre*) at the summit of Mt. Sumeru, to take his rightful place. The text of the *Tattvasaṃgraha* discusses the rituals and mystic circles (*maṇḍala*) focussing on enlightenment and concludes, some twenty-six chapters later, with Vajradhātu turning the wheel of dharma and returning to the tree of awakening to perform the acts of the Buddha in accordance with the worldly understanding of the Buddha's progress. Most importantly, Chapter 6 introduces what was to become perhaps the most influential myth of esoteric Buddhism—the subjugation of Śiva (Maheśvara).

As described in Chapter 6 of *Tattvasaṃgraha*, all the *Tathāgata*s requested the Bodhisattva Vajrapāṇi, the master of mysteries, to produce the divinities of his clan (*kula*) for the *maṇḍala* on the peak of Mt. Sumeru. Vajrapāṇi, however, declined, saying that there yet existed 'criminals', such as Maheśvara and other gods. So Vairocana uttered the *mantra* '*oṃ suṃbha nisuṃbha huṃ... vajra huṃ phaṭ*' and forms of Vajrapāṇi issued forth from the hearts of all the assembled *Tathāgata*s, coming together to create the body of Mahāvajrakrodha. Vairocana intoned the *mantra* '*huṃ ṭakki jjaḥ*', which is known as the disciplinary *ankuśa* (goad) of all the Tathāgatas. By this utterance, the 'criminals', Maheśvara and the like, were all dragged to the Adamantine Jeweled Palace on Mt. Sumeru. Vajrapāṇi then commanded them to accomplish the Buddha's teaching by taking refuge in the Buddha, Dharma, and the Saṅgha, and by obtaining the spiritual mysteries of omniscience. But Maheśvara replied to Vajrapāṇi, 'Hey, you're just a local spirit (Yakṣa); I am the creator and arranger of the triple worlds, the master of all spirits, the God of gods. Why should I do as you, a local ghost, command?' So Maheśvara turned to Vairocana, 'Just who does he think he is, giving orders to God?' Vairocana responded, 'I'd do what he says, friend, and go for the refuges! Don't make Vajrapāṇi, this cruel, mean, angry spirit, destroy the whole world with his flaming *vajra*.'

Maheśvara, however, decided to show Vajrapāṇi what fear was, so he displayed his great wrath and cruelty in the form of Mahābhairava, flames spurting out of him, accompanied by Mahāraudra's laughter, together with all of his minions: 'Hey, I'm the Lord of the triple worlds! You shall do what I command!' They then exchanged more mutual challenges and insults and Vajrapāṇi returned to Vairocana. 'Well, Lord, he's not paying homage to the teaching, being God and all. Now what do I do?' Again Vairocana intoned the *mantra* '*oṃ śuṁbha niśuṁbha huṁ phaṭ*', and Vajrapāṇi added his own adamantine '*huṁ*'. Immediately, all the gods, including Maheśvara, fell down on their faces, uttering a cry of pain, and went for refuge to Lord Vajrapāṇi. Maheśvara alone remained fallen on the ground, unconscious, and there he perished. Vairocana lectured the other gods about the virtues of the Buddhist perspective and they became entirely restored, happy and virtuous. Then Vairocana addressed Vajrapāṇi: 'If we revive His deadness, he could become a real person.' So Vajrapāṇi intoned the correct *vajrayuh* and Maheśvara was immediately brought back to life.

### *Subjugation of Maheśvara by Heruka in* Cakrasaṃvara Tantra

The above myth of *Sarvatathāgatatattvasaṃgraha* (seventh century CE) of subduing of Maheśvara by Vajrapāṇi was repeated later in Chapter 41 of the *Yoginītantra* of *Cakrasaṃvara* (tenth century

CE) where Heruka subdues Maheśvara. As Ronald Davidson says, 'Maheśvara occupies the place of Māra of early Buddhism in the Mantrayāna tradition' (Davidson 1991: 202). In the *Cakrasaṃvara Tantra,* Heruka imitates the system of the opponents in order to destroy them. In the story of imitation and destruction of Maheśvara and his system lies the story of the adaptation of Śaiva practices and an attempt by the Buddhists to make their religion more *laukika* and attractive at the expense of Śaiva-Śākta system. Cakrasaṃvara's story is quite interesting because it refers to Oḍra, Kaliṅga and Kośala as the place of emanation of the Bhairavas created by Maheśvara to rule different parts of Jambudvīpa while he was in deep embrace with Umā on mount Kailāśa. The story runs thus. At the beginning of this *Kali Yuga* there was mutual slaughter and blood bath; out of the blood clouds developed from the cloud, rain came; the rainwater led to the rise of eight rivers and ... then, to the south of Sumeru, in the continent of Jambūdvīpa, Maheśvara's emanation arose. Thereafter arose 24 self-originated places from which 24 ferocious Bhairavas arose. Out of these 24 Bhairavas, one appeared in Oḍra ( in north coastal Odisha), one in Kalinga (southern Odisha) and one in Kośala (western Odisha). Following the emanation of these 24 Bhairavas and their consorts, Mahādeva arose on the peak of Mt. Sumeru, having four heads, twelve arms, fully naked, black in complexion, with his hair tied up in matted locks and body smeared with ashes. His consort, Umā Devī, was with one face and two arms, and they were in a sexual union. In conjunction with Maheśvara, his four Umās and eight Mātṛkās emanated. As a shrine *(caitya)* for each of these Bhairavas, Maheśvara gave them 24 *lingaṃas* in the form of self-produced stones. Once established in Jambūdvīpa, Maheśvara and his minions began to conduct themselves in a most irregular manner. For food, they ate human flesh and drank human blood. They made ornaments out of human bones—circlets, earrings, necklaces, bracelets, and belts—all smeared with the ashes of human bones. From human hair, they wove their Brahmanical threads and fashioned garlands of human skulls. Now, in order to bring them under control, the 'causal form of Vajradhāra—the experiential body (*saṁbhogakāyā*) in Akaniṣtha heaven—manifested sixty-two varieties of the Emanated Bodies (*nirmāṇakāyā*) as of Vajradhara.' In opposition to Maheśvara and Umā Devī emerged Heruka and his consort. The story goes on to repeat the subduing of Maheśvara by Heruka. Thus, the *Cakrasaṃvara Tantra* talks of the replacement of Maheśvara-Umā *maṇḍala* by the Buddhist *maṇḍala* of Heruka-Vajravarāhī.

In this story of origin and subduing of Maheśvara in the *Cakrasaṃvara Tantra,* lies the story of competition between the Śaiva-Kāpālikas and Mantrayāna Buddhism. Heruka replaced Maheśvara as the result of Śaiva-Kāpālikas' antinomian behaviour, such as the making of ornaments of human bones. The myth, on the one hand, represents subordinate integration of the Śaiva elements as Maheśvara and 24 Bhairavas find a place in the Buddhist scheme of things, including Śiva and Umā (Kālarātri), who find a place under the feet of Heruka. It seems that *Cakrasaṃvara Tantra* was produced in a setting where there was a strong Śaiva presence. The myth illustrates the state of hostile interdependency between Śaivism and Buddhism and vice versa, where elements of the Śaivas, such as the iconographic forms of Śiva, were borrowed by the Buddhists. This hostile interdependency also occurred in a contested space. For example, the *Saṃvara Maṇḍala* which Heruka created, replaced the Maheśvra *Maṇḍala*. Both are in Mt. Sumeru on which Kailaśa is located. The adaptation of the Śaiva forms and rituals by Heruka led to the blurring of lines in some contested spaces. One can cite the example of Nepal *Maṇḍala* in which there are deities such as Guheśvarī and Mahākāla, whose Buddhist or Śaiva associations are difficult to trace. In Odisha too, there is such blurring of lines between Buddhist and Śaiva divinities as in the case of Mahākāla of Ratnagiri and Vajravarāhī/Varāhī at Ajodhya in Balasore district of Odisha where the divinities are considered to be both Buddhists and Śaivas.

The *Cakrasaṃvara Tantra's* claim of the subduing of Maheśvara by Heruka may be an allusion to the Buddhist attempt to dominate at the expense of the Śaiva Kāpalika. The victory of the Buddhists over the Śaiva order has been represented in the iconography of many Buddhist divinities from Odisha, such as Heruka, Vajrahunkāra and Saṁvara, who have been represented trampling upon Bhairava and Rati. Jajpur was the capital of Oḍradeśa or Utkaladeśa in the seventh-eighth century CE, and the *Cakrasaṃvara Tantra*'s reference to the emanation of Maheśvara and Bhairavas in Oḍra, Kaliṅga and Kośala refers to the expansion of Śaivism in Odisha by eighth century CE. The subduing of Maheśvara and Bhairavas by Cakrasaṃvara is a reference to Buddhist attempts to compete with an expanding Saivism by making numerous innovations in Mantrayāna Buddhism.

## Buddhist-Śaiva Animosities in Early Medieval Odisha: Buddhist Sculptural Evidence

The Buddhist adaptation of Śaiva-Śākta order—*maṇḍalas*, initiation rituals for kings, protection rituals, and incorporation of folk and autochthonous elements into Buddhism—made Buddhism more *laukika* (laity-oriented). *Maṇḍala* sculptures, *dhāraṇīs* and temples dominated the Buddhist landscape of Odisha, but the Śaiva-Śākta order had already expanded considerably by ninth-tenth century Odisha. The Śaiva-Śākta order with its Purāṇic and tantric mixture, has its locus in temples and monasteries (*maṭhas*), with a dedicated group of ascetic tradition (Pāśupatas and Kāpālikas) and for many other innovations which have been outlined by Sanderson, became quite salient in the religious landscape of early medieval Odisha (Sanderson 2007). This is amply attested by the existing temples, sculptures and epigraphic data from Odisha of the sixth and tenth centuries CE. On the other hand, the Buddhist adaptation and integration of Śaiva practices provided an opportunity for the Śaivas to make inroads into the Buddhist establishments of Odisha. At the Buddhist site of Ratnagiri, we find Śivaliṅgas and Śaiva-Śākta divinities such as Gaṇeśa and Mahiṣamardinī Durgā. The precise date at which the Brahmanical pantheon began to enter the Buddhist sites of the Jajpur district cannot be ascertained with certainity but on the iconographic styles, these deities belong to the ninth century CE. The process may have started earlier. This is indicated by an analysis of sculptural data from some important Buddhist monastic sites. An early iconic repre-sentation of Viṣṇu, dated eighth century CE, has been reported from the Buddhist monastic site of Lalitgiri. Similarly, a sculpture of Mahiṣamardinī Durgā, datable to the late eighth century CE, has been reported from the monastic site of Udayagiri.

The expansion of Śaiva-Śākta order and the Buddhist attempts to appropriate, adapt and integrate Śaiva-Śākta elements—while simultaneously portraying the Śaiva divinities in an inferior light, often being trampled upon by Buddhist divinities—resulted in animosities. These animosities between the two started in the late eighth century CE but gained greater prominence from the tenth century onwards when Somavaṃśis united coastal Odisha with Western Odisha by defeating the Bhaumakaras and shifted their capital from Vinitapura (Sonepur) to Jajpur, which was renamed as Yayātinagara in the name of its ruler Yayāti I (922-55 CE). Unlike the Bhaumakaras, who patronized all religions, the Somavaṁśis were strong Śaivites. They are credited with the resurgence of Śaivism-Vaiṣṇavism in Jajpur. Yayāti Keśari was credited with the famous *yajñas* on the bank of river Vaitaraṇī in Jajpur to which he invited 10,000 Brāhmaṇas from Kanauj. He constructed many temples, including an auspicious pillar which symbolized his victory over Buddhism.

Iconography offers glimpses of this conflict in Jajpur and other regions in Odisha. Sculptures 'on the ground' were an active participant in the ongoing social life of its communities (Davis 1997: 263) and reflect social processes. The conflicts between Buddhism and the Śaiva-Śākta order are represented in numerous sculptures from Odisha. From the ninth century onward, Buddhist sites innovated many fierce deities of *Yoginī tantras,* often depicted trampling on Bhairavas and Kālarātri (Figs. 2.1 and 2.2). Mention may be made of Saṃvara of Ratnagiri, Vajrahunkāra from Achyutarajpur hoard in Puri district and

Figs. 2.1 & 2.2: Saṃvara from Ratnagiri and Vajrahunkāra from Achyutarajpur trampling on Bhairava and Kālarātri, Puri District, tenth century CE. *Source:* Photograph by the author.

several other images such as Heruka and Yamāri from Ratnagiri, Udayagiri. Debala Mitra, in her commentary on the Vajrahunkāra image from Achyutarajpur, suggests that the image was deliberately designed and created with a specific purpose. It is pertinent to quote her:

> It appears that the Buddhists of this establishment being apprehensive of the mustering strength of the followers of the Brahamanical cults, particularly Śaiva and Śākta ... installed the icon, a flagrant example of ill-feeling towards the Brahmanical faith, with the object of combating with the all absorbing forces of Brahmanism which was apparently in the ascendancy and of drawing the people to the Buddhist fold by showing the impotence of the Brahamanical deities under the feet of the Buddhist god. The overcoming power of this two-armed Buddhist deity is emphasized in a dramatic way by the depictions of the scattered weapons of the muti-armed Brahmanical gods and goddess (Mitra 1978: 84-5).

Another sculpture reflecting this animosity is found in Buhalo in the Nischintkoili block in the Chitroptola River Valley

Fig. 2.3: Buddha in *bhūmisparśamudrā*, Fakirpatna, Buhalo, *c.* 10th–11th centuries CE. On the dexter, Brahmanical deities Śiva, Viṣṇu, Indra, and Brahmā are depicted in *tarjanīmudrā*, symbolizing an attack on Buddha; on the sinister, these deities are depicted in *vandanāvinayīmudrā*, symbolizing their acknowledgment of Buddha's authority. *Source:* T.E. Donaldson, 2001.

of the Cuttack district. This image depicts Buddha in *bhūmisparśamudrā,* flanked by Maitreya and Avalokiteśvara (Fig. 2.3). He is framed by a trefoil-shaped *haṃsa* or swan) *toraṇa* (arch) with a miniature *rekha deula* at the apex. The four Brahmanical gods—Indra, Brahmā, Viṣṇu and Śiva—are represented as four *māras* or evil forces. Twice on the upper right half, the principal set of hands displays *añjaḷimudrā*, as prescribed in the *Dharmdhātuvāgīśvara maṇḍala* of the *Niṣpannayogāvalī* byAbhayākaragupta, implying that they are paying homage to the victorious Buddha (Bhattacharyya 1972: 65). The frontage of *Viśvapadma* is marked by a Vajra. This dramatic sculptural representation, as described in the *Dharmadhātuvāgīśvaramaṇḍala,* signifies the degree of subordinate integration of Brahmanical divinities and their subordinate position within the Buddhist pantheon structure.

## Śaiva Animosities towards Buddhism: Sculptural and Literary Evidence

The Brahmanical texts of Odisha also refer to the growing conflict between the followers of Buddhism and Śaivism. The *Ekāmra Purāṇa*, a Śaiva *Sthalamahātmya* on Bhubaneswar dated to the thirteenth century CE, describes a fierce war waged by Śiva against the *asuras* on the banks of river Gandhavatī for control over *Ekāmra*-Bhubaneswar. The Gandhavatī River corresponds to the modern Gangua stream, which flows through Bhubaneswar. Hiraṇyākṣa, the demon king, advised by his guru Śukrācārya, attempted to stop the yajña that the *devatās* intended to perform on the river bank.

At first, the *asuras* succeeded in defeating the *devatās*. However, Śiva's intervention ultimately led to the defeat of Hiraṇyākṣa (*Ekāmra Purāṇa* 1986: 211). K.C. Panigrahi, a scholar renowned for his unbiased judgement of historical and religious facts, supported by his deep knowledge of Brahmanical traditions, observed that the *devāsurasangrāma* at Ekāmaravana mirrored 'a conflict between the Śaivas and the Buddhists'. As a Śaiva text, it preferred to label the Buddhists as *asuras* and the followers of Śiva as *devatās*. This process reflects the Śaiva attempt to establish dominance over Bhubaneswar at the expense of Buddhism. K.C. Panigrahi refers to numerous pieces of evidence demonstrating such transitions. Bhāskareśvara *liṅgam*, is, in fact, according to Panigrahi, an Aśokan pillar that was converted to a Śaiva *liṅgam* during the eighth to ninth century CE (Panigrahi 1986: 310 ).

The *Dharmapūjā-vidhāna*, a thirteenth-century text, refers to the *sadharmis* and the Buddhists of the Jajpur region of Odisha who are said to have been persecuted by the Brāhmaṇas (Bhattacharyya 1994: 334). The *Caitanya Bhāgavata* composed by Iśwara Dasa towards the end of the sixteenth century, records tradition as to how Anangabhīmadeva sided with Brahmins and clubbed to death 32 Buddhists when they failed to satisfy him in answering a test (Panigrahi 1986: 312). The Somavaṁśī king, Yayāti II opposed Buddhism and killed 616 Buddhists (Mukherjee

1940: 53 ). The *Madalāpāñji* (a Jagannātha Temple chronicle of sixteenth century) records a similar story of the persecution of the Buddhists by Madana Mahādeva, who is represented in the text as a brother of Codagangadeva (Mohanty 2001: 17). The text states that Buddhists lived in 84 hills and caves of Odisha, such as in Aragarh, Dhauli, etc. There was once a wager between the queen and the king regarding the level of knowledge of Buddhists and Brahmins. The queen sided with the Buddhist monks while the king considered the Brahmins to be more knowledgeable. In the ensuing test, Brahmins proved victorious. Thereafter, the king ordered the beheading of the Buddhist monks. The Buddhist monks fled their *kandara* (caves and hills) and went to the forest. In the *Bhakti Bhāgavata* of Kavi Dinḍima Jivadeva, it is stated that Brahmin Bhāvadeva, who was the family priest of Somavaṁśī King Udyotakeśari, lifted the world when it was submerged in the ocean of *tantras* (Panigrahi 1986: 312).

The sculptures of the period also reflect this conflict between the *Śaiva*s and Buddhists. One instance of this conflict is the representation of the Buddha in the sacrificial *yūpa* just outside the entrance of the Śaiva-Kāpālika Vaitāla Temple (Fig. 2.4),

Fig. 2.4: Stele with Buddha used as sacrifice post by Kāpālikas, Vaitāla Temple, eighth century CE. *Source:* Photograph by the author.

dated eighth century. Outside the temple, just in front of the entrance to the *Jagamohana* (porch), there is a worn out, reworked Buddhist sculpture serving as the base of a *yūpa* (the socket on the top was made to insert another stone on a wooden figure) testifying to the sacrifices offered to Goddess Cāmuṇḍā. Through an analysis of textual sources, K.C. Panigrahi has shown that the Cāmuṇḍā of the Vaitāla deul, was originally a shrine of the *kāpālika*s. Its name is derived from the *vetāla*s or spirits with the help of which they attained their *siddhi*s (Panigrahi 1961: 234-5). This sacrificial *yūpa* symbolizes the sacrifice of the Buddha at the hands of *kāpālika*s, thereby representing the ongoing conflicts between the Śaiva-Buddha traditions.

The connection between the sacrificial *yūpa* and the representation of Bhairava and Goddess Cāmuṇḍā aspect have been discovered in Odisha, in which Bhairava and Cāmuṇḍā are shown standing/sitting on a corpse resembling the Buddha – such as elongated ears and curly hair (Fig. 2.5). The elongated

Fig. 2.5: Cāmuṇḍā sitting on a corpse. With elongated ears and curly hair, the corpse looks like a Buddha figure, Trilocaneśvara Temple, Jajpur, eighth-ninth century CE.
*Source:* Photograph by the author.

ears and curly hair are associated with the sculptural representation of the Buddha in Odisha. Is there a connection between the sacrificial *yūpa* with Buddha representation and Cāmuṇḍā or Bhairava standing on corpses, whose hair and ears resemble the representation of the Buddha? The *Ekāmra Purāṇa* assigns a role to Pārvatī, who in the *Ekāmravana* kills the demons Kirti and Vāsa, who wanted to enjoy her. Pārvatī in her Cāmuṇḍā aspect and Śiva in his Bhairava aspect emerged as the embodiment of battlefield. The *Agni Purāṇa* provides a number of impressive innovations to address Cāmuṇḍā in order to obtain victory in the battle. In the *Kālikā Purāṇa,* she is worshipped with bloody rituals during the new moon night of autumn.

In another mode of representing the corpse, he is shown as a dead warrior, as shown in certain cases by the short sword in the sheath that he wears slipped onto his waist belt. In some cases, as in a late tenth-century stele from Devagrāma in Balasore district, the dead man is depicted as a richly clothed person wearing a necklace and bracelets, easily identifiable as a tribal *rājā*. There are steles from Odisha and Bihar where Bhairava is represented trampling on shaven heads or the head of the Buddha (Verardi 2011: 286-7). Such instances are used by Verardi to argue that the Śaiva assertion during the Somavaṁśī period, from the middle of the tenth century CE onwards, was marked by Śaiva opposition to not only common Buddhists but also to local *rājās* of tribal origin. These *rajās* resisted the persecution of Buddhists by the kings of the Somavaṁśī dynasty. They also resisted the political domination of the Somavaṁśī rulers. The arrival of Brāhmaṇas as owners of agricultural land, as reflected in the Yayāti tradition of 10,000 Brahmins brought from Kannauj to Jajpur, led to clashes between the new Brahmin settlers and the old local *rājā*s who were owners of lands. The Bhairava and Cāmuṇḍā sculptures of Odisha, which show Bhairava/ Cāmuṇḍā sitting on the corpse of the local *rājā*s, may indicate the usurpation of land of the local Buddhist *rājā*s of tribal origin and the status that Buddhism enjoyed in the Bhaumakara period.

## Vaiṣṇava Domination over Buddhism: Import of Gayāsura Myth of the *Vāyu Purāṇa* to Jajpur in the Fourteenth Century

The Somavaṃśī period (tenth-eleventh century) saw the assertion of the Śaiva-Śākta tradition and the growing animosities between the Buddhists and Śaiva-Śāktas. The mutual borrowing and adaptation gave way to open display of antagonism in Jajpur region. The *Kapila Saṁhitā (*composed in the thirteenth century*)* and *Ekāmra Purāṇa* (fourteenth-fifteenth century) also refer to the gradual expansion of Śaiva-Śākta tradition in the Jajpur region. Kṣetra *Mahtāmya* refers to Śaiva centres Khilāteśvara, Varuṇeśvara and Beleśvara forming the three vertices of the inverted triangle of Virajā Kṣetra.[1] Explorations have revealed the presence of tenth-eleventh-century Ūmā-Maheśvara images at Beleśvara and Khilāteśvara, coming up on the Buddhist ruins. Images of Heruka and other Buddhist gods are found along the ruins of the Khilāteśvara Temple. In the Jajpur region, many Śaiva establishments such as Mukteśvara, Trilocaneśvara, and Akhandaleśvara temples came up also during the period. Śaivism also expanded to the tribal-dominated Keonjhar area during the period. Moreover, the *Kapila Saṁhitā* for the first time refers to the Nābhi Gayā tradition. In the fourth century CE at least, the fact that the Pāṇḍavas performed *śrāddha* on the bank of the Vaitraraṇī River in the Virajā Kṣetra points out the earlier origin of Jajpur as a centre for performing *śrāddha* rituals for the dead. But, for the first time, the *Kapila Saṁhitā* brought in the *Vāyu Purāṇa* theme of the Nābhi Gayā. As described in the *Vāyu Purāṇa*, Gayāsura's head touched the Kolāhala hill in Gayā, his navel touched Virajā Kṣetra and his feet touched the Mahendra mountain in Piṣṭapuram in the south. Gadādhara Viṣṇu tried to keep him still with his mace.[2] In return for this great sacrifice, his wish was to be remembered as *pitṛ tīrtha*. In this way, *trigayā* (three Gayās) originated. The *Virajākṣetramahtāmya* of the *Brahmāṇḍa Purāṇa* repeats the same story: 'To the north-east of the Virajā is situated the Nāvi Gayā. Those who offer *piṇḍa* to their ancestors here ... release twenty-one generations of their ancestors from hell (*Virajākṣetramahtāmya*, 25.11). The Gadādhara image of Viṣṇu is found affixed to the western inner wall of the Nābhi Gayā (ibid.).

The composition of the *Kapila Saṁhitā* is ascribed to the thirteenth century and the *Virajākṣetramahtāmya* to the fourteenth century. At what time did the Vaiṣṇava theme of Nābhi Gayā appear in Jajpur? In our view, starting with the Yayāti II in the latter half of the tenth century, Vaiṣṇavism began to gain ground in Jajpur. The antiquity of Viṣṇu worship in Jajpur is much earlier and dated to early seventh century CE, but from the tenth century CE onwards, Viṣṇu images proliferated in the Jajpur region. The theme of Nābhi Gayā entered Jajpur in this period of Vaiṣṇava expansion and domination. Further, the fame of Jajpur as a centre for performing rituals for the dead is older, but what is new in the religious landscape of Jajpur in the twelfth century is the tradition of Nābhi Gayā, a tradition which attempted to place it on equal footing with Gayā in Magadha. We are not limited by historical questions concerning the antiquities of the Buddhist Bodh Gayā *versus* Viṣṇupāda Gayā.[3] What is important to understand is the context of the emergence of Vaiṣṇava theme of Nābhi Gayā in Jajpur. This occurred in twelfth-thirteenth century in the period shortly before the composition of *Kapila Saṁhitā* when the Vaiṣṇava order emerged as the most important cult with the active patronage of Jagannātha of Puri as a form of Viṣṇu by the ruling Ganga dynasty from the twelfth century onwards.

## Kandarāsura Myth: Allusion to Śaiva Domination over Buddhism

Another myth which is found in the undivided Cuttack district, where Buddhism had quite a substantive presence, was the myth of the killing of the demon Kandarāsura by Lord Balabhadra. It is worth mentioning that Balabhadra is considered a form of Śiva, and the killing of Kandarasura is a case of Śaiva domination.

The *Tulaṣi kṣetra Māhātmya,* which presents the glory of Kendrapara, named after Kanadarāsura, states that the demon lived near Lalitagiri—Alatigiri and was the destroyer of yajñas (sacrifices), was ruling over the area surrounding Lalitagiri and Assia mountain ranges. In fact kandarā means small hillocks. The Madalāpāñji, the temple chronicle of the Jagannath Temple of Odisha, to which allusion has already been made in connection with the Buddhist persecution by Ganga King Madana Mahādeva, refers to the fact that the Buddhists of Odisha were living in 84 *gumhā* (caves) and kandarās (hillocks) and fled to forest as the king beheaded and persecuted them. The *Sthala Māhātmaya, Tulaṣi kṣetra Māhātmya* states that Lord Balabhadra defeated him in a fight at Lalitgiri and as a result of which he left the place, went to Kapilas mountain which was a prominent Śaiva centre during the Ganga period. Lord Balabhadra thoroughly searched every nook and corner of the hill. Balabhadra killed the demon Kandarāsura in a fight and threw his slain body all over nearby places by cutting it into pieces. The scattered body was believed to have fallen at Asureswar, Balagaṇḍi, Kamar Khandi, Navi Khaṇḍa. These places are named after the head, body part (Ganḍi of Aswa) waist (Kamar-Khaṇḍa) and navel (piece of Nāvī) of the demon Kandarāsura respectively. It is also believed that the Śiva temples of Swapneswar at Kantia, Lankeśwara of Gualisingh, Bileswar of Kagal were founded by Baladeva over the face, neck and waist of the demon respectively (Kendraparā). According to his name, the place name 'Kandaraparā' or 'Kendrapara' has been derived. This myth has a striking similarity with the Gayāsura myth of the *Vāyu Purāṇa* and *Brahmāṇḍa Purāṇa* where Gayāsura was a cultural allegory of superimposition of Vaiṣṇavism over Buddhism. The Kandarāsura myth, with its allusion to Lalitagiri, an important Buddhist centre as the seat of demon Kandarā is a similar allegory of the domination of Saivism over Buddhism. The area where the slain parts of *Asura* fell of became important Śaiva centres. There were many Buddhist centres such as Brahmāvana, Fakirpatna and others which existed in the belt where Kandarasura myth was quite popular.

## Cult of Jagannātha as *Rāṣṭradevatā* and Jagannātha as Buddha

The emergence of Jagannātha under the Anantavarman Coḍagangadeva in early twelfth century and subsequent declaration of the Ganga kings as merely the *rāuta* (servant) of the *rāṣṭradevatā*, Jagannātha, who is the real ruler of Utkaladeśa (Odisha), marked a decisive shift in its religious landscape. Jagannātha, who is regarded as a form of Viṣṇu emerged as the most important cult of Odisha by the thirteenth century. Most likely, it was during this period of Vaiṣṇava assertion that the Vaiṣṇava theme of Nābhi Gayā entered to Jajpur. The Vaiṣṇavas also made inroads to *Ekāmrakṣetra* by constructing the Ananta Vāsudeva Temple in the thirteenth century under the active patronage of the Ganga kings and queens. For the first time, Vaiṣṇava temple in the form of Ananta Vāsudeva came up in the long evolution of Bhubaneswar as a Śaiva *Kṣetra*. *Ekāmra Purāṇa* and *Ekāmra Candrikā* prescribe for visiting the Vaiṣṇava shrine of Ananta Vāsudeva first before obeisance to the central shrine of *Ekāmra Kṣetra* i.e. Liṅgarāja (*Ekāmra Candrikā* 1995: 3).

The emergence of Nābhi Gayā tradition and expansion of Vaiṣṇava order in Jajpur, the patronage of Vaiṣṇava Jagannātha as the state cult under the Gangas and Gajapatis from twelfth century onwards, the construction of Ananta Vāsudeva Temple by the Ganga queen in the last quarter of the thirteenth century marking the inroads of Vaiṣṇavism into the Śaiva centre of Ekāmra were marked by not only the decline of Buddhist centres in Odisha but the identification of Buddha with Jagannātha. Many Vaiṣṇava poets of Odisha of fifteenth-sixteenth centuries equated Jagannātha with Buddha. Saralā Dāsa, the Śūdra poet who composed Odia *Mahābhārata* in the fifteenth century, gives a curious account of the origin of the Buddha image. According to the Odia*Mahābhārata*, Kṛṣṇa's dead body was thrown into the sea near Dwārakā. It came floating to Puri and remained in the custody of the Śavara tribe for some time to become later mysteriously a tree out of which a stature was carved in the form of Buddha; this being the incarnation of Viṣṇu which follows immediately that of Kṛṣṇa. Saralā Dāsa in many of his verses in the Odia *Mahābhārata* equates Buddha with Jagannātha.[4] Jagannātha replaced Buddha as the ninth *avatāra* of Viṣṇu in the *dasāvatāra* panel painting found inside the *Jagamohana* (porch) of the Puri-Jagannātha temple. G.C. Tripathi argues that both Buddhism and Jagannātha cult existed beyond the pale of Purāṇic Hinduism and therefore, it was easy to dislodge the heterodox Buddha by Jagannātha:

> The Buddha incarnation came here handy, as it stood outside the pale of Brahmanism but still loosely connected with it and further, the iconography of the different forms of Buddha was not so well known to Hindus that they would have hesitated to accept his identity. Besides, this was the incarnation of Viṣṇu which could have been most easily dislodged for the sake of Jagannātha from the classical scheme of the incarnation since it was not so firmly established in Hinduism (Tripathi 1978: 477-90).

There were two trends at work in Odisha during the period from the thirteenth to the fifteenth century CE. The decline of Buddhism was followed by the identification of Jagannātha with Buddha. Secondly, there was evidence of the taking over of the Buddhist establishments by Śaiva ones. The pattern is also visible in the Buddhist establishments of Ratnagiri and Udayagiri of Jajpur district. In Ratnagiri, a Śaiva temple called Vajra Mahākāla temple was constructed in the thirteenth century. The presiding deity is the Buddhist god Mahākāla, but he is being worshipped as a form of Śiva. *Vajra Mahākāla vrata* is observed in the locality on the bright fortnight of the month of *Kārtik* (November), considered to be a special day of Lord Śiva. Similarly, Vajra Mahākāla Temple and Śaiva monastic establishment came up in Udayagiri, coming as they are on the ruins of the Buddhist establishment. In Jajpur, many Śaiva establishments came up on the ruins of the Buddhist establishments in twefth century CE. The Buddhist establishment of Solampur was now reconfigured in the new Purāṇic narrative of *Virajākṣetramāhātmya* as the starting point of the pilgrimage of *Virajā Kṣetra*. Any devotee who is interested to go round the pilgrimage of the *Virajā Kṣetra*, should start the pilgrimage on the 14th day of the new moon of Vaiśākha or Māgha month (April and January respectively) by taking a dip in the *tīrtha-dvāra* (gateway) which is located to the east of the Varāha temple on the northern bank of river Vaitraraṇī. Verse 21 of Chapter 4 of the *Virajākṣetramāhātmya* elaborates that the pilgrim should go to the goddess Santeśvarī and worships her after taking a dip at *tīrtha dvāra*. Goddess Santeśvari is still worshipped as the *Iṣṭadevī* (presiding goddess) of the village Solampur. Thus, the village Solampur was reconstituted as part of the pilgrimage field of *Virajā Kṣetra*. Buddhism thus finally ended in Odisha with Śaiva and Vaiṣṇava take over. The process seems to have ended in the fourteenth century when Vajramahākāla Temple was constructed at Ratnagiri. In the next century Buddha was identified as Jagannātha in the regional tradition of Odisha.

## Conclusion

This paper shows how myths provide important clues to understanding the historical processes of the past. The myth of the subjugation of Maheśvara in the *Cakrasaṃvara Tantra* was an allusion to the hostile interdependency between Saivism and Buddhism and vice versa. Other myths such as the Gayāsura myth of the *Vāyu Purāṇa* and the *Brahmāṇḍa Purāṇa* and Kandarāsura myth are cultural allusion to the superimposition of Vaisnavism and Savism respectively on Buddhism in the early medieval Odishan context. Juxtaposed with the literary and sculptural evidence from medieval Odisha, these myths reflect the ascendancy of Saivism and Cult of Jaganānth at the expense of Buddhism whereas Buddhism had tried subordinate integration of Śiva.

## NOTES

1. '*Santi bhagavantaḥ satvāḥ maheśvarā diduṣṭasatvā, ye yuṣmābhirapi sarvatathāgatairavineyāḥ, teṣāṃ mayā kathaṃ pratipattavyam!*' // Chapter 6 of *Tattvasaṃgraha*.

2 Subhakarasimha, who studied in Ratnagiri Mahāvihārā of Odisha took *Mahāvairocana Sūtra* and *Sarvatathāgatatattvasaṁgraha* to China (Yamamoto 1990).

3. The subduing of Maheśvara in the Buddhist text of *Cakrasaṃvara Tantra* is dealt in by Ronald Davidson and David Gray (Davidson 1991: 197-235; Gray 2007: 495-8).

4. This episode of subjugation of Maheśvara has been dealt with by David Gray. See Gray (2007).

5. Coastal Odisha was known as Utkala and Oḍra deśa in seventh-eighth century CE. This is known from two inscriptions of Somadatta issued in his 15th and 19th regnal years. He was ruling over northern Odisha as a rāgnal (chief) in seventh century CE. See *EI* XXIII: 202 and Rajaguru, *OHRJ*, vol. XI, no 4, 226.

6. According to Chapter 41 of the *Cakrasaṃvara Tantra*, the 24 Bhairavas occupied 24 sites out of which three are Kaliṅga, Odra and Kosala, indicating the strong Śaiva Bhairava-Kāpālika presence in Odisha. This is borne from archaeological evidence of the strong presence of Śaivism in early medieval Odisha. The 24 sacred sites listed in CST, ch. 41. The twenty-four places are divided into ten different categories, The first circle which is associated with cittacakra of the Cakrasamvara to Chapter, consists of the following sites: Pitha: 1. Pulliramalaya, 2. Jālandhara, 3. Oḍḍiyāna 4. Arbuda; Upapiṭha: 5. Godvari 6. Rāmeśvarī 7. Devikoṭī 8. Mālava. The second circle, corresponding to the earth and the vākcakra, are kṣetra: 1. Kāmarūpa, 2. Oḍra, upakṣetra 3. Triśakuni, 4. Kośala. Chandoha: 5. Kaliṅga, 6. Lampaka Upachandoha: 7. Kāñcī, 8. Himālaya. The third circle which corresponds to the underworld and the Kāyacakra, are melāpaka 1. Pretapuri, 2. Gṛhadevatā, upamelaka: 3. Saurāṣṭra 4. Suvarnadvipa, śmaśāna: 5. Nāgara, 6. Sindhu; upśmaśāna: 7. Maru 8. Kulūṭa (Gray).

7. Verses 39-40 of chapter 3 of the *Virajakṣetramāhātmya* state that the Virajā Kṣetra extends up to 5 *kosas* (one *kosa* is 2 miles) is located Khilateśvara, on the south Varuneśvara and on the western vertice of the inverted triangle of Virajā Kṣetra is located the Beleśvra Temple. Khilateśvara (also pronounced as Kilalateśvara) is located on the bank of Kalindi river in the Alinagar village of Bhadrak district whereas Belesvara is located 5 km away from the Jajpur town near Kampagaḍa.

8. *Akrāntamdaityamjaṭharamdharmeṇa virajādriṇa Nabhikūpasamipetū-*

*devīyāvirajāsthitā/tatrapiṇḍādikrtsaptakulanuddharatenarah/ Mahendragiriṇātasyapādausuniscalaau*...(*Vāyu Purāṇa*, II, 44.85-6).

9. Both the *Gayāmahātmya* and *Virajākṣetramāhātmya* state that both the *Kṣetras* extend up to 5 *koṣas*.
10. '*Boloi Jagannātha Nilagiribasi/Bauddharupe/Nilakandarechantiisi.// (Madhya Parva); DvāparaJugeśeṣare Deva Jagannātah/Bauddha-rupare Bije Karibe je ethi// (Sabhā Parva); Balabhadra Subhadra o Krṣṇatinirupa/Baudharupareheleemantasvarūpa// (Vāna Parva); Jaya Nilādrivihārī he Jagannātha/Bauddharupe Kaliyugeahimebikhyāta.// Kaliyugerahibakukichidinaiccha/Bauddhāvatāraenisceviharibu.//*' (Sāralā Dāsa's Odiā *Mahābhārata* (Reproduced from Tripathi 1978: 479)

## REFERENCES


Bhattacharyya, B. (1967 rpt.) (ed.). *The GuhyasamājaTantra or Tathāgataguhyaka,* Gaikwad Oriental Series 53, Baroda: Gaikwad Oriental Institute.

Chandra, Lokesh (ed). *Sarvatathāgatatattvasamgraha*, Satapitaka Series, New Delhi: IAIC.

Davidson, Ronald. 1991. 'Reflections on the Maheśvara Subjugation Myth, Indie Materials, Sa-skya-pa Apologetics, and the Birth of Heruka', *The Journal of the International Association of Buddhist Studies*, vol. 14, no. 2, 197-235

Donaldson, T.E. 2001. *Iconography of the Buddhist Sculptures of Orissa*, 2 vols., Delhi: IGNCA/Aryan Books.

*Ekāmra Purāṇam*. 1986. Ed. U.N. Dhal, Delhi: Nag Publishers.

Eschmann, A., H. Kulke and G.C. Tripathi (eds). 1978. *The Cult of Jagannath and the Regional Tradition of Odisha*, New Delhi: Manohar.

Gellner, D.N. 1996. *Monk, Householder, and Tantric Priest-Newar Buddhism and Its Hierarchy of Rituals*, New Delhi: Cambridge University Press.

Giebel, R.L. 2005.tr. *The Vairocanābhisambodhi Sūtra*, Berkeley: Numata Center for Buddhist Translation and Research.

Gray, David. 2007. The *Cakrasaṁvara Tantra: A Study and an Annotated Translation*, American Institute of Buddhist Studies: Columbia University.

*Kapila Samhitā*. 2005. Edited by Pramila Mishra. Delhi, New Bharatiya Book Corporation

Kinnard, J.N. 2000. 'The Polyvalent Pādas of Viṣṇu and the Buddha'. *History of Religions*, vol. 40(1), 32-57.

Krag, U.T. 2011. 'Appropriation and Assertion of the Female Self: Materials for the Study of the Female Tantric Master Laksmi of Uddiyana', *Journal of Feminist Studies in Religion* 27(2): 85-108.

*Madalāpāñji* (ed. Artaballav Mohanty). 2001, 1st pub. 1932, Bhubaneswar: Odisha Sahitya Akademi.

Mayer, Robert 1998. 'The Figure of Maheśvara/ Rudra in the rNin-ma-Pa Tantric Tradition', *International Association of Buddhist Studies*, vol. 21.2: 271-310.

Mukherjee, Prabhat. 1940. *The History of Medieval Vaisnavism in Orissa*, Calcutta: R. Chatterjee.

*Vāyu Purāṇa*, Annotated and translated by G.V. Tagare, Delhi: Motilal Banarsidass, 1987

Verardi, G. 2011. *Hardships and Downfall of Buddhism in India*, Delhi: Manohar.

*Virajākṣetramāhātmya* (*The Glory that was Virajā kṣetra*). 1984. ed. U.N. Dhal, Delhi: Nag Publishers.

Weinberger, Steven Neal (2003). 'The Significance of Yoga Tantra and the Compendium of Principles (TattvasaṃgrahaTantra) within Tantric Buddhism in India and Tibet'. PhD dissertation, University of Virginia: Department of Religious Studies.

# PART II

# ENCOUNTERS WITH ISLAM AND ISLAMIC POWERS IN MEDIEVAL INDIA

CHAPTER 3

# Representations of the Ghurids in a Twelfth Century Sanskrit Mahākāvya

## A Contextual Analysis of the *Pṛthvīrāja Vijaya*

JAY VARDHAN SINGH

## Preliminary Insights

The interaction between Islam and Hinduism has a long history, dating back to the end of the seventh century CE. It was trade that led to the first interaction, albeit an indirect one, between these two cultures. But with the expansion of Arab power in the East, especially after the Sassanids' fall (CE 651), these two cultures, for the first time, came into direct contact. This was the period of the seventh century. The Rashidun Caliphate (CE 632-61), had destroyed the last remnants of the once-great Sassanid Empire (CE 224-651), and now the Caliphate came in direct contact with the Indian cultural sphere. It were the regions of Afghanistan and parts of Central Asia which were part of the Indian cultural sphere during the seventh century CE that first came into direct contact with Islamic culture.[1] The seventh century was also the phase when the Caliphate armies tried to make inroads into the Indian subcontinent. With the arrival of the Ummayads (CE 661-750), the Arabs were successfully able to establish their ruler in the bordering regions, especially Sindh. But in the heart of the Indian subcontinent, apart from some raids, no significant inroads were made in the eighth or ninth century. It was only with the establishment of the Turkic power in Afghanistan in the tenth century that we see that, for the first time, significant inroads were made deep into the subcontinent, and the Islamic rule expanded eastwards. The process culminated around the end of the twelfth century when the armies of Shihāb al-Dīn Ghūrī were able to successfully establish their rule over large parts of northern India. Thus, from the Arab conquest of the Sindh to the establishment of the Delhi Sultanate, the interaction that happened between the two cultures was a complex one. One way to understand this multi-layered interaction would be to analyse how these two cultures depicted each other in their texts. In the literary tradition of both cultures, we see that this interaction has been recorded. In the Arabic literary sources, India was described as *Al-Hind*, and the people of *Al-Hind* were called *Hindus*.[2] In the Sanskrit literary sources, not only we find the use of different terms to denote Muslims in general, but there are also qualities, both negative and positive, that are ascribed to them. The present study aims to understand the perception of the Muslims through how the Ghurids are depicted in a twelfth century Sanskrit text: *Pṛthvīrāja Vijaya*.

## About the Text

*Pṛthvīrāja Vijaya* belongs to the Sanskrit Mahākāvya tradition, and because of it, the Sanskrit that is used in this text is ornate. The text tells us about the achievements and glories of the Chauhāna kings of Ajmer, but the special focus is on Pṛthvīrāja III, who is popularly known as Pṛthvīrāja Chauhāna. The present text which we have was first discovered by German Indologist Georg Bühler in 1876 in Kashmir. The original manuscript was in *Śāradā* script. However, its condition when it was found was poor. It was damaged in some places, and the last pages of the manuscript are not available.[3] Thus, the text only has twelve cantos available. On reading the twelfth canto, it is clear that this is not the last canto. From what survives, it is extremely difficult to say how many cantos were part of the complete text. Even the cantos that survive are not complete. In some cantos, there are missing verses, and as we move towards the twelfth canto, the number of these missing verses increases.[4]

The question of who was the author of the text is also somewhat debated. Generally, it is believed that Jayānaka, a Kashmiri poet, authored this text. This assertion is based on the fact that Jayānaka is himself mentioned in the text.[5] The dating of the text is also a matter of debate. Although there is no agreement on when the text was composed, it is believed that the text was composed between CE 1191 and 1193.[6] One reason behind this assertion has to do with the title itself. The title of the text—*Pṛthvīrāja Vijaya*—suggests that the text was composed to celebrate a great victory of the Chauhāna king Pṛthvīrāja III. This victory, according to Cynthia Talbot, was the famous victory of Pṛthvīrāja III over Shihāb al-Dīn Ghūrī in the First Battle of Tarain.[7] Since the battle took place in CE 1191 and the Second Battle of Tarain took place in CE 1192[8] suggests that the text was composed during the interval between the first and the second battle.[9] Chandra Prabha[10] and Sheldon Pollock[11] are also of the opinion that the text was composed between CE 1191 and 1193. But Audrey Truschke rejects this dating and believes that the text was written after the Second Battle of Tarain in the late 1190s.[12] She argues that the interval between the two battles of Tarain 'leaves a rather narrow window in which Jayānaka is supposed to have written his robust poem.'[13] This, in our view, is not a substantive argument to argue that the text was written in the later 1190s.

## *Pṛthvīrāja Vijaya* and the Debates Surrounding Identity Formation

Since *Pṛthvīrāja Vijaya* is one of the earliest Sanskrit *Mahākāvyas* where Muslims are depicted, the text has been analysed by some scholars to understand how the Muslims were perceived by a certain section of the society in twelfth-century northern India. One such scholar is Sheldon Pollock.[14] In his analysis, Pollock argues that *Pṛthvīrāja Vijaya* was written at a particular moment in Indian history when *Rāmāyaṇa* had moved away from literary discourse and occupied an important place in the political discourse. As per him, it was between the eleventh and fourteenth century CE in western and central India that *Rāmāyaṇa* came into the 'public political discourse.' Pollock believes that the reasons behind the transition of *Rāmāyaṇa* from a literary sphere to the 'public political discourse' were mainly two. First, during this period, i.e. between the eleventh to the fourteenth century CE, those who were the makers of elite culture, realized what value *Rāmāyaṇa* as a text had to offer to the kingship of this period in the process of legitimization. Second, this was also the period which saw, for the first time, the emergence of an 'Other' that could not be assimilated into the broader Indian culture, or it was thought that they could not be assimilated into the broader Indian culture. For Pollock, this 'Other' was the Muslims and it was their imagined or real unassimilable 'quality' that exposed them to the 'demonising formulation' that *Rāmāyaṇa* provided. According to Pollock, before the twelfth century, Rāma cult was not present in the cultural milieu of India. There existed representations in the form of sculptures which depicted different scenes from the *Rāmāyaṇa*, but Rāma cult was not there. It was only in the twelfth century, and because of the historical events that are associated with this period, mainly the establishment of Muslim power in the Indian subcontinent, we see that the Rāma cult became popular in India. Pollock opines that the use of *Rāmāyaṇa* in the political sphere and the emergence of the Rāma cult, which can be seen in both textual and epigraphical sources, was a reaction against the encounter of the Indian powers during this period with the polities of Central Asia and later the Indo-Muslim power that established their base in India. For Pollock, *Pṛthvīrāja Vijaya* is a text where this paradigm can be seen fully developed. Brajadulal Chattopadhyaya rejects this view of Pollock. According to Chattopadhyaya, 'there were different ways of making comparisons' and a comprehensive analysis of both literary and epigraphical sources of this period would reveal that imagining the kings as Rāma and his adversaries, in the case of *Pṛthvīrāja Vijaya*—Ghurids, as demons are one of the many ways through which the image of a king was constructed.[15] Audrey Truschke has also analysed how the Ghurids are represented in *Pṛthvīrāja Vijaya.*[16] For Truschke, the Ghurid representation in the text should not be seen through the lens of 'us' and 'them'. The way Ghurids are represented, Truschke argues, is not very different from how other political opponents of Pṛthvīrāja are perceived.

## Ghurid Representation in *Pṛthvīrāja Vijaya*

Through a comprehensive analysis of how the Ghurids are represented in *Pṛthvīrāja Vijaya*, the present study will try to challenge some of the assertions that the abovementioned scholars make. Since the text was composed during a period when the Chauhāna rulers were fighting against the Ghurids, the Ghurids enjoy a central role in the narrative of *Pṛthvīrāja Vijaya* as the foremost adversary of Pṛthvīrāja. Even the terms that are used to denote Ghurids in general are also diverse. On the one hand, we have familiar terms like *turuṣka* and *mleccha*, but less common terms like *mātaṅga*, *janaṅgama* and *pulinda* are used in the text for the Ghurids. These terms are generally used in Sanskrit literature to denote outcastes. Apart from these general terms, the term *gori* appears in the text, but it is not used for a single person but instead used to describe the Ghurids as a whole.[17] The later Ghaznavid ruler is also mentioned, but he is not named. He is just called the 'Lord of Horses' (*hayapati*).[18]

The term *mleccha*, which appears in *Pṛthvīrāja Vijaya*, is the most common term used in Indian tradition for outsiders. The term appears for the first time in a later Vedic text—*Śatapatha Brāhmaṇa*—where it is used to describe someone whose speech was impure.[19] Aloka Parasher has argued that during the time when the early Dharmaśāstras were being written, the meaning of the term was broadened. The inability to pronounce Sanskrit as a quality of the *mlecchas* was kept, but now it also included those who did not follow the *varṇāśramadharma*.[20] According to B.D. Chattopadhyaya, *mleccha* as a category provided a 'timelessness', i.e. what was essential in considering someone as *mleccha* was whether these groups were outside the *varṇāśrama-dharma* or not. Chattopadhyaya believes that it is this reason why we see that old terms like *mleccha* are used for the Muslims in texts like *Pṛthvīrāja Vijaya*. Not only the terms but, in Chattopadhyaya's opinion, the qualities that were assigned to the 'early' *mlecchas* were now being assigned to the Muslims who now became the 'new' *mlecchas*. These *mlecchas*, whether 'old' or 'new', were regarded as a threat to the Brahmanical social order. This was the case with early Brahmanical texts, and it is also true for the early medieval Sanskrit texts like *Pṛthvīrāja Vijaya* as well. To buttress his argument, Chattopadhyaya argues that Sanskrit sources like *Pṛthvīrāja Vijaya* could have used the term *musalamāna* for the Muslims. The use of this term would have shown that these early medieval Sanskrit sources were concerned about religious differences. But that is not what we see being used in *Pṛthvīrāja Vijaya* or other Sanskrit texts of the early Medieval period. The Muslims in the Sanskrit sources are portrayed as a group that is ethnically different and belongs to a different land. This description is similar to how the early texts described Indo-Greeks, Indo-Scythians or Indo-Parthians. The use of generic terms like *mleccha* was another way the Sanskrit texts tried to show how the Muslims do not follow the same social order, i.e. *varṇāśramadharma*. Thus, in Chattopadhyaya's analysis, the description of the attack on temples and beef-eating, which are attributed to Muslims, was not a display of 'xenophobia' or a way to religiously differentiate the Muslims; instead, these descriptions were used to show how the *varṇāśramadharma* was under attack. As per Chattopadhyaya, these Sanskrit sources do not attempt to highlight the religious or territorial differences of the Muslims.[21]

Although it is true that *Pṛthvīrāja Vijaya* does not talk about the religion of the Ghurids or the later Ghaznavids, the way the Ghurids especially are represented in the text does suggest that there existed a major difference between how the early 'outsiders' were perceived and how the Muslims are being perceived. The qualities and the actions that are ascribed to these Ghurids in

*Pṛthvīrāja Vijaya* suggest that the author of the text was not just concerned about the attack on the social order.

Broadly, the description of Muslims in *Pṛthvīrāja Vijaya* can be classified into two categories. On the one hand, the text has a certain sense of awe for the Ghurids and, to a lesser extent, for the Later Ghaznavids, especially regarding the military strength of their armies. On the other hand, Ghurids are viewed as inherently impure. This negative attitude towards the Ghurids is based on their diet and their practice of destroying and desecrating sacred places and temples.

In *Pṛthvīrāja Vijaya*, the military strength of both the Ghurids and the later Ghaznavid is highlighted, and there is a sense of awe that can be seen regarding it. The Turkic armies are described as having plenty of horses.[22] The later Ghaznavid ruler, who is not named in this text, is described as *hayapati*. We are also told that 'the Lord of Horses, the ruler of *Garjani* [Ghazni], is supreme amongst the kings of north-west who are as powerful as the wind.'[23] In the next verse, we are told that 'this Lord of the Horses was defeated and lost his kingdom of Ghazni to the evil Ghoris'. Then the verse goes on to tell us that 'the *Gori* strove to become Eclipse itself, to darken the royal fortune of the entire circle of Kings'.[24] This *Gori* was no other than Shihāb al-Dīn Ghūrī. The fact that he is described in such a way in *Pṛthvīrāja Vijaya* suggests that the military might of Shihāb al-Dīn was well appreciated. Apart from associating horses with the Turkic armies, the text also describes the *turuṣkas* as wearing heavy metal armour.[25] This is an important detail because, generally, it is believed that the Turkic armies were only equipped with light-armed cavalry or mounted archers. But this was not the case. Although light-armed cavalry was an important part of Turkic armies, but these armies also employed heavy cavalry as well. These heavily armoured troops were tasked to charge at the enemy infantry and break their lines. How important the cavalry was for the Turkic armies can be seen from the fact that when Bakhtiyār Khalajī conquered Bengal, the coins which were issued depict a Turkic cavalryman.[26]

As mentioned above, the text also provides negative descriptions of the Ghurids. These descriptions are based on their diet, especially the fact that they ate beef, desecrated temples and how they were inherently impure.

In *Pṛthvīrāja Vijaya*, there are multiple representations where the Ghurids are described as beef-eaters. Even the name Ghurids is itself Sanskritized to mean 'enemy of the cows'. A verse tells us that 'the name *gori* is given to the Ghurids because they are the enemies of the cows'.[27] In other words, because they eat beef, they are considered the enemy of the cows. The same verse also describes them as 'eating foul foods'. The text also mentions the arrival of a Ghurid ambassador to the court of Pṛthvīrāja III.[28] One verse describes him as bald with a broad forehead, and we are told that this was intentionally done by God as if to inscribe on it a large number of cows he had slain.[29]

The text also talks about the practice of temple desecration. It begins by describing the sacredness of the pond of Puṣkara, and this sacred pond, we are told, is under the control of the *Mātaṅgas*.[30] There is no evidence to suggest that the region of Puṣkara ever came under the control of the Ghurids during the time of Pṛthvīrāja III. But one could argue that these descriptions are memories of early Muslim raids in which Puṣkara became a target. One verse mentions that the *mlecchas* are destroying the sacred temples of Puṣkara.[31] The text tells us that the actions of the *mlecchas* were not restricted to destruction alone. There are multiple references that describe the different acts of desecration of the sacred pond of Puṣkara. One verse describes how the *mātaṅga mlecchas* have taken captive *vipras* (Brahmins) at the sacred pond of Puṣkara, and now, because of their tears, the Puṣkara region has become warm.[32] It is also mentioned that 'because of the evil deeds that are being done by the *mlecchas* at the sacred pond of Puṣkar, these *mlecchas* will now get the *avīci* hell not only in their afterlife but while living as well.'[33]

The reference to *mlecchas* as being impure often appears in *Pṛthvīrāja Vijaya*. In the first canto itself, the text describes how the sacredness of Puṣkara is being destroyed because now it is controlled by the inherently impure *mlecchas*. One verse uses the term *janaṅgama* alongside *mleccha*.[34] This term *janaṅgama* means *caṇḍāla*, i.e. those who are outcastes. The verse tells us that 'these *janaṅgama mlecchas* are polluting the sacred waters of Puṣkara by throwing their waste into it. A different verse describes how, in the waters of Puṣkara, where even the *apasarās* did not bathe, now the menstruating *mleccha* women are bathing and desecrating the sacred waters of Puṣkara.[35] This depiction of desecrating the sacred waters of Puṣkara pond appears often in the text. At one instance, we are told that 'once the *devās* used to drink the sacred waters of Puṣkara pond, but now this sacred water is being used for bathing the carts, horses and camels of the *mlecchas*'.[36] The next verse uses the term *pulinda* instead of *mleccha*, and we are told that 'once where [in Puṣkara] *saptarṣī* used to make *pāyasa* from the milk of Kāmadhenu at that very place where now the *pulindas* are cooking fishes that were caught from the sacred pond of Puṣkara'.[37] The term *pulinda,* in early texts, is associated with outcaste tribes and is generally used alongside *mlecchas*.[38] All of these references about the sacredness of Puṣkara and how it is being desecrated appear in the first canto. As it is mentioned earlier, these descriptions do not describe any historical events. But these imageries of the desecration of Puṣkara do have a purpose. The text uses it to establish the reason for the coming of the Cāhamāna, the mythical person from whom the Cāhamānas originated. We are told in the second canto that 'in order to destroy the *mlecchas* on earth, Lord Viṣṇu has established this Cāhamāna'.[39] Thus, in a way, the presence of the *mlecchas* and their actions of desecration of Puṣkara is the main reason for the appearance of the mythical Cāhamāna.

In the tenth canto of *Pṛthvīrāja Vijaya*, when the Ghurid ambassador visits the court at Ajmer, there are multiple references where he is described as impure. We have already highlighted how the text describes the ambassador as bald with a broad forehead.[40] It is also mentioned that 'because of the fear of sins this person has committed, the colour black has shunned his beard, his eyebrows, even his lashes'.[41] In other words, his colour was very pale, and even his beard, eyebrows and lashes were not black. In the next verse, the whole body of this ambassador is called impure.[42] The verse then goes on to tell us that even his speech was impure because he could not pronounce *mūrdhanya varṇas*, such as *ṛ, ṭa, ṭha, ḍa, ḍha, ja, ra* and *ṣa*.[43] There is also a verse that comments on the clothes of this ambassador. We are told that 'just like an impure person wearing good clothes spoils the clothes and does not make him look good, the same was the case with this ambassador'.[44] In the same verse, it also mentioned that 'it looked like this ambassador was not wearing any clothes. Instead, it seems as if his sins have engulfed him'. These descriptions make it clear that, for the text, the Ghurids were considered impure. There is one instance where the text explicitly calls the Ghurids demons when it describes them as 'demons with the bodies of men' (*nṛtanubhir asruraiḥ*).[45]

## Historiographical Implications and the Beginning of Identity Formation

The variegated descriptions of the Muslims in *Pṛthvīrāja Vijaya* show that, at the end of the twelfth century, Indian powers like the Chauhānas had a clear understanding of what was happening in the north-western part of the subcontinent, particularly the region that was under the control of the Ghaznavids. The rise of the Ghurids and how a particular section of Indian society viewed them is also apparent in the text. The descriptions associated with the Ghurids in the text challenge some of the conclusions made by B.D. Chattopadhyaya. The fact that the text explicitly mentions that the impurity of the Ghurids arises because they were the enemy of the cows and they eat beef seems to suggest that it was not the attack on *varṇāśramadharma*, as Chattopadhyaya has argued, which led Sanskrit texts to depict Muslims as impure. For *Pṛthvīrāja Vijaya*, it was the actions of the Muslims, particularly the Ghurids, that made them impure.

The negative qualities that are assigned to the Ghurids in *Pṛthvīrāja Vijaya* also contradict Chattopadhyaya's assertion that the use of the term *mlecchas* for the Muslims shows that there was no difference between the Muslims and the earlier outsiders like the Greeks, Indo-Parthians or Indo-Scythians. Similarly, Truschke's assertion that the characterization of the Ghurids as inherently impure and beef-eaters was not very different from how other kinds of outcastes are identified[46] also does not hold any ground when we look at the description of other outcasts or 'older *mlecchas*'. There is no mention of them desecrating sacred sites or killing cows. Instead, we find that in both the epics, *Mahābhārata* and *Rāmāyaṇa*, the origin of the *mlecchas* are mentioned where Nandinī, the divine cow of Vasiṣṭha, created a *mleccha* army to combat the army of Viśvāmitra.[47] However, such narratives are absent in *Pṛthvīrāja Vijaya*. The author of the text does not make any attempt to incorporate these 'new *mlecchas*' as the early Indian texts had done. It is true that in these descriptions of the Ghurids, there is no mention of the religion of the Ghurids and how their religious practices are different from the Chauhānas. But these negative qualities that are attributed to the Ghurids do become a basis on which a distinction is made between the Ghurids and the Chauhānas. The text employs the term *mleccha* because it was the general term that was used for the 'outsiders'. But there was a clear distinction between these 'new outsiders' and the 'older' ones. What made these 'new outsiders' different from the 'older' ones was their actions. It is these actions, beef eating and temple desecration, that would eventually become a marker of distinction between 'us' and 'them'. In the fifteenth-century text *Kānhaḍade Prabandha,* which recounts the struggle of the Chauhāna ruler of Jālor–Kānhaḍade with 'Alā' al-Din Khalajī, these same qualities are assigned to the army of 'Alā' al-Din Khalajī.[48]

## NOTES

1. For an analysis of socio-religious situation in eastern Afghanistan and adjoining regions of north-western India, see Giovanni Verardi, 'Buddhism in North-western India and Eastern Afghanistan', *Zinbun*, Kyoto University, vol. 43, 2011, pp. 147-83. Verardi has argued that all areas to the south of the Hindukush

mountains were parts of the Indic sphere as late as early eleventh century (p. 148).

2. André Wink, *Al-Hind,* vol. 1: *Early Medieval India and the Expansion of Islam 7th–11th Centuries*, Leiden, 1991, p. 5.
3. Jayānaka, *The Pṛthvīrājavijaya of Jayānaka*, ed. Gaurīshaṅkar Hīrāchand Ojhā and Chandradhar Sharma Guleri, Ajmer, 1941, p. 1.
4. Chandra Prabha, *Historical Mahākāvyas in Sanskrit, Eleventh to Fifteenth Century AD,* New Delhi, 1976, p. 145.
5. Jayānaka, *Pṛthvīrāja Vijaya Mahākāvyam*, Jodhpur, 2022, XII.63, p. 269.
6. Chandra Prabha, op. cit., p. *146*.
7. Cynthia Talbot, *The Last Hindu Emperor: Prithviraj Chauhan and the Indian Past, 1200–2000,* Cambridge, 2016, p. 36.
8. Ibid., p. 42.
9. Ibid., p. 37.
10. Chandra Prabha, op. cit., pp. 146-7.
11. Sheldon Pollock, 'Ramayana and Political Imagination in India', *The Journal of Asian Studies* 52 (2), 1993, p. 274.
12. Audrey Truschke, *The Language of History: Sanskrit Narratives of Indo-Muslim Rule,* New York, 2021, p. 47.
13. Ibid., p. 47.
14. Pollock, op. cit., pp. 274-7.
15. Brajadulal Chattopadhyaya, *Representing the Other?: Sanskrit Sources and the Muslims (Eighth to Fourteenth Century)*, Delhi, 1998, pp. 112-13.
16. Truschke, op. cit., pp. 44–65.
17. Jayānaka, *Pṛthvīrājavijaya Mahākāvyam,* Jodhpur, 2022, X.38-42, 49, 50, pp. 224-8.
18. Jayānaka, *Pṛthvīrājavijaya Mahākāvyam,* Jodhpur, 2022, X.39, pp. 224-5.
19. Aloka Parasher, *A Study of Attitudes towards Mlecchas and Other Outsiders in Northern India (c. A.D. 600),* London, 1978, p. 91.
20. Ibid., pp. 7-12.
21. Chattopadhyaya, op. cit., pp. 86-90.
22. Jayānaka, *Pṛthvīrāja Vijaya Mahākāvyam,* op. cit., VI.14, p. 134.
23. Ibid., X.39, pp. 224-5.
24. Ibid., X.40, p. 225.
25. Ibid., VI.4, p. 132.

26. Richard M. Eaton, *The Rise of Islam and the Bengal Frontier, 1204–1760*, Berkeley, p. 33.
27. Jayānaka, *Pṛthvīrājavijaya Mahākāvyam,* op. cit., X.40, p. 225.
28. Ibid., X.42, p. 225.
29. Ibid., X.43 pp. 225-6; Sheldon Pollock, 'Ramayana and Political Imagination in India', *The Journal of Asian Studies* 52 (2), 1993, p. 276.
30. Jayānaka, *Pṛthvīrājavijaya Mahākāvyam,* op. cit., X.49, p. 227.
31. Ibid., I.50, pp. 22-3.
32. Ibid., I.52, p. 23.
33. Ibid., I.56, p. 24.
34. Ibid., I.51, p. 23.
35. Ibid., I.53, p. 23.
36. Ibid., I.54, p. 24.
37. Ibid., I.55, p. 24.
38. Aloka Parasher, op. cit., pp. 237-46.
39. Jayānaka, *Pṛthvīrājavijaya Mahākāvyam,* op. cit., II.67, p. 49.
40. Ibid., X.43, pp. 225-6.
41. Ibid., X.44, p. 226.
42. Ibid., X.45, p. 226.
43. Ibid., X.46, p. 226-7.
44. Ibid., X.47, p. 227.
45. Ibid., X.50, p. 228.
46. Truschke, op. cit., p. 57.
47. Parasher, op. cit., p. 12.
48. Padmanābha, *Kānhaḍade Prabandha,* Jaipur, 1953, I.33, p. 7; III.31, p. 106; III.236-III.239, pp. 154-5; Padmanābha, *Kānhaḍade Prabandha*, New Delhi, 1991, op. 4, 49 and 68.

## REFERENCES

Chattopadhyaya, Brajadulal. 1998. *Representing the Other?: Sanskrit Sources and the Muslims (Eighth to Fourteenth Century)*. New Delhi: Manohar.

Eaton, Richard M. 1993. *Rise of Islam and the Bengal Frontier, 1204–1760*. Berkeley: University of California Press.

Jayānaka. 1941. *The Pṛthvīrāja Vijaya of Jayānaka*, ed. Gaurīshaṅkar Hīrāchand Ojhā and Pandit Chandradhar Sharma Guleri. Ajmer: Vedic Yantralaya.

———. 2022. *Pṛthvīrāja Vijaya Mahākāvyam*, ed. Gaurīshaṅkar Hīrāchand Ojhā and Pandit Chandradhar Sharma Guleri. trans. Manmohan Sharma. Jodhpur: Rajasthani Granthagar.

Padmanābha. 1953. *Kānhaḍade Prabandha*. ed. K.B. Vyas. Jaipur: Rājasthān Purātattva Mandira.

———. 1991. *Kānhaḍade Prabandha*. tr. V.S. Bhatnagar. New Delhi: Aditya Prakashan.

Parasher, Aloka. 1978. *A Study of Attitudes towards Mlecchas and Other Outsiders in Northern India (c. A.D. 600)*. London: University of London. https://eprints.soas.ac.uk/id/eprint/29097.

Pollock, Sheldon. 1993. 'Ramayana and Political Imagination in India'. *The Journal of Asian Studies* 52 (2): 261-97.

Prabha, Chandra. 1976. *Historical Mahākāvyas in Sanskrit, Eleventh to Fifteenth Century A.D.* New Delhi: Meharchand Lachhmandas.

Talbot, Cynthia. 2016. *The Last Hindu Emperor: Prithviraj Chauhan and the Indian Past, 1200–2000*. Cambridge: Cambridge University Press.

Truschke, Audrey. 2021. *The Language of History: Sanskrit Narratives of Indo-Muslim Rule.* New York: Columbia University Press.

Verardi, Giovanni. 2011. 'Buddhism in North-western India and Eastern Afghanistan, Sixth to Ninth Century AD.' *Zinbun,* Kyoto University, 43: 147-83.

Wink, André. 1991. *Al-Hind*, vol. 1: *Early Medieval India and the Expansion of Islam 7th-11th Centuries*. Leiden: E.J. Brill.

CHAPTER 4

# The Making of the 'Self' and the 'Other'

## The Representations of Hindus and Muslims in a Fifteenth Century Prākrit Text

BIRENDRA NATH PRASAD
JAY VARDHAN SINGH

## Introduction

Identity formation in pre-modern India as a field of study has gained considerable attention in recent times. Recent scholarship on the issue of identity formation and expression regarding Hindu and Muslim socio-religious groups is usually built on literary evidence. One of the first detailed studies about how Sanskrit sources depict Muslims was done by Brajadulal Chattopadhyaya.[1] In his work, Chattopadhyaya not only used some literary sources, but also epigraphical sources. Apart from Chattopadhyaya, Audrey Truschke[2] has also dealt with few of the same questions. Compared to Chattopadhyaya, whose analysis of literary sources ends in the fourteenth century CE, Truschke's work is broader in scope. Truschke has analysed literary sources that were composed between the twelfth century CE and eighteenth century CE. Despite the difference in the period under analysis, what is similar in both these works is the type of literary source they have analysed. Both Truschke and Chattopadhyaya have focused on texts that were written in

Sanskrit. When it comes to the question of identity formation, the focus is mainly on Sanskrit texts. This approach has certain limitations, as it does not provide us with a comprehensive perspective. From the eighth century CE onwards, we have non-Sanskrit Indic sources that can provide us with a different perspective. The current scholarship has largely ignored these non-Sanskrit textual narratives. One such significant non-Sanskrit text is *Kānhaḍade Prabandha.* The present paper aims to understand how the two socio-religious groups—Hindus and Muslims—are represented in this text.

## The Text, its Author, and its Context

*Kānhaḍade Prabandha* belongs to the *Prabandha* tradition. The *Prabandha* tradition is part of the Jain historical tradition, and as a literary tradition, it emerged in the late first and early second millennium CE.[3] The author of the text was a Nāgara Brāhmaṇa named Padmanābha. It was composed in CE 1455.[4] Padmanābha, at several instances, tells us that the language in which he has composed this *Prabandha* is Prākrit.[5] According to the editor of the text, K.B. Vyas, the language of the text 'embodies a stage when Gujarātī and Rājasthānī were just beginning to evolve their distinctive characteristics from the common source—the post-*Apabhraṁśa*'.[6] Although the text belongs to the *Prabandha* tradition, there are important differences between *Kānhaḍade Prabandha* and other Jain *Prabandhas*. The main difference has to do with the influence of the Rājapūta courts.[7] The major themes of the text are bravery, valour and martyrdom, which make the text different from other texts of the *Prabandha* tradition.

The text chronicles the glories of the Chauhāna ruler of Jālor—Kānhaḍade—and his struggle with Alauddin Khilji. It was composed at the request of Akhairāja, who was the fifth descendant of Rāval Kānhaḍade. Although the narrative is historical, this is not a *Carita*. Padmanābha tries to portray this text as a religious text, and at the end of the text, he writes that 'those who listen to this account with attention, all their sins will be washed off'.[8] In another verse, the text is compared to the Purāṇas, and we are told that those who listen to this text will earn the same reward which one gets by listening to the recitation of the Purāṇas.[9]

Since the main narrative revolves around the struggle of the Chauhāna ruler of Jālor—Kānhaḍade—against Alauddin Khilji, we find that the text has become an important source for scholars to understand the perception of the Delhi Sultanate in the early Rājapūta literary tradition. Ramya Sreenivasan[10] has used this text to understand the literary portrayal of Alauddin Khilji in medieval Rājapūta courts. Romila Thapar[11] has also used this text in her work on Somanātha Temple. But in her analysis, her focus is not primarily on the process of identity formation. Thus, there has not been a significant attempt to understand how the two socio-religious groups, Hindu and Muslims, are portrayed in *Kānhaḍade Prabandha*. Since the text provides us with some of the earliest literary examples where a clear Hindu self-representation and equal representation of Muslims are present, an analysis of how these identities are represented can help us better understand the phenomenon of identity formation in pre-modern India.

## Representations of the Muslims in *Kānhaḍade Prabandha*

The central narrative of the text revolves around the struggle of the Chauhānas against the army of the Delhi Sultanate, and because of it, we find that there are ample references to the Muslims. The text employs multiple terms to depict Muslims. Only in one verse do we find the mention of the term *Musalmāna*,[12] otherwise, the most common term used for Muslims is *turaka*[13] and *mleccha*.[14] The term *turaka* means Turks, and most likely, it is derived from the term *turuṣka*, which appears in the Sanskrit texts of the early medieval period to denote Muslims.[15] The term *mleccha*, however, is much older. It first appeared in a later Vedic text called *Śatapatha Brāhmaṇa*.[16] In texts that were composed later, i.e. after the Vedic period, *mleccha* as a term was used to denote outsiders. But in *Śatapatha Brāhmaṇa*, its meaning is rather limited. Here, the term is used for those whose speech is impure.[17] According to Aloka Parasher, *mleccha* as a social category gradually evolved, and, in early Indian texts, it is used for those groups that do not follow the *varṇāśrama dharma.*[18] In these early Indian literary sources, *mleccha* as a term was not only used for foreign groups like the *Yavana, Śaka, Pahlava, Kuṣāṇa* and *Hūṇa,*[19] but it was also used for groups that lived within India.[20] For Muslims, *mleccha* as a term was used in a generic sense in early medieval sources.[21] Apart from these general terms, we have some unique terms as well that is used in *Kānhaḍade Prabandha* for Muslims. One such term is *Sillāri.*[22] According to V.S. Bhatnagar, *Sillāri* probably means 'one who keeps a *Selha* or *Sela* (spear)'. He points out that the term has been used for Muslims in other Rājasthanī texts.[23] Since the text focuses on the struggle of the Chauhāna ruler Kānhaḍade and Alauddin Khilji, Alauddin too is mentioned in person. He is called *Alāvadīna.*[24] Three terms are generally used by the text to address Alauddin: *Suratrāṇa,*[25] *Asapati,*[26] and *Pātisāha.*[27] The term *Suratrāṇa* was derived from *Sultāna*, whereas *Asapati* comes from the Sanskrit term *aṣvapati*, which means Lord of the Horses. The term *Pātisāha* is derived from the Persian term *pādaśāha. Sultāna* and *Pātisāha* are not standalone examples of the use of Persian and Arabic terms in the texts. Multiple terms like *nīsāṇa*[28] for *niśāna, mīra*[29] for *amīra, phuramāṇa*[30] for *farman, pāyaka*[31] for *pāik, bandīṣāna*[32] for *bandikhānā, silāma*[33] for *salāma, phoja*[34] for *fauja, lasakara*[35] for *laśkara, dīwāṇa*[36] for *dīwān,* etc., that are derived from Persian and Arabic, have been used in the text. Interestingly, the term '*gorī*' is also used for Alauddin and his army.[37] The use of *gorī* suggests that the memories of the Ghurid attacks still lingered, and with time, this term was used for any Sultāna and his army.

In the text, there are multiple verses that show that the author had some idea about the religious beliefs of Muslims. For instance, we are told in one verse that before going on the campaign against Kānhaḍade, Alauddin paid obeisance to his *wali.*[38] According to Bhatnagar, this *wali* could be either Sheikh Nizamuddin Auliya or the heir apparent.[39] There is also a reference to the Muslim call to prayer in one verse. The term which is used in this verse for *azāna* is *bāng*.[40] Even mosques are mentioned in the text. The term *masīta* is used for mosques, and we are told that the Sultanate army, as it moved to different places, also built *masītas*.[41] It appears that the author was also aware of the fact that eating pork was taboo among the Muslims, which is why Kānhaḍade dares the envoy of the Sultan that 'if he [Sultāna] doesn't invade Jalor with all his force, he will be taken to have eaten pork (*sūara*)'.[42]

In *Kānhaḍade Prabandha*, there are also multiple references to the desecration of temples done by Alauddin's army. The most important being the destruction of the temple of Somanātha. It was in the year CE 1298 that a Sultanate army under Ulugh Khan desecrated the temple of Somanātha.[43] *Kānhaḍade Prabandha* provides us with a detailed description of this episode.[44] After the temple was destroyed, we are told that 'Ulugh Khan (*alūṣāna*) then gave orders (*phurmān*) to despatch the idol (*bhūta*) to Delhi (*Ḍhīlī*), where it will be crushed and made into lime.'[45] Later, when Alauddin's army began the siege of Jālor, the residents of the fort entreated Kānhaḍade that he should not think that the supply in the fort has run out because if the fort fell, then the enemy would destroy the temples.[46] In this narrative, when the Sultanate army is about to conquer the fort of Jālor, Goddess Āsāpurīdevī tells Kānhaḍade that she is now going to leave her abode in the fort. Apart from Āsāpurī, Gaṇeśa, Kṛṣṇa, and Brahmā also say the same thing to Kānhaḍade.[47] The abandonment of the fort by the gods and goddesses is not only meant to show that the fort was about to fall, but it was possibly a harbinger of the destruction of the temples that would commence with the fall of Jālor. Later, the desecration of temples did take place as we are told that during the siege of the fort, the temple of Kānha Swāmī was destroyed by Alauddin's army.[48] Another verse tells us what happened after the fall of the city of Aṇahalapura in Gujarat. We are told that 'where once stood temple now the prayers (*bāng*) of *Sillāri* could be heard'.[49] *Sillāri*, as noted earlier, was used to denote Muslims. This reference suggests that after destroying the temples, mosques were sometimes built in their place.

Apart from references to the desecration of temples, there are also references to the practice of taking prisoners by the Sultanate army. For instance, we are told that after the destruction of the Somanātha Temple, the Sultanate army 'took captive—Brāhmaṇas and children, and women, in fact, people of all the eighteen *varṇas*'.[50] V.S. Bhatnagar believes that in this verse, *varṇa* has been used in the sense of *jāti*.[51] These prisoners were placed in prisoners' quarters (*bandīṣāna*).[52] There is also a reference to the practice of forced conversion to Islam in the text. In one verse, the prisoners who were taken captive by Ulugh Khan following the destruction of the Somanātha Temple worriedly exclaimed 'if however, Kānhaḍade does not come to our deliverance, then we all will definitely be made *Turakāṇai*'.[53] Apart from converting the prisoners to Islam, there are references to suggest that some were sold into slavery as well. The text mentions that when the Sultanate's army marched towards Jālor, it was accompanied by sellers of captives (*niṣāsa*).[54] According to Bhatnagar, 'the actual term is *nakhkhās*, and these were sellers of captives or cattle taken as plunder'.[55] There are also references to the slaves of the Sultāna (*suratāṇī vandā*) in the text.[56]

In the text, Alauddin and his army are portrayed as being extremely hostile towards Brāhmaṇas and cows. One verse tells us that while attacking a fort, the Sultāna ordered: 'cut down the Brāhmaṇas (*vipra*) wherever they may be performing *homa* or mulching cows! Kill the cows—even those which are pregnant (*vyāhaṇā*) or with newly born calves!'[57] This is a complete contrast to how the Rājapūtas are portrayed in the text. When the Sultāna's army seeks permission from Kānhaḍade to pass through his territory, Kānhaḍade refuses. Among the reasons that Kānhaḍade provides for his refusal is the fact that if he allows the passage of the Sultāna's army, it will lead to the torture of Brāhmaṇas (*vipra*) and cows.[58] This verse not only paints the

Rājapūtas as the protector of Brāhmaṇas and cows, but also projects Alauddin's army as their enemy. This contrasting imagery appears again when the daughter of Alauddin goes to Kānhaḍade's son Vīramade to request the release of prisoners. Prince Vīramade tells her that 'if the Pādashāh (*Pātasāha*) agrees to what we say, then what you have desired will be fulfilled. He should refrain from violating the sanctity of the temples and breaking idols and inflicting suffering on Brāhamaṇas (*vipra*) and cows.'[59]

## Representations of Hindus in the *Kānhaḍade Prabandha*

*Kānhaḍade Prabandha* is one of the earliest texts where we find that the term 'Hindu' is used for a socio-religious group. The text uses it to denote a collective group[60] and also for the army of Kānhaḍade.[61] Hindu as a term is used interchangeably with terms like *Rāuta*[62] and *Rājapūta*.[63] There is one verse in the text where Ulugh Khan, who has been called *alūṣāna*, addresses a soldier of Kānhaḍade as Hindu.[64] In another verse, the warriors of Kānhaḍade who attacked the army of the Sultan are addressed as *Balawantā Hindū*.[65]

The text tries to project Hindus as superior to Turks. This is best reflected in the episode when the daughter of Alauddin —Pīroja—wanted to marry Kānhaḍade's son Vīramade. In this narrative, Alauddin first tells her that 'marriage between a Hindu (*Hindū*) and a Turk (*turaka*) does not take place.'[66] She responds by listing out the differences between Hindus and Turks—'Hindus alone know how to enjoy good things of life, like Indra. They are wise in speech and conversation—sweet and intelligent at the same time. They have such variety of food preparations and they bedeck themselves with finery and ornaments in a most beautiful and graceful manner.'[67] This sense of superiority is again highlighted when Pīroja proposes to Vīramade. Prince Vīramade rejects this marriage proposal and argues that if he were to marry a Turk (*turakaṁṇai*), then it would not only be a blot on the glorious line of the Chauhānas (*cāhūāṇa*), but it would also incur shame on the 36 royal clans of the Rajpūtas. Even his father will be ashamed of this act.[68]

When it comes to the struggle between the Rājapūtas and Alauddin's army, we see that in many instances it is portrayed as a struggle between the *deva*s and the *asura*s. The Sultanate army is described as *asura*s, especially during episodes of temple desecration.[69] In one verse, the clash between the Rajāpūta army and Alauddin's army has been compared to the fight between Rāma and Rāvaṇa or the battle between the *deva*s and the *asura*s.[70] The same allegory of the battle between the *deva*s and the *asura*s appears again during the final siege of Jālor.[71] The reference to the *Rāmāyaṇa* also appears again when Vīramade tell his troops that the 'final fight with the *mlecchas* will be reminiscent of *Rāmāyaṇa*'.[72]

The use of the term *asura* can also be contrasted with how Kānhaḍade is portrayed in the text. One verse describes him as an incarnation (*avatāra*) of Ādipuruṣa.[73] In another verse, we are told that when Kānhaḍade rescued the idol of Somanātha, he was proclaimed by the people as an incarnation of Kṛṣṇa.[74] The next verse tells us that it was only because of the *puṇya* earned by the Chauhāna clan that Kānhaḍade was able to destroy the *mlecchas*.[75] Later, Kānhaḍade is described as an incarnation of Rāma and Kṛṣṇa,[76] who in Kaliyuga 'had lightened the burden of the earth by destroying the *mlecchas*'.[77]

## Concluding Observations

The variegated descriptions of Hindus and Muslims in *Kānhaḍade Prabandha* show that two distinct socio-religious identities had emerged by the fifteenth century CE. The term 'Hindu', which earlier was used by Persian and Arabic sources for the non-Muslims of the Indian subcontinent, was now begun to be adopted by the non-Muslims themselves. With the emergence of a collective Hindu identity, Muslim as a separate socio-religious identity also emerged within the Indic literary tradition. Although many of the intricacies of the Islamic faith were not understood by these non-Muslim sources as yet, there was some broad understanding. This emergence of two distinct socio-religious identities was the result of the consolidation of the Delhi Sultanate. This consolidation had some fundamental repercussions as perceived in *Kānhaḍade Prabandha*: desecration of temples, flight of deities, slaughter of Brāhmaṇas and cows, forced conversions to Islam, and forced enslavements. It was this deepening of the rule of the Delhi Sultanate and its concomitant repercussions that hastened the formation of an apparent Hindu self-representation.

## NOTES

1. Brajadulal Chattopadhyaya, *Representing the Other?: Sanskrit Sources and the Muslims (Eighth to Fourteenth Century)*, New Delhi: Manohar, 1998.
2. Audrey Truschke, 'The Language of History: Sanskrit Narratives of Indo-Muslim Rule', in *The Language of History* (Columbia University Press, 2021).
3. Romila Thapar, *The Past Before Us* (Harvard University Press, 2013), p. 651, https://www.jstor.org/stable/j.ctt6wpq6f.
4. Padmanābha, *Kānhaḍade Prabandha*, trans. V.S. Bhatnagar (New Delhi: Aditya Prakashan, 1991), p. vii.
5. Padmanābha, *Kānhaḍade Prabandha*, ed. K.B. Vyas (Jaipur: The Director, Rājasthān Purātattva Mandira, 1953), vv. 1.1, 1.11, 4.352.
6. K.B. Vyas, op. cit., p. 1.
7. Romila Thapar, *Somanatha: The Many Voices of a History*, New Delhi: Penguin Books India, 2008, p. 125.
8. *Kānhaḍade Prabandha*, 1953, v. 4.345; *Kānhaḍade Prabandha*, 1991, p. 104.
9. *Kānhaḍade Prabandha*, 1953, v. 4.345-4.346; *Kānhaḍade Prabandha*, 1991, p. 104.
10. Ramya Sreenivasan, 'Alauddin Khalji Remembered: Conquest, Gender and Community in Medieval Rajput Narratives', *Studies in History* 18, no. 2 (1 August 2002), pp. 275-96.
11. Thapar, op. cit.
12. *Kānhaḍade Prabandha*, 1953, v. 3.124.
13. Ibid., 1953, vv. 1.14, 1.31, 1.55, 1.67, 1.73, 1.85, 1.106, 1.118, 1.136, 1.146.

14. Ibid., vv. 1.17, 1.52, 1.56, 1.84, 1.91, 1.126.
15. Chattopadhyaya, op. cit., pp. 40-3.
16. Aloka Parasher, 'A Study of Attitudes towards Mlecchas and Other Outsiders in Northern India (c. A.D. 600)', PhD thesis, University of London, 1978, p. 91. Available online: https://eprints.soas.ac.uk/id/eprint/29097.
17. Ibid., p. 95.
18. Ibid., 7, 12.
19. Ibid., p. 275.
20. Romila Thapar, 'The Image of the Barbarian in Early India,' *Comparative Studies in Society and History* 13, no. 4 (1971): 432-3.
21. Chattopadhyaya, op. cit., p. 30.
22. Ibid., 1953, v. 1.65.
23. Ibid., 1991, p. 119.
24. Ibid., 1953, v. 1.19, 1.38.
25. Ibid., 1953, v. 1.11, 1.19, 1.30, 1.34, 1.36, 2.19.
26. Ibid., 1953, v. 1.28, 1.119, 1.127.
27. Ibid., 1953, v. 1.20, 1.28, 1.35, 1.38, 1.66, 1.109, 2.19.
28. Ibid., 1953, *v. 1.47, 1.72, 1.78.*
29. Ibid., 1953, v. 1.37.
30. Ibid., 1953, v. 1.36.
31. Ibid., 1953, v. 1.80.
32. Ibid., 1953, v. 1.105.
33. Ibid., 1953, v. 1.140, 1.142.
34. Ibid., 1953, v. 3.76.
35. Ibid., 1953, v. 1.29, 1.135.
36. Ibid., 1953, v. 1.19.
37. Ibid., 1953, v. 2.154, 3.153.
38. Ibid., 1953, v. 2.31.
39. Ibid., 1991, 32.
40. Ibid., 1953, v. 1.65; 1991, 7.
41. Ibid., 1953, v. 4.83; 1991, 79.
42. Ibid., 1953, v. 3.12; 1991, 47.
43. Richard H. Davis, *Lives of Indian Images*, New Jersey: Princeton University Press, 1999, p. 191.
44. *Kānhaḍade Prabandha*, 1953, v. 1.93-1.96; 1991, 10.
45. Ibid., 1953, v. 1.98; 1991, 10.
46. Ibid., 1953, v. 4.134; 1991, 84.
47. Ibid., 1953, v. 4.198-4.200; 1991, 90.

48. Ibid., 1953, v. 4.251; 1991, 95.
49. Ibid., 1953, v. 1.165; 1991, p. 7.
50. Ibid., 1953, v. 1.104; 1991, p. 11.
51. Ibid., 1991, 128.
52. Ibid., 1953, v. 1.105; 1991, p. 11.
53. Ibid., 1953, v. 1.176; 1991, p. 18.
54. Ibid., 1953, v. 4.79; 1991, p. 78.
55. Ibid., 1991, p. 194.
56. Ibid., 1953, v. 3.84, 3.94; 1991, pp. 52-3.
57. Ibid., 1953, v. 3.31; 1991, p. 49.
58. Ibid., 1953, v. 1.33; *Kānhaḍade Prabandha*, 1991, p. 4.
59. Ibid., 1953, v. 3.236-3.239; 1991, p. 68.
60. Ibid., 1953, v. 1.27.
61. Ibid., 1953, v. 1.132, 1.201, 1.205, 1.207.
62. Ibid., 1953, v. 1.208, 2.42.
63. Ibid., 1953, v. 2.28.
64. Ibid., 1953, v. 1.150.
65. Ibid., 1953, v. 2.53.
66. Ibid., 1953, v. 3.123; 1991, p. 56.
67. Ibid., 1953, v. 3.125-3.126; 1991, pp. 56–57.
68. Ibid., 1953, v. 3.133-3.135; 1991, p. 57.
69. Ibid., 1953, v. 1.96, 1.122, 1.248, 2.131, 2.155.
70. Ibid., v. 2.165; 1991, p. 45.
71. Ibid., , 1953, v. 4.259; 1991, p. 96.
72. Ibid., 1953, v. 4.297; 1991, p. 100.
73. Ibid., 1953, v. 3.119; 1991, p. 56.
74. Ibid., 1953, v. 1.223; 1991, p. 25.
75. Ibid., 1953, v. 1.224; 1991, p. 25.
76. Ibid., 1953, v. 4.292; 1991, p. 99.
77. Ibid., 1953, v. 4.293; 1991, p. 99.

## REFERENCES

Chattopadhyaya, Brajadulal. *Representing the Other?: Sanskrit Sources and the Muslims (Eighth to Fourteenth Century)*. New Delhi: Manohar, 1998.

Davis, Richard H. *Lives of Indian Images*. Princeton, NJ: Princeton University Press, 1999.

Lorenzen, David N. 'Warrior Ascetics in Indian History', *Journal of the American Oriental Society*, vol. 98(1), 1978.

Padmanābha. *Kānhaḍade Prabandha*. Edited by K.B. Vyas. Jaipur: The Director, Rājasthān Purātattva Mandira, 1953.

———. *Kānhaḍade Prabandha*. Translated by V.S. Bhatnagar. New Delhi: Aditya Prakashan, 1991.

Parasher, Aloka. 'A Study of Attitudes towards Mlecchas and Other Outsiders in Northern India (c. A.D. 600)'. University of London, 1978. https://eprints.soas.ac.uk/id/eprint/29097.

Pinch, W.R. *Warrior Ascetics and Indian Empires*, Cambridge: Cambridge University Press, 2006.

Thapar, Romila. *Somanatha: The Many Voices of a History*. New Delhi: Penguin Books India, 2008.

———. 'The Image of the Barbarian in Early India'. *Comparative Studies in Society and History*, vol. 13(4), 1971: 408–36.

———. *The Past Before Us*. Harvard: Harvard University Press, 2013.

Truschke, Audrey. 'The Language of History: Sanskrit Narratives of Indo-Muslim Rule', in *The Language of History*. Columbia University Press, 2021.

# PART III

# NĀTHA SAMPRADĀYA IN ITS INTERACTIONS WITH SOCIAL-ECONOMIC PROCESSES AND INSTITUTIONS

CHAPTER 5

# The Construction of a Monastic 'Empire'

## Ascetics, State and Peasants in the Twentieth Century Himachal Himalayas*

MAHESH SHARMA

Recent historiography demonstrates that 'asceticism' in India was more than a spiritual institution. It participated actively in the daily lives of people, particularly in the late medieval Indian polity. The 'monastic orders' were cash-rich organizations sustained by a network of long-distance trade and protected by ascetic soldiers.[1] This interest in trade perhaps turned the monastery into a militant 'seminary', an instrument through which 'moral order' was upheld and 'social order' manipulated. This has recently been reiterated by Pinch & Lorenzen, who navigated the career of one Anupgiri, the Gosain 'ascetic'(?) from Bundelkhand in central India.[2] This is supported by incidents of sectarian rivalry leading to monastic militarization, as narrated by Abu'l Fazl, the chronicler of Akbar, and the contemporary European travellers. These trading-soldier-ascetics legitimated and sustained polity, the Mughals included, by providing both arms and cash. In turn, the state patronized them, thereby creating a symbiotic relationship of dependence and collaboration. This relationship, between the pre-colonial

* Editor's Note: Diacritical marks have not been used in this chapter, which is regretted.

state and militant 'ascetics', was resisted by the British colonial rule leading to the revolt of the 'moral order'—of the Sanyasis and Faquirs. It is, however, argued that while the British successfully disbanded them militarily, these ascetics collaborated with the nationalist forces and provided leadership to the popular peasant reform movements in the early twentieth century. In the process, the questions of social status and religious identity, which, as Pinch argues, with the 'nineteenth-century withdrawal of the state from the popular spectacle', became 'such a crucial public arena'. This was the arena in which, as Freitag has argued, larger community identities were expressed with greater political urgency as nationalist ideology became pervasive.[3] By associating themselves with the nationalist movement, the ascetics gained access to the 'newly emergent power base, namely—the urban middle-class' Hindus. This association had long-term ramifications: the partition that 'further embedded the communalist understanding of the Indian past'; and, the Ramajanamabhoomi movement (a movement to reclaim the birth place of Hindu warrior-hero Rama at Ayodhya)—the culmination of 'the longer history of warrior asceticism'.[4] This is, of course, premised by the reformist role played by these 'ascetics', particularly the Ramanandis in Awadh, to Sanskritize the lower-caste peasants—from Shudras to Kshatriyas—during the British rule.[5]

Contrarily, this paper—geographically restricted within the confines of the north Indian state of Himachal Pradesh—delineates the mechanism by which the Shaivite 'ascetic' monasticism—the Jogis and Gosains—controlled the agrarian space, not as reformers but by perpetuating caste hierarchy during 1850-1960. These organizations competed and appropriated land from peasants, aided by the legal and land settlement regime. They were aided by the British administration that, anxious to curb the mobile tendency, settled and perhaps even domesticated them to deflate the potential conflict or 'sedition' that they saw in the itinerant ascetic 'classes'. The nexus curbed the radical peasants during the height of the national movement, drawing them into the larger fold of 'Hinduism': the customs and rituals. The point that I wish to emphasize is that what the British saw as legal problem was 'realized' as an opportunity to assert its influence by the 'moral order'. There are thus debates about family, marriage and legality, caste and its norms, purity and pollution, and life cycle rites; or debates about propriety of customary and religious sanction based on sastric-scriptural legal digests. These debates tacitly take from and support the legal perspective, particularly the issues of succession and inheritance, of uniform social system and hierarchy therein that restrains and contains the problems of law and order. These debates are also tacitly supported by the local colonial officials in the law courts, land settlement offices, or by such offices/officials that control the everyday lives of people. Therefore, we need to probe the role of actors or agents involved in perpetuating 'colonial rule', who filled the space of 'public arena' or 'spectacle' with that of public office. In fact, they propelled this 'office' into the psyche of the rural localities to perpetuate the 'rule' and the 'traditional' or 'Hinduized' social order. The office of land settlement was one such arena by which the British rule tacitly strengthened the 'moral order' and sustained it through the instruments of local and traditional authority.

## Appropriating Localities; Creating Ascetic 'Empires'

Colonial intervention in the Himachal hill states, while effecting institutional change—particularly in the land settlement, legal, and forest departments—did not alter significantly the local polity that was based on clan allegiance to the Raja—who continued to be socially significant (as in Chamba)—and to the clan deity, the *kulaja*. This relationship between the deity and ruler, which determined identity and polity, remained intact even as the political structure was transformed due to institutional changes effected by colonial rule. The social life, therefore, continued to revolve around the village 'moral order' that consisted of both the Sanskritic and local deities, each having a role in regulating the social and economic life in its locality—the appropriation or colonization of space that evolved culturally over time and socialized through ritual activities. The political construction of locality, as also argued by Appadurai, was invoked by linking it with the broader 'cosmological' and 'moral' order, embedded in the social system and economic agency—the organization of kinship and social interaction or stratification and the agricultural or shepherding cycle, for example.[6] It is at this level of locality that the significance of the 'ascetic' agency in creating local 'empires' needs to be appreciated.

Landgrants played a prominent role in the ascetics' appropriation of locality and the eventual creation of 'monastic empires'. Let us take the example of the Jogis of Jakhbar, who first received 200 *bigha*s of land as a *madad-i-ma'ash* grant from Akbar on the banks of river Ravi in Pathan *pargana* in CE 1571 (Doc. I).[7] By 1578 another grant of 10 *bigha*s was added in the *pargana* of Kathuah, in the name of another Jogi (Doc. III). As the land would be denuded by river Ravi, the Jogis got themselves relocated to village Narot, replacing the Jakh shrine—usually constructed in the middle of the fields, a common territory—and building the famed monastery, Jakhbar. This was a prime irrigated property that the Jogis ensured got water from the Shah Nahr to 'its orchard and cultivated land' (Doc. XVA). Even the colonial functionaries were directed to give water free of charge to the Mahant, though the cultivators were charged for irrigation.[8] By the middle of the eighteenth century, the tentacles of this shrine had spread to Jammu and the Himachal hills, the *pargana*s of Shahpur, Jwalamukhi, Gumtal and Sarol (Doc. XV). Since the Jogis succeeded through the agency of spiritual brotherhood, *gurubhais*, a close tab was kept on the activities of the sub-centres that were coming up due to these land grants. It would be worthwhile to point out that the grants were made by various functionaries—the emperor, governor, *faujdar*s, down to the *jagirdars* or *zamindars* of the area. Thus, each of these sub-centres got further entrenched in villages, having close ties with the local functionaries. For instance, by 1725-6, the Jogis of Jwalamukhi already controlled the areas around the shrine of the goddess, a prominent pilgrimage site, as well as the forests of Pathiar, Droh, Tiara, Tanauli Chak, and Mahadev Balakrupi. Thus, while maintaining the vertical linkage with Jakhbar, the Jwalamukhi Jogis were horizontally spreading out in the lower hills—creating a kind of network of monastic institutions linked to the main shrine at Jwalamukhi—who could control the spiritual and commercial traffic to this pilgrim site. In the urban areas, they were provided with different kinds of prerogatives. For example, Muhammad Shah provided one *tunkah-i-Alamgiri* per shop to the Jogis of Jakhbir from the bazaar of the *qasba* Muhiuddin Pur in 1728-9 (Doc. XIII). Similarly, Bhag Singh, the governor in the early nineteenth century provided octroi rights to the Jogis of Sujanpur (Doc. XVII). No wonder George Foster, in his travelogue, wrote of the Nurpur 'ascetics' that they were rich, and exercising their influence as merchants, soldiers and statesmen.[9]

Similar examples are there about the Vaishnava ascetic establishments as well. The documents available from Pindori seat, for instance, inform that one Shaikh Mahbub Alam of Batala provided grant of a well-irrigated land for five years at Rs. 88 in 1695, which was attached to the Pindori seat (Doc. I).[10] The Maliks of Yadgarpur sold their entire possession for Rs 700 in 1711 to the Vaishnavas (Doc. II); while the *darogha*s of Shahnahr offered the village Talibpur to Gosain Ramdas of Pindori in 1732 (Doc. III). Similar offerings were made in village Jaitopur, villages in *pargana* Nurpur, Paniyal, Pathan, etc. Like the Jogis, the Vaishnavas too were patronized by all classes of officials.

These examples are only representative of the mechanism by which the 'ascetic' establishments spread horizontally, entrenching themselves in narrow units and, finally, the villages, for a couple of centuries. The role of the state in a horizontal proliferation of the 'ascetic' establishments should, however, be emphasized with caution. For instance, unlike the Jogis of Jakhbar, the Vaishnavas in Panjab were provided with properties which were purchased by the devout and handed over to the main seat, which operated through its agent in the area. We thus have a fair idea about the mechanism by which these ascetic institutions spread over space, linked horizontally to each other through the spiritual lineages and vertically to the parent shrine—in this case, the seat of Pindori. The state, however, asserted its control over these 'ascetic' agencies, as is evident from Chamba records, by reordering the grants and actively intervening in monastic successions, as it could ill afford inimical elements detrimental to its interest. The state could arm-twist, and force its choice as it regulated and maintained the shrines-*dehras* and monasteries through land grants and annuities. The ascetics' influence was also disciplined by defining and re-adjusting their territorial domain or hinterland (*vrita* or *vratesari*). Moreover, the state induced and settled most of these 'ascetics' and turned them into householders—married with children—and these organizations became their personal properties. Such householders were, however, placed lower in the caste hierarchy as the society looked down upon them, but they continued to play significant roles derived from their genealogy with the mystic cults that they belonged to, such as the Jogis of Chamba, who continued to derive benefits from their association with the paradigmatic Nath cultic figure, Charpatnath. Their seats or *deras* consequently played a similar role as monasteries and competed for state patronage along with other organizations, the Giri *akhara* in the case of twentieth century Chamba.

Let us consider the example of the Charpat Jogis of Chamba—Charpatnath being one of the paradigmatic Nath Siddhas who is allegedly associated with the Chamba state in the seventeenth-century royal *vamshavali* (genealogy) to gauge the influence of the ascetic agents over rural scape. This is reflected in the detailed collection sheets that we have access to, particularly those belonging to the early twentieth century. The annual/biannual collection that the Jogis received is also significant because of its size, indicative of things that worked at the level of 'locality'. The proceeds are complex, in a sense that it is not a simple collection of money, but also of produce—grains, pulses, wild products like incense and honey—and domestic animals, particularly sheep and goat; or animal-related produce like *ghee*, etc. The collections were made bi-annually at the end of each harvest. But, as most of the land under agriculture was not conducive for double cropping or was left fallow (*khila*), every alternative year/crop to reclaim fertility, mostly single annual collections, were made. The size, perhaps, is not important, even if the symbolism is. These collections, mostly from each household in a given locality, are indicative of the type of influence that the ascetic agents exerted, how pervasive their hold was, and how entrenched they were in the locality.

Within this structure, the ascetics were in a position to radically manipulate the local polity. They used their influence to control land and power and in the process became landed magnates or landlords, with vested interest in upholding the social order of caste so as to safeguard and even augment their possessions and influence. Thus, these ascetic organizations created 'local empires' for themselves, conniving with the colonial institutions and administration.

The Jogis of Charpat, who were householders and not renunciants—though being the Mahants of the shrine, formed a significant spiritual order. It is an example of how the Jogis replaced local tillers and peasants. Madho Jogi, the Mahant in the first half of the twentieth century, obtained ex-party decrees in his favour against two low-caste tenants of the barber (*nai*) profession and caste in Pihura *pargana* in 1925 (case nos. 438 & 439 both filed in 1923 and awarded in 1924); and a widow of fellow Jogi member from Sarol in 1943 (case no. 200) along with 'cost' of Rs. 10 respectively in each case. All three ex-party decisions are significant as the tenants could ill afford the cost of litigation and its wherewithal, and may be seen as the beginning of the process of land accumulation by forced occupation, manipulation of records by the nexus between the revenue officials and the Jogis, and finally by litigation.

These two examples are only illustrative of the strategy that the Jogis used for their social and economic empowerment at a time when there was peasant unrest in the hill states (discussed later). It must be pointed out that the colonial Superintendents made changes in the titular arrangement of land on the lines of settlement in Panjab (*mahalbandi* or demarcating revenue estates) to leverage revenue collection in Chamba. These changes confirmed the dominance of local magnates, both secular and religious, to appropriate them in the bureaucratic hierarchy that the colonial administration felt comfortable to relate with. Like Panjab, land was central to the conception of honour, status and brotherhood (*biradari*).[11] The ownership of land, thus, provided both control and status.

In 1874, Col. Blair Reid started the measurement of the cultivated area according to possessions, accounting for the revenue to be paid. The old system of levying *bacch* or cash and *sal* or kind payments bi-annually, at the end of each harvest, was also partly replaced by cash payment. Cash being rare in Chamba added to the woes of peasants to such an extent that there are numerous instances where land was sublet to the tenants on the condition of payment of rent to the authorities, alienating thereby its proceeds totally to the occupant tenant. Later, in 1891, formal revenue rates were fixed at Rs. 4 per acre on irrigated land and Rs. 2 per acre on non-irrigated land respectively.[12] The settlement was resisted, for instance in 1895 in Bhattiyat. As the peasant unrest spread in the 1920s in Kangra, the fertile area of Bhattiyat was also affected. The fixed revenue, enhanced to Rs. 7.50 in 1910-11, was beyond the means of occupant-cultivators or owners of marginal acreage. In many cases, the tillers reclaimed the land from the owners on a long-term basis on the surety of revenue payment. In fact, it was an accepted practice in Chamba, even by 1910, to cede land on a long-term basis on surety of revenue payment by the occupant-tenants. Occasionally, a rupee or two was demanded to assert ownership rights (*haq malikana*), which was also upheld/imposed by the Court whenever such disputes came forth.[13] That the Jogis could benefit from such an arrangement by using protracted revenue receipts, occupant status (*kabiz*) and the judicial process to their advantage underwrites their dexterity. It may be pointed out that the householder Jogis, who formed the ritually low castes in hierarchy, became landed caste by such manipulation. Thus, when the first regular settlement of Chamba was initiated in 1951-8, the Jogis (populated throughout the erstwhile Chamba state) had a titular claim over 4,494 *bighas* of land (one acre was about five standard *bighas* of land), about 0.07 per cent of the total area in the Chamba state. Out of this,

3,466 *bighas* was cultivated, which was about 0.7 per cent of the total cultivated area in Chamba.[14] The land ownership estimates are, besides their claims as *kashtkars* or tenants, the actual tillers of soil. Could this revision have been possible without the connivance of the land settlement and revenue officials?

That the spiritual agencies manipulated the 'new' instruments of land settlement and the judicial process to assert ownership, appropriation of land claiming power and status in connivance with local *zamindars* is well documented. In the Balakrupi shrine of *tika* Har in Kangra, for instance, the low-caste servitors of the shrine were geographically distanced to appropriate the prime land. They were ritually excluded from the shrine by manipulating genealogy, mythology and consequent Sanskritization of the 'peasant deity' as it became an economically vibrant centre. This shrine too falls in the orbit of Siddha Nath Jogis, who colluded with the local officials to entrench themselves as the local landed magnates of the area. That such assertions were legitimized legally undergirds the mechanism by which the state instruments connived with spiritual leaders.[15]

## Peasant Protests and 'Ascetic' Ascendancy

The most significant change that the colonial regime implemented in the hill states was the settlement of land, which secured the dominant local bonds by recognizing the politico-religious landed relationship, while creating a class of ownership that could trade in land as a commodity. The commodification of land enhanced the traditional association of prestige, honour and power with land. By making land a private enterprise, like the British landlords, the colonial state sought to break the bond between the Raja and subjects. Moreover, the land belonging to the shrines came within the political orbit of priests and ascetic agents. This would change the social-political dynamics at the level of locality, in particular.

The introduction of Western education, legal institutions, and the ascendant 'national' movement, however, politicized these localities, challenged by the peasants in the 1920s. The challenge was aimed at Sanskritizing (upward social mobility) their community-caste status as well as to economically negotiate the emergent social status in the transformed local structure. It is in this struggle that the role of 'ascetics', both the individual householders(!) and the monastic establishments, becomes significant as they see this as an opportunity to entrench themselves economically and politically. The response of the 'moral order' emphasizes the competing caste hierarchy based on denial to the immediately lower *jati* (sub-caste)—unlike Pinch, who considers the larger *varna* category and calls all peasants as Shudras and therefore blur the boundaries of the coercive competing hierarchies within this larger social category, which he conveniently places at the bottom of the ladder (though the bottom itself is nuanced, and bitterly ranked and laddered, which is not taken into account)—as well as its connivance with the agents of state and the high castes that catapulted the monastic order into the centre of local power. While Pinch's formulation renders all peasant castes as untouchables, we shall argue that there were 'clean' and 'unclean' castes within the Shudra hierarchy, the touchable and untouchable and that this was flexible.[16] At the height of the peasant revolt, the monastic agency is used to Sanskritize certain castes and therefore render some untouchable castes as 'clean' castes, particularly the artisans, the upgrading of the status necessary to create a class of domestic household workers, the status which was earlier enjoyed by the dominant peasant castes like Ghirths, Batwals and Kanets in the Himachal hills. Whether it was also accompanied with caste-derogation of peasants is contested and uncertain. What our evidence, however, suggests is that the monasteries and ascetics were not reformers and at the forefront of the nationalist movement as has been argued, not at the level of locality at least. Rather, they entrenched themselves in the rural agricultural areas during this time, where they had interests in land and therefore in the caste dynamics, and were tacitly aided by the colonial instruments to assume the locality leadership instead of opposing or distancing them.

## Peasant Revolt and the Landed Classes

There seems to be a major realignment of class order at this time, based on landed interest and services. While the peasants were alienated from the landholding Rajput-warrior caste, the artisan classes were Sanskritized and aligned with the landholders. The relationship between ascetics and Jogis as well as the dominant landed class, the Rajputs, may be comprehended in their shared class consciousness as landholders. While the Brahmans, the custodians of the ideological sector and therefore the local 'power source', largely depended upon and drew their power from service rendered to the colonial administrative structure—particularly those associated with writing and liaisoning (as clerks, chefs, advisors); the Rajputs were the local political leaders and dominant landed class. Significantly, they served in the colonial military (the hillmen formed the Dogra regiment), which at this time of two world wars was of critical importance. It is against this backdrop that the peasant rebellion of the 1920s assumes a greater significance.

By 1926, the Ghirths—the dominant touchable low caste cultivators and marginal landholders—revolted against the restrictions imposed by the dominant landed community, the Rajputs. The symbols of ritual impurity and social distance became the attributes of resistance. They refused to cultivate at the prevailing terms of tenures and rates.[17] Their movement and leaders were also sympathetic to the larger nationalist movement led by Congress, which was now making inroads into the hills, sensitizing and organizing the peasants. Also, almost simultaneously, the Kolhis, the untouchable service caste, upped their attempts to move up the ritual hierarchy. They reformulated their caste genealogy such that they were originally Rajputs who were derogated because of a 'minor breach of caste orthodoxy'. It is interesting to observe that invariably all inversion myths claim Kshatriya-Rajput or warrior ancestry, which Pinch terms as Vaishnavization based on the perceived status equated to Rama—the Kshatriya warrior hero-god. None of these claim the apex Brahminhood? In the vernacular material logic, the

Brahmana signified the relations of dependence, while the Kshatriya-warrior caste is the status of ruler, patron, and upholder of the society. Moreover, the Brahmana as a 'sacred' symbolized Sanskrit as a language, discourse, and cultural code that could not be appropriated; though, one could 'Sanskritize' the way of life. So, unlike Pinch's argument, the struggle was to appropriate the symbols of the ruler, which had a bearing on caste hierarchy as well. Thus, Kolhis reclaimed upward status by Sanskritizing their way of life by eliminating widow inheritance, bride price, and reciprocal exchange marriages—practices that the British frowned upon. The institutional change is also influenced by the 'civilization discourse' in which both the colonial administration and Hindu textualists (the monastic ideologues) were interested—both arguing that there were cultural aberrations that needed to be corrected. Marriage, rituals and forms were the significant reforms advocated. For the British, such definitions were significant from a legal perspective, involving rights to property and assessing revenue liability, etc.; for the 'spiritual sector', it was an attempt to homogenize while adding to the growing population of Sanatana Hindus.

Yet significantly, the Kolhis had to defy the numerous restrictions imposed on them by the high castes, like playing musical instruments in their weddings, using gold ornaments, assuming the sacred thread; privileges of the high castes. Parry writes, 'in the face of bitter high-caste opposition, they have attempted to do all these things with varying degrees of success'. The high-caste opposition was aimed at the denial of symbols of ritual purity. The Brahmanas refused to give them the sacred thread, and 'the Kolhis were reduced to stealing the sanctified threads with which the high caste women festoon the sacred *bar* (Ficus) tree'.[18] Obviously, the ascetic agents, particularly the Giris and the Jogis, played a significant role in legitimizing their upward rise by providing them sanctity, for instance, the symbolic right of using the sacred thread.

In the local caste hierarchy, the Kolhis were placed ritually lower to the Ghirths. The Rajputs and the landed monastic orders (the king and the ascetic), therefore, used the Kolhi pretensions to clean caste status to blackmail the Ghirths into a more submissive attitude. In this case, the Kolhis acquiesced.[19] The Ghirth movement had left many high castes in a quandary since traditionally 'Ghirths had been their domestic servants', while being their tenant cultivators. As they were of the clean caste, they could perform various duties, like fetching water or cleaning cooking utensils, which could not be done by the lower artisanal castes. However, in their attempts to claim higher status, the Ghirths refused to do this kind of menial work. At the face of such a revolt, the Kolhis were moved up the ladder so that they may become a ritually clean caste in order to carry on the domestic jobs earlier being handled by the Ghirths.[20] In the process, not only the notions of caste, touch and hierarchy were altered, implying the flexibility and control within the institution, but also the relationship between the peasant and artisanal classes was significantly changed. This change would, thereafter, define the varied interests in land and agriculture, as well as the regulation of both peasant and artisan classes, drawing authority from the 'ascetic' moral order and charisma associated with it. This charisma rested in the ascetic's power to control nature and elements (*siddhis*). While the protest against the ruler could threaten existence, any protest against the 'moral order' threatened the 'after life' as well.

In this process of social change, the role of the Brahmanas is critical, since they are perceived as the regulators of caste society. As also noted by Parry, the caste regulation or change, however, was the prerogative of the Rajput-warrior kingship; even in the 1930s, as the *Gazetteer of Kangra* points out.[21] Much against the wishes of the Brahmanas, thus, the Kolhis were moved up in the caste ladder. How was such social engineering legitimized? Equally critical is the role of the colonial administration that, obviously, was not sympathetic to the peasant revolt, and also because it feared that the revolt may become a tool for the nationalist movement. This again returns the focus on the monastic order and how it extended its 'local empire' aided by the colonial instruments represented by the dominant warrior castes.

## Monastic Credit: The Instrument of Control

The role played by the ascetic agencies in derogating and uplifting the caste status of particular communities at the time of the peasant unrest, was also an attempt to dislodge the peasants from their tilling rights and create a new class of tillers constituting of the members of the artisanal castes, who would be totally dependent upon the landed class for their survival. The subtle reorienting of landed demography may be appreciated better against the backdrop of changing markets during the period of the world wars, 1914–45. Local changes are significant in this context. For instance, while the general weighted agricultural price index declined through 1920s and 1930s, the local prices almost doubled during this time.[22] Thus, there was a sharp decline in both money and real wages in Panjab as well in the adjoining hill states. How the ascetics were instrumental in shaping the change in the rural scape, we will demonstrate by using evidence from a Śankarite monastery of Giri ascetics from Thor in the present-day district of Sirmaur in Himachal Pradesh. These monasteries, as in Thor, were not only the landlords in their localities but were also capital-intensive establishments that employed all range of artisans and other service providers to facilitate their landed and trade interests.

The decline in money wages may have made little difference to peasants, but the artisans who got fixed dues or were paid in cash, suffered.[23] Most of these artisans were landless agriculture labour, tied to the village through service relations or *sep/jajmani*. These artisans contributed rent (*khudi kamiani*) and non-proprietary resident's cess (*kuri kamiani*) to the village headman, a contribution that tied them to the village agriculture economy; a condition where artisanal services and labour became dependent upon the landowners for sustenance.[24]

Given the declining wages, why did the artisans continue producing for the monasteries or the landowners? Possibly, the artisans wanted the reciprocal exchange or *jajmani* relations to continue because they valued the payment in kind at the end of each harvest season for artisanal services, particularly when rural manufactures had a very small urban market.[25] By 1916, there were only two large population centres in the state of Sirmaur: Nahan, with a population of 6,859 and Shamsherpur with a population of 949.[26] Other small towns like Rajgir or Renuka, had a population of less than 500 each. These towns, which served as redistribution centres, particularly for agricultural commodities, had scarce need of such craft commodities as compared to the villages. Since most of the villages had their own artisans, the scope of production outside the *jajmani*-exchange network was minimal. In such circumstances, the artisans in Panjab sought alternative employment, mostly as agriculturists.[27] In Himachal, where agricultural productivity continued to be poor and there was no industrialization, such possibilities were remote. If the artisans barely met with their subsistence needs, there was little left to meet such needs as the purchase of cattle, treatment, festivities, etc.[28] As the state refused credit or alternative ways to help meet their needs, they were forced to borrow from the moneylenders at exorbitant interest.[29] The loans contracted were difficult to return.[30] For instance, in 1961, in Moginand, it was established that there were eighteen indebted artisan families owing Rs. 2,870 at the rate of 12½ per cent per annum.[31] The Mahants, however, ostensibly advanced interest-free loans.

The *modus operandi* of raising loans was simple.[32] The borrower usually became the bonded labour of the monastery whenever the amount was more than Rs.100. His dependants were obliged to work for the Mahant at the current agricultural wages, performing domestic chores or farm labour. The craft speciality was also the prerogative of the Mahant, who received the manufactured goods against food supplied by the monastery, without any customary or monetary payment. The labour only accounted for the interest and it was obligatory to return the principal. In order to guarantee the principal, usually an assurance was required, both in person and in terms of material objects. The Mahant, however, was not fastidious about the material assurance. In most cases, only personal assurance, provided by the borrower's witness, was required. The amount of loan was not always handed over in cash, particularly when it was a successive loan, but paid in the form of wages. Thus, when Balaki contracted a successive loan of Rs. 140, to be added to an outstanding amount of Rs. 15, he accepted the payment in daily wages for the work done. This was despite the fact that he mortgaged the 'gold ring' of his father and provided a personal assurance of one *ghanu*. In other words, the successive loan in this particular case signifies only a change in position from an unpaid labourer to a paid labourer, the payment being made out of the principal. As the payment was made at the rate of the current wages from the principal, the work done may be deemed as an interest. Thus, the interest was as high as 100 per cent. Indeed, the loans contracted were seldom returned in entirety. Apparently, the Mahant was not even interested in the principal being returned. A flow of cheap labour was thus ensured to work upon the sizeable land and for other economic interests of the monastery, like running the water mill or the flourmill, etc.

The loan contracted was hereditary. In case of death, the next of kin inherited the loan, for which a separate deed was signed. Thus, the widow of one Sadhu, a basket-maker, inherited a debt of Rs. 312 and promised to work for the Mahant along with her family. Moreover, there are also instances of the loan being transferred to the person providing assurance.

People of neighbouring villages also took monastic loans. On such occasions, the Mahant forced the debtors to shift themselves along with their family and goods. Thus, a leather worker, Khadku, migrated with his family and cattle to the monastic estate when he borrowed Rs.100 to return an outstanding debt. Such migrations were welcome as they uprooted the immigrant from their social environment, and at the same time, pressurized the local artisans/peasants to acquiesce, as the migrants competed to share the limited resources controlled by the Mahants. It would not be out of place to observe here that the monasteries always attempted to change the demographic and hierarchical landscape of the local society to create alternatives by redistributing the largesse in terms of grants, offerings or employment, to perpetuate hegemony and assert their dominance. For instance, in Nurpur, Foster observed in 1790 that in order to conduct their business gainfully, the monasteries employed Kashmiris, who were dextrous in all works, such as weaving, dyeing, tailoring, etc., preferring them than a local potential.[33] That this was a common practice is evident from the fact that the tea planters hired Kashmiri porters as farm hands, replacing the protesting locals in 1914 in Palampur.[34] Obviously, the Kashmiris would be less inclined to protest as the local society might, just as Mahants asserted control by ignoring the local potential. That they rigidly transformed the local demographic profile is evident from the fact that by 1845, Hugel wrote that of the total Nurpur population of 6,000, 'two-thirds are Kashmiris, who have been settled here for more than a generation'.[35]

The Mahant was also entitled to 'free help' from the debtors as a right whenever the need arose. Therefore, a debtor promised in writing that, 'whenever such occasion arises, he will leave his own work, how so important it may be, and accord primacy to the job of the Mahant'. These workers operated the flour and water mills, performed tilling, threshing and harvesting, rearing of the monastic livestock, irrigation and manufactured for agricultural and ritual purposes.

All the credit documents were legal contracts, signed on the Promissory Note of the Sirmaur state and was worth an *anna* or 3 *annas*. An official scribe wrote all the contracts; all of them were accompanied by a personal guarantee; in some cases, material guarantee was also sought. The borrowers signed the contracts or their thumb marks were imprinted. Two types of witnesses were also required, comprising mostly *lambardars*, *zaildars*, or the village headman. All the contracts were between the artisans and the Mahant. Unlike Panjab, there is not an instance of loan being contracted by any peasant cultivator.[36] It was, obviously, not in the interest of the monastery to advance loans to the peasants. At this time, the nationalist movement was picking up in Nahan, a nearby town, and Kanet cultivators were its vocal participants. 'Land for the tillers' was one of the slogans raised by the cultivators.[37] They were the first to defy the local niche of power enjoyed by the Mahants in this area. But the Mahants, by ensuring access to artisan labour, gained influence over the cultivators in that they could reduce the cultivator-tenants' share in output or evict them that much more easily, as was done by the Jogis of Chamba. A similar strategy was followed by the Rajput warrior castes in Kangra, who tacitly supported the Mahants to legitimize their raising an alternative group that would replace the tenant-cultivators.

The involvement of the village functionaries is notable from a legal perspective. The illiterate artisans always feared the written word, as they had no way of knowing the exact wording of the contract or its nature and implications. The involvement of these functionaries heightened the fear because of the notion of power that they wielded. Writing, throughout the sub-continent, was a symbol of power, due to its ritual and legal usage. The basis of fear was amply substantiated as these functionaries, the high caste landowners, and, to an extent, the state, connived with the Mahants in marginalizing the artisans.[38] Since these artisans were non-proprietary residents, they were at the mercy of the village functionaries. The *lambardar* was not only the collector of revenue, but 'a strong man, who feels that he will be able to exercise influence in restraining a doubtful character from committing an offence'.[39] The Mahants invoked his office for protection against any non-complying artisan who borrowed from them. Indeed, the *lambardar* seems to be more powerful than the headman, and hence was used mostly as a witness by the Mahant. Moreover, the Mahants and the *lambardar* complemented each other because the former also had the right to collect revenue as the landowners but were in turn assessed by the *lambardar* after the deduction of all dues and payments not only to the artisans and agricultural labour but also the tenants.[40] The Mahants used the office of the headman not only to seek protection against the non-conforming artisans and agricultural labourers, but also the tenants. Both the *lambardar* and headman received 5 per cent of the net output from the

Mahant as well as the artisans or other tenants.[41] Nevertheless, the Mahant always had something extra for these officials.

The colonial officials as well as the state connived with the moneylenders in general and Mahants in particular, to extend their local niche of power. They intervened directly in the 1930s when the prices of agricultural goods were declining. Consequently, those getting cash payments stood to advantage as against those receiving the payment in kind. The artisans receiving cash payments were forced to accept a 25 per cent cut in their wages. At the same time, an adjustment was made between the debtor and the creditor, as well as between the landowner and the government, as in both cases, cash payment was insisted. The negotiations were such that it doubled the 'burden of agriculture debt'. Thus, a peasant who could clear his debt in 1929 by selling 100 maunds of produce had to sell 200 maunds or more in 1934.[42]

The social status of artisans who were associated with the monastic enterprise was promoted to compete with the Kanet peasants, much like the Kolhis against Ghirths in Kangra. This is where the monastery as a space beyond the community, yet interacting and binding on the community, acquires significance. Theoretically, monasticism imparted a sense of communitas and a feeling of liminal subversion of hierarchy. Practically, it empowered the caste community. Thus, the social status of some members of the Lohar community was raised, who henceforth became Giris (a Dasanami order to which the monastery belonged), though continuing with their ancestral occupation of smithy. These Gir-Lohars could serve inside the monastery, as well as against the Dumnas or Chamars or even other Lohars who served only in the fields. Yet, these 'Sanskritized' Lohars continued to marry within their parental castes and were forced to observe commensal-dietary taboos with the high castes as earlier, while forming the upper echelon of their parental caste. Such social mobility, within the community was welcomed by the high-caste Rajputs. It did not affect their high caste status but became an effective tool to control the low castes, as the

Rajputs of Kangra used against the Ghirths by promoting the Kolhis and other artisan castes.

The Mahants of Thor were not the only ones to raise an alternative 'community' of artisans as tillers or agricultural labourers, but perhaps all major land-owning religious establishments fostered such change in landed relations. In Devi Kothi, for instance, by the 1930s, four Lohar families were added to the list of cultivators, as against 12 'others'. By 1956, this had increased to 15, while the original cultivators stood at 11 only. A new class of landless agriculturists was thus being raised. This is reflected in the village land productivity relations as well. By 1960, as many as 14 Lohars, 3 Chamars and 5 Dhakis owned land from 0.5 acre to 2 acres. While the land qualified them as well as raised their status as agriculturists, it could barely meet their requirements. All these households were also the tenants or agricultural labour, particularly of the shrine of Chamunda, working for other landed castes as well. Consequently, their dependence on their artisan expertise declined. The caste genealogy of these Lohar-blacksmiths was consequently reformulated, formally admitting them as a peasant caste. Within a span of thirty years (1930-60), they replaced the Batwal peasants, the major land cultivating class of the area. In the process, the high castes, through the intervention of the religious establishments, asserted their dominance by sustaining change.[43]

## Conclusion

There are two blurs in recent historiography that should be addressed. One, the way asceticism as an institution has been depicted, without distinguishing between those who give up the world altogether, and the householder-ascetics (a misnomer in itself) or those who settled at some point in time but continue to be loosely associated with the ascetic group (and therefore called 'ascetics') that becomes its identity marker. Thus, we have Sanyasis, Gosains or Jogis as caste names as well as renunciants. It must, however, be understood that when 'ascetics' (characterized by abstention of all kinds, who are socially dead) become householders, they are looked down upon and therefore punished by placing them low in the caste ranking. For example, the Nath monasteries or *dera*s were revered places and were places of power, however, the householder Naths were frowned upon. Consequently, in order to draw prestige and status that was associated with the renunciant classes, the eponymous householders continued to associate with them, holding an in-between position and exhibiting associated markers. Thus, Nath householders would wear Nath 'horns' and sometimes the 'earrings' as well to lay claim to the history of their association with the sect and the specific lineage therein. By such association and appropriation of cultic history, these householders assumed a leadership role in a given rural locality. In fact, the distinction between the Nath ascetics, the novice Aughar renouncers (some continued as novices throughout their lives) and the householder Naths, provide us with differing dynamics both within the sect and 'order' as well as their relations of power with the local society. Thus, the social history woven around 'ascetics' and their institution becomes more challenging and nuanced, and it is imperative to qualify and make distinctions where applicable, given the commonsensical understanding and standardization of the term 'ascetic'. This has been demonstrated by Kasturi as well.[44] She argues that the Anglo-Hindu law on succession was used by the state and the 'spiritual orders' to assert masculinities within these 'orders' to claim succession and properties. Thus, by defining 'asceticism' literally as an institution that is beyond and against sexuality and bonds or kinship obtained thereof, many 'orders' tried to reconstruct or purify their genealogies and sought the intervention of legal system on this premise. Based on the commonsensical reading of the term (refracted through the prism of European understanding of the terms 'ascetic', 'monk' and 'monastery') the law courts created a picture of pristine ascetic orders which was simplistic and did not take into account the complex ways by which the local society dealt with the issues of domestication and caste fixation, sexuality, relationships and social bonding. This anomaly needs to be addressed at length.

Second, did the colonial state withdraw altogether from the 'public arena', a space that was allegedly filled by the 'ascetics', who would then motivate and influence the national movement? The communal colour, therefore, is tacitly sprayed into the Indian national movement and the consequent rise of right-wing politics after Independence. Interestingly, the 'public arena' is the *mela*s and fairs (*kumbha* at Prayag or Haridwar, for instance), which were always the meeting point for various ascetic factions, which also became the rallying points for nationalists. The hijacking of the national movement in such arenas, as has been argued, in fact, would be contradictory to the well-accepted fact of ascetic militarization. Militarization of the ascetic sects and flaring tempers and battles in such gatherings would rather point to the contested space—both ideas and geography—instead of convergence of militarized sects into right-wing politics. This argument, however, is too simplistic and needs more clear and careful enunciation.

It would be interesting to interrogate that which sects were coloured black by the colonial state and which they continued to colour white. Which among the sects were actually demonized? Moreover, how did the colonial state control and influence the 'public space' through its agents would be another question. As far as this paper is concerned, we have observed that the 'agents' or officials of the colonial state connived with the 'spiritual sector'—the monasteries and the householders—to influence and control the localities. The colonial state, in fact, refurbished the axiomatic symbiotic relationship between the king and the ascetic, in this case, both were the 'involved' 'outsiders' who could effectively deflate the potential threats while bringing about marked changes by normatively 'Hinduising' the society. In the process, the local 'spiritual order' was leveraged to create a 'local empire' and assume a leadership role. At the level of locality, our evidence demonstrates how religious establishments, mirroring and safeguarding the interests of landed high caste 'community', maintained control of and access to rural labour through capital control and effected change in the caste-occupational and demographic profile of the local society. The caste manipulations were effected to check the bargaining power of the peasant castes. Acting as the 'rural local bosses', the monastic system regulated and controlled caste hierarchy.[45] By manipulating its temporal and spiritual-ideological authority, it effected and legitimized changes in the rural social-economy, thus deflating the protest or unrest, as in Kangra or Chamba. In the process, these establishments extended their 'local empires' that the hinterland of these establishments represented. This extension of their niche of power and their role as 'local bosses' reaffirmed their social, economic and ideological dominance. They were aided by the colonial agents, who occupied various offices and ranks—schools, judiciary, land revenue and settlement or forests—whose role and influence necessitates a closer scrutiny. It is through them that the colonial state influenced and acted in the 'public arena' as well as in the rural localities.

## NOTES

1. B.S. Cohn, 'Role of Gosains in the Economy of Eighteenth and Nineteenth Century Upper India', *Journal of Social Research*, 17, 1974, pp. 88-95; D.H.A. Kolff, 'Sanyasi Trader-Soldiers', *Indian Economic and Social History Review* (*IESHR*), 8, 1971, pp. 213-18; also, S.N. Gordon, 'Comment', *IESHR*, 8, 1978, pp. 219-20; Pinch writes that these 'ascetics', 'exercised broad political and economic influence as merchants, bankers, and, most importantly, soldiers. Powerful Mahants (abbots) speculated in real estate and engaged in extensive moneylending activities in order to diversify monastic endowments in urban centers throughout the north, thus facilitating links between the increasingly regional political economies of the late Mughal era.' W. R. Pinch, *Peasants and Monks in British India*, Berkeley: University of California Press, 1996, p. 24.
2. W.R. Pinch, *Warrior Ascetics and Indian Empires*, Cambridge: Cambridge University Press, 2006; David N. Lorenzen, 'Warrior Ascetics in Indian History', *Journal of the American Oriental Society*, 98, p. 1, 1978.
3. S. Freitag, 'Contesting in Public: Colonial Legacies and

Contemporary Communalism', in David Ludden, (ed.), *Contesting the Nation: Religion, Community, and the Politics of Democracy in India*, Philadelphia: University of Pennsylvania Press, 1996, pp. 211-34.

4. The history of and leading to the movement is long with, P. van der Veer, *Gods on Earth: The Management of Religious Experience and Identity in a North Indian Pilgrimage Center*, New Delhi: Oxford University Press, 1989, just before the demolition of the structure and James G. Lochtefeld, 'The Vishva Hindu Parishad and the Roots of Hindu Militancy', *Journal of the American Academy of Religion*, 62, 2, 1994, pp. 587-602, just after the event.
5. Pinch, *Peasants and Monks in British India*, op. cit., particularly chapter 3: 'Being *Vaishnava*, Becoming *Kshatriya*', pp. 81-115.
6. Arjun Appadurai, 'The production of Locality', in, *Counterworks: Managing the Diversity of Knowledge*, ed. Richard Fardon, London, 1995, pp. 204-5; for comparative African example, Ute Luig, 'Constructing Local Worlds: Spirit Possession in the Gwembe Valley, Zambia', in *Spirit Possession: Modernity and Power in Africa*, ed. Heike Behrend and Ute Luig, Madison, 1999, pp. 124-41.
7. B.N. Goswamy and J.S. Grewal, *The Mughals and Jogis of Jakhbar*. Simla: Indian Institute of Advanced Study, 1967. This and subsequent document number are given in parenthesis from this collection.
8. Veena Sachdeva, 'Agrarian Production', Punjab Language and Culture Akademi, p. 289.
9. George Foster, *A Journey from Bengal to England: Through the Northern Part of India, Kashmir &c*, vol. I, Calcutta, 1790, Chandigarh: Punjab Language and Culture Akademi (rpt.) 1970, p. 267. The widowed Rani of Bilaspur was observed to be influenced by her favourite 'sunassee', the ascetic, p. 248.
10. B.N. Goswamy and J.S. Grewal, *The Mughals and Sikh Rulers and the Vaishnavas of Pindori*. Simla: Indian Institute of Advanced Study, 1968. This and subsequent document number are given in parenthesis from this collection.
11. For Panjab see, R.G. Fox, *Kin, Clan, Raja and Rule: State-Hinterland Relations in Preindustrial India*, Berkeley: University of California Press, 1971.
12. T.S. Negi, *Settlement Report of the Chamba District (First Regular Settlement 1951-58)*. Simla: Government Press, 1961. p. 13.

13. *Chamba State Gazetteer, 1904. Part A. Lahore: Civil and Military Gazette Press, 1910*, p. 231.
14. Negi, *Settlement Report of the Chamba*, Table 14, p. 11.
15. Mahesh Sharma, 'Marginalisation and Appropriation: Jogis, Brahmins and Sidh Shrines', *IESHR*, 33(1) 1996, pp. 73-91; also *The Realm of Faith: Subversion, Appropriation and Dominance in the Western Himalaya*. Shimla: Indian Institute of Advanced Study 2001, pp. 100-15.
16. Parry, who studied the Kangra Rajput-warrior castes, uses this binary to emphasize those who could provide household-related domestic service and those who could not enter a high-caste household, Jonathan P. Parry, *Caste and Kinship in Kangra,* Delhi: Vikas, 1979; for caste as colonial construct subsuming diverse identities and the rise of caste-based movements, N.B. Dirks, *Castes of Mind: Colonialism and the Making of Modern India*, Princeton: Princeton University Press, 2001.
17. *Punjab District Gazetteer, Part A: 1924-25, Kangra District* (*KDG*), vol. II, Lahore: Govt. Press, 1926, pp. 173-4.
18. *Caste and Kinship in Kangra*. 1979, pp. 115-28.
19. H.A. Rose informs that the Raja of Bilaspur accepted the clean status of Kolhis because he needed soldiers to fight, while the Katoch Raja of Kangra refused because he did not. *A Glossary of the Castes and Tribes of the Punjab and North-West Frontier Province*, Lahore: Govt. Press, 1919, vol. I, p. 44.
20. *Caste and Kinship in Kangra*. pp. 121-5.
21. J.P. Perry, 'The Koli Dilemma', *Contributions to Indian Sociology*, vol. 4, Dec. 1970, p. 99; *KDG,* p. 152.
22. On general price index, see Michelle McAlpin, 'Price Movements and Fluctuations in Economic Activity', in Dharma Kumar, ed., *The Cambridge Economic History of India, 1757-1970*, Cambridge: Cambrdige University Press, 1982, p. 904.
23. By 1912, 58 per cent of the villages paid only in cash, 4 per cent partly in cash and partly in grains; while only 2 per cent of the villages continued to make customary payments in grains, *Report on the Moral and Material Progress of the Punjab, 1901-11*, Lahore, 1915, p. 5. See also M. L. Darling, *Wisdom and Waste in the Punjab Village*, London: Oxford University Press,1934, p. 316.
24. O.P. Aggarwala, *Punjab Land Revenue Act, 1887*, Lahore: Lahore Law Depot & Lahore Law Agency, 1936; Delhi, 1991 rpt.

(hereafter *PLRA*), p. 51. These were to be paid at the end of the agricultural year, which commenced from every 16th of June, pp. 52, 54.

25. The Mahant, like other landowners, supplied the raw material required for production. For the days that the artisans worked for a particular family, it provided them with food. However, the payment was made at the end of the seasonal harvesting, called *faslana* or *sakta*. This seasonal payment was linked to the amount of land tilled, generally measured in the 'number of ploughs one owned'. If a *zamindar*, for instance, owned a plough of land in 1961, he paid 20 *seers* of cereals, 1 *seer* jaggery, 1 *seer* cotton or 10 *seers* of sugar cane juice. At that time, wheat cost Rs. 24-40 kg; a metre of cotton cloth cost Rs. 1-3; and 40 kg jaggery cost Rs. 27-45. *Census of India*, 1961, XX, (Part VI) no. 8, *Village Survey of Moginand*, p. 44.
26. *Census of India*, vol. II, 1901, *General Tables for Provinces and Feudatory States*, p. 28.
27. H.C. Sharma, 'Changing World of the Artisans', in *Five Punjabi Centuries: Polity, Economy, Society and Culture, c.1500-1900*, ed. Indu Banga, Delhi: Manohar, 1997, p. 500.
28. C.A.H. Townshend, Director of Civil Supplies, Punjab, has provided a comparative cost of living for a family of a worker or an artisan between 1914 and 1918. The base income is considered Rs. 50 per month as in 1914. The calculations show that subsistence and other basic needs accounted for almost the whole of income. See Ravinder Kumar, 'The Rowlatt Satyagraha in Lahore', in his *Essays in the Social History of Modern India*, New Delhi: Oxford University Press, 1983, p. 187.
29. In 1961, loans could be obtained at *takina byaz*, i.e. after paying the fee of an *anna* per rupee (16th part of the loan as fee) over and above the yearly interest of 12½ per cent. Sometimes the loan was contracted at 12½ per cent per men sum. Census of India, 1961, XX, (Part VI) no. 17, *Village Survey Rajana*, p. 39.
30. For different reasons than in Thor, during the inter-war period, the scale of moneylending and debts expanded in rural Punjab. In this expansion, the vulnerability of the debtor may have played a role. In general, however, it is believed that it was creditworthiness that encouraged moneylending and debts. In 1922, Calvert concluded that the number of moneylenders assessed to tax in Punjab increased from 8,400 in 1902-3 to 15,035 (out of the total

number of moneylenders, 40,690) in 1917-18. At the same time the 'money on loan' increased from Rs. 130 to 280 in this period. (H. Calvert, *The Wealth and Welfare of the Punjab*, Lahore: Printed by the *Civil and Military Gazette*, 1922, p. 129.) Darling concluded that by 1934 the average debt per proprietor in Panjab (43,733 proprietors) was Rs. 463, which was 12 times the land revenue due from them. In contrast the average debt of small proprietors was Rs.310 and occupancy tenants (12,000 tenants) Rs. 210. Thus, the more propertied a person, the more indebted he was. (Malcolm Darling, *The Punjab Peasant in Prosperity and Debt*, New Delhi: Oxford University Press, 1947, pp. 4, 14.) Darling in 1934 concludes that 'debt follows credit', and that 'those who have no credit will have no debt.' Thus, in Jhang area where 'cultivation was uncertain, the people nomadic', there was no credit. Similarly, Ludhiana with 'weak soil and little irrigation' was free from debt. Nevertheless, the rich districts were more indebted as the moneylender was ready to make more investments (ibid., p. 211). In these districts, the price of land was higher, thus the value of land as security was higher. The rate of interest for secured loans was also lower, being 12 to 18¾ per cent as against jewellery. Only 5 per cent of loans were secured thus. The rate of interest against land without possession was 12 per cent; but when possession was also given, the rate, measured in produce, figured only 6 to 9 per cent. The rate of interest on unsecured loans in Punjab, as in the case of grain loans, ranged from 12 to 25 per cent. Malcolm Darling, *The Punjab Peasant*, pp. 180-1.

31. *Census of India*, 1961, XX, (Part VI) no.8, *Village Survey Moginand*, p. 42.
32. The main source for this section is the *bahi*-account book, that was recovered from the Shaivite *Dasanami math* (monastery) of Giri order from the village Thor (*Hadbast* no. 131, or revenue boundaries), in *tahsil* (revenue circle) Rajgarh, district Sirmaur. This *bahi* was recovered from the Mahant of Thor and is presently in the possession of Himachal Archives, Shimla. It is written in Pahari–Hindi using Devanagari script in black ink; signed by the witnesses in Devanagari, occasionally in Urdu, and rarely in English. It is bound in red cloth cover in the form of an account book, similar to those maintained by merchants and moneylenders. The folios are unnumbered but contain the contracts signed by the artisans with the Mahant of Thor between 1926 and 1934.

The *bahi* is of significance in not only providing us with information regarding the economic relations between the artisans and Mahant, but also on the income and expenditure pattern of the artisans. Significantly, it acts as an authentic inventory of castes in an area on which there is otherwise little information. Moreover, the contracts contained implicitly emphasize the nexus between the State functionaries and the religious establishment.

These documents detail the terms of contract arrived at with the Mahant, authenticated by two witnesses and occasionally accompanied by a mortgage. The contract, for example, specified that 'the borrower will plough the lands of Mahant (without wages) and one person of his family will sow for Mahant on the payment of daily wages'. Moreover, they were required to 'perform all the domestic chores of the Mahant, working as unpaid labour, and tending to the water mill'. If the borrower refused or showed a lack of interest, he was charged interest, penalty, or both, though explicitly the Mahant agreed not to charge interest. The contract is followed by the balance sheet, showing both receipts and subsequent loans advanced.

33. Foster, *A Journey from Bengal to England: Through the Northern Part of India, Kashmir & c*, vol. I, op. cit., p. 268.
34. G.M. Boughey, *Preliminary Assessment of the Palampur Tehsil of the Kangra District*, Lahore: Civil Press, 1914, p. 14.
35. Baron C. Hugel, *Travels in Kashmir and the Punjab*, tr. J.B. Jervis, London: J. Petheram, 1845, p. 55.
36. Contrary to Thor, in Punjab, Malcolm Darling concludes that 'those who have no credit will have no debt', *The Punjab Peasant in Prosperity and Debt*, Delhi, 1947, p. 211.
37. *Himachal Pradesh District Gazetteer – Sirmaur*, Aligarh, 1961, second chapter.
38. An example has been discussed about Himachal. See Mahesh Sharma, 'Marginalisation and Appropriation: Jogis, Brahmins and Sidh Shrines', *IESHR*, 33 (1), 1996.
39. Punjab Land Revenue Act (PLRA) 1887, p. 54. IOPR 1890 (revised).
40. *PLRA*, pp. 52, 54.
41. Veena Sachdeva, 'Agrarian Production and Distribution in the late 18th Century', in *Five Punjabi Centuries: Polity, Economy, Society and Culture, c.1500-1900*, ed. Indu Banga, New Delhi: Manohar, 1997, p. 288.

42. Darling, *Wisdom and Waste*, p. 316.
43. *Jamabandi-Consolidation Report*, 1956, Devi Kothi, Chamba District. Patwari record of Devi Kothi.
44. Malavika Kasturi, '"Asceticising" Monastic Families: Ascetic Genealogies, Property Feuds and Anglo-Hindu Law in the late Colonial India', *Modern Asian Studies*, 43 (5), 2009, pp. 1039-83.
45. D. A. Washbrook contends that the rural local bosses farmed their estates by the hired labour while acting as the moneylenders at the same time. He shows that for them, 'economic considerations always were subordinate to, and an instrument of, political activity', *The Emergence of Provincial Politics: The Madras Presidency 1870-1920*, Cambridge: Cambridge University Press, 1976, p. 83.

## REFERENCES

Aggarwala, O.P. 1936. *Punjab Land Revenue Act, 1887*. Lahore: Lahore Law Depot & Lahore Law Agency.

Appadurai, Arjun. 1995. 'The production of Locality', in Richard Fardon (ed.), *Counterworks: Managing the Diversity of Knowledge*: 204-25. London: Routledge.

Boughey, G.M. 1914. *Preliminary Assessment of the Palampur Tehsil of the Kangra District*. Lahore: Civil Press.

Calvert, H. 1922. *The Wealth and Welfare of the Punjab*. Lahore: Printed by the Civil and Military Gazette.

*Chamba State Gazetteer, 1904. Part A*. 1910. Lahore: Civil and Military Gazette Press.

Cohn, B.S. 1964. 'Role of Gosains in the Economy of Eighteenth and Nineteenth Century Upper India'. *Indian Economic and Social History Review*, vol. 1, no. 4: 175-82.

Darling, M. L. 1934. *Wisdom and Waste in the Punjab Village*. London: Oxford University Press.

Darling, Malcolm. 1947. *The Punjab Peasant in Prosperity and Debt*. New Delhi: Oxford University Press.

Dirks, N.B. 2001. *Castes of Mind: Colonialism and the Making of Modern India*. Princeton: Princeton University Press.

Foster, George. 1970 (rpt). *A Journey from Bengal to England: Through the Northern Part of India, Kashmir, Afghanistan, and Persia, and Into Russia by the Caspian Sea*, vol. I. Chandigarh: Punjab Language and Culture Academy.

Freitag, S. 1996. 'Contesting in Public: Colonial Legacies and Contemporary Communalism', in David Ludden (ed.), *Contesting the Nation: Religion, Community, and the Politics of Democracy in India*: 211-34. Philadelphia: University of Pennsylvania Press.

Gordon, S. N. 1971. 'Comment'. *Indian Economic and Social History Review*. 8: 219-20.

Goswamy, B.N. and J.S. Grewal, 1967. *The Mughals and Jogis of Jakhbar*. Shimla: Indian Institute of Advanced Study.

_____. 1968. *The Mughals and Sikh Rulers and the Vaishnavas of Pindori*. Shimla: Indian Institute of Advanced Study.

Hugel, Baron C. 1845. *Travels in Kashmir and the Punjab*, tr. J.B. Jervis. London: J. Petheram.

Kasturi, Malavika. 2009. 'Asceticising' Monastic Families: Ascetic Genealogies, Property Feuds and Anglo-Hindu Law in the late Colonial India'. *Modern Asian Studies*, vol. 43, no. 5: 1039-83.

Kolff, D.H.A. 1971. 'Sanyasi Trader-Soldiers'. *Indian Economic and Social History Review*, vol. 8, no. 2: 213-18.

Kumar, Ravinder. 1983. *Essays in the Social History of Modern India*. New Delhi: Oxford University Press.

Lochtefeld, G. 1994. 'The Vishva Hindu Parishad and the Roots of Hindu Militancy'. *Journal of the American Academy of Religion*, vol. 62, no. 2: 587-602.

Lorenzen, David N. 1978. 'Warrior Ascetics in Indian History'. *Journal of the American Oriental Society*, vol. 98, no. 1: 61-75.

Luig, Ute. 1999. 'Constructing Local Worlds: Spirit Possession in the Gwembe Valley, Zambia', in Heike Behrend and Ute Luig (eds.), *Spirit Possession: Modernity and Power in Africa*: 124-41.Madison: University of Wisconsin Press.

McAlpin, Michelle. 1982. 'Price Movements and Fluctuations in Economic Activity', in Dharma Kumar (ed.), *The Cambridge Economic History of India, 1757-1970*: 878-904. Cambridge: Cambridge University Press.

Negi, T.S. 1961. *Settlement Report of the Chamba District (First Regular Settlement 1951-58)*. Shimla: Government Press.

Parry, Jonathan P. 1979. *Caste and Kinship in Kangra*. New Delhi: Vikas.

_____. 1970. 'The Koli Dilemma', *Contributions to Indian Sociology*, vol. 4, no.1: 84-104.

Pinch, W.R. 1996. *Peasants and Monks in British India*. Berkeley: University of California Press.

_____. 2006. *Warrior Ascetics and Indian Empires*, Cambridge: Cambridge University Press.

*Punjab District Gazetteer, Part A: 1924-25, Kangra District*, vol. II, Lahore: Superintendent, Govt. Printing Press.

R.G. Fox. 1971. *Kin, Clan, Raja and Rule: State-Hinterland Relations in Preindustrial India.* Berkley: University of California Press.

*Memorandum on the Moral and Material Progress in the Punjab During the Years 1901-02 to 1911-12.* Lahore: Superintendent, Government Printing, Punjab, 1914.

Rose, H.A. 1919. *A Glossary of the Castes and Tribes of the Punjab and North-West Frontier Province*, vol. 1. Lahore: Govt. Press.

Sachdeva, Veena. 1997. 'Agrarian Production and Distribution in the late 18th Century', in Indu Banga (ed.), *Five Punjabi Centuries: Polity, Economy, Society and Culture, c.1500-1900:* 285-306. New Delhi: Manohar.

Sharma, H.C. 1997. 'Changing World of the Artisans', in Indu Banga (ed.), *Five Punjabi Centuries: Polity, Economy, Society and Culture, c.1500-1900*: 496-508. Delhi: Manohar.

Sharma, Mahesh. 1996. 'Marginalisation and Appropriation: Jogis, Brahmins and Sidh Shrines'. *Indian Economic and Social History Review*, vol. 33, no.1: 73-91.

_____. 2001. *The Realm of Faith: Subversion, Appropriation and Dominance in the Western Himalaya*. Shimla: Indian Institute of Advanced Study.

van der Veer, P. 1989. *Gods on Earth: The Management of Religious Experience and Identity in a North Indian Pilgrimage Center*. New Delhi: Oxford University Press.

Washbrook, D.A. 1976. *The Emergence of Provincial Politics: The Madras Presidency 1870-1920*. Cambridge: Cambridge University Press.

CHAPTER 6

# Temple Ascetics and Community Formation

## Three Case Studies from the Jāṭa Localities of Delhi

MIHIR KESHARI

### Introduction

Despite all their diversities, contradictions, and the general nature which defies any attempt towards straightforward theorization, Hindu temples are arguably the most prominent marker of Hindu identity, culture and religiosity. Hence, modern academic studies concerning Hinduism have paid great attention to studying and understanding Hindu temples, through varied disciplinary approaches ranging from History, Archaeology, Art History, to even Ethnography. This article, through ethnographic studies of specific temples in Jāṭa localities of Delhi, aims to locate and explore temples as spaces which facilitate the interaction of ascetic traditions with the larger society and the subsequent socio-cultural possibilities that this presents. The article is broadly divided into three sections. The first section deals with the current dominant historiographical trends in the academic understanding of temples and argues for the necessity to revisit it, the second section analyses the debates surrounding Hindu asceticism and argues for the linkages between temples and Hindu ascetic traditions, tracing them back from the early historical to late-medieval period, and the third presents specific case studies, which are later analysed to understand the socio-historical and cultural implications of the phenomenon of temple asceticism, including the phenomenon of community formation.

## Major Trends in the Historiography of the Social History of Hindu Temples

The academic scholarship on Hindu temples is extensive. Unfortunately, what unites studies about Hindu temples is the common insistence on situating temples in the domain of politics and power in one way or another.[1] Hence, not only have temples come to just represent and mark monarchies but also their very classification has been done on monarchical dynastic lines. This mode of understanding temples has virtually thwarted any possibility of analysing them in their broader socio-cultural context. Salila Kulshreshtha, in her analysis of the historiography of Hindu temples, observes that studies on temples have relegated them to the exclusive domain of politics and royalty, where temples are simply seen as under the control of the Brāhmaṇa priest and as tied to royal patronage, which she shows has been done basically through three methodological approaches.[2]

The first approach bases its analysis of Hindu temples to a significant extent on textual sources and architectural treatises concerning temples, in supplement to archaeological/architectural observations; within this approach, Kulshreshtha places the work of scholars like A.K. Coomaraswamy and Stella Kramrisch. This approach, she argues, continues not only to attribute the construction of temples to royal initiative alone, but also to view ancient historical treatises concerning temples as some sort of a 'rulebook' which governs and facilitates the construction of temples as the material manifestation of theological or ideational principles as codified by the Brāhmaṇas.[3] The second approach locates temples within the process of state formation. The third approach has been identified as the 'art historical' method, where not just the construction of temples but more importantly, their architecture and iconography are viewed as suggesting royal propaganda. However, the second is more important, given the wider implications of its theorization. Hence, it will be discussed below in some detail.

The second approach is of special significance because it does not limit its analysis to the mere materiality of the temple and questions regarding its construction, but rather places the temple within a broader structure and the processes which it entails. The broader understanding remains largely the same across different interpretive modes: it looks at the linkages between temples and royalty, where temples under the patronage of royal power and under the control of the Brāhmaṇa priest helped to establish royal authority.

For R.S. Sharma and other proponents of the Indian feudalism model, the increasing royal patronage in the form of land grants to temples and other such religious institutions, and to individuals, in early-medieval India represented a process through which royal authority and revenue was decentralized in favour of local/regional power structures to the detriment of centralized polity, which led to formation of a feudalized political structure.[4] Even for scholars who argue against the feudal model of Sharma and others, temples continue to be an institution particularly aligned with the cause of royalty.

In Burton Stein's Segmentary model for the south Indian states, temples continue to represent a political force, royal patronage to temples and brāhamaṇas being seen as a mechanism through which control over different segments of the polity was maintained.[5] Similarly, for the proponents of the integrative model of early-medieval Indian polities, such as Hermann Kulke (1993), B.D. Chattopadhyaya (1994) and B.P. Sahu (2003), royal patronage to temples is seen in the context of local/regional state formation, where such religious institutions provided legitimacy to the local/regional state, and hence helped in its consolidation.[6]

To demonstrate how donations to Brāhmaṇas were tied to specific local-tribal shrines, which were afterwards Brahmanized by associating the deity of the shrine with a member of the pan-Hindu pantheon, Chattopadhyaya (2004) cites many cases where local deities like the 'Goddess of the Forest' (*Araṇyavāsinī*),

'Goddess of the Pot' (*Ghaṭavāsinī*), 'Goddess of the Tree' (*Vaṭayakṣiṇī*), or elsewhere the 'Goddess of the Pillar' (*Stambheśvarī*), etc., were associated with Durgā.[7] According to Chattopadhyaya, local kings made these donations to strengthen and legitimize their reign by providing patronage to organizations such as temples.

What is clear from the above brief discussion of some important academic studies of Hindu temples is the dominant inter-relationship between temples and royalty on which these studies build their understanding. This excessive emphasis on linkages between temples and royalty has eclipsed an alternative theoretical understanding of Hindu temples, where temples are not limited to the domain of power but can be understood as social institutions where the role of the larger community can be taken into consideration. This is something which has been highlighted by scholars like Prasad (2011).[8]

Moreover, the exclusive focus on large temple structures for identifying linkages between temples and royalty has ignored the analysis of smaller village shrines and their social implications. This is significant because both textual and archaeological evidence points in the direction of the existence of such shrines at local levels, having local support bases which were understandably non-royal in nature.

## Temples and Ascetics

In general, the ascetic or renouncer can be understood as an individual who has chosen to live a life of penance, either as a wanderer or by joining an institution made for such purpose; this stands against the choice to live as a householder, and is done for the attainment of certain goals, which in the Indian religious context can range from *mokṣa/nirvāṇa* to attain certain *siddhis*.

Romila Thapar (1978) identifies an ascetic as someone 'who has opted out of society'; moreover, she draws a distinction between ascetics and renouncers, where ascetics are individuals concerned solely with liberation of their own self, while a renouncer on the other hand is more of a 'social being' concerned with the liberation of others as well, and apparently is part of an alternative social system, which can be thought of as representing a 'counter culture'.[9]

The notion that ascetics/renouncers 'opted out' of society has been popularized by Dumont (1980), for whom the way of the ascetic/renouncer was a way out of the world of Brahmanical caste order, and hence society.[10] However, this only holds if our idea of society is limited to the world of the householder, as pointed by Burghart (1983), who asserts that the view of Dumont and others on asceticism is from the perspective of the householders and not from that of the ascetics themselves, who in any case have diverse positions on both caste structure and the householder tradition.[11] Moreover, scholars like Patrick Olivelle, through textual analysis, have traced the evolution of the ascetic/renouncer traditions within Brahmanism.[12]

From this brief discussion, what becomes clear is that a lot of discussion around the contrast between the householder and the renouncer/ascetic tradition is 'ideational' in nature, in the sense that it is concerned with marking distinctions within the sphere of ideas. However, this leaves unstudied the interactions between these two supposedly different structures, and the possible sociological and historical implications of this interaction.

The distinction between ascetic and renouncer is questionable, since ascetics do not exist in isolation but have at least some initial or eventual link with what can be termed as renouncer-like institutions which impart at least some unified teaching, which enables us to categorize these traditions as distinct from each other. Further, individual wandering which is generally associated with ascetics is also practiced by renouncers. Moreover, other scholars like Hausner do not appear to maintain this distinction and use the terms 'ascetic' and 'renouncer' interchangeably.[13]

Hsuan-Tsang noted the presence of many non-Buddhist ascetics, identified as *Pāśupata*s and *Kāpālika*s in what he called '*deva* temples'.[14] This has been interpreted by scholars like Ghurye

(1953) and Thapar (1978), as indicating the relatively late period in which we can see the organizations of Hindu ascetic traditions into unified *maṭha*-like institutions.[15]

However, to our understanding this must be seen at least in some sense as marking the distinctness of Hindu asceticism/monasticism, where wandering together with the association of ascetics with temples, always remained important. This is reflected in the variety of sources, across many periods, in which ascetics are mentioned. In the *Kathāsaritsāgara*, an early-medieval Kashmiri text, we find references to ascetic groups residing in temple premises (as discussed in Malhan, 2023).[16] Similarly, Himanshu Prabha Ray in her article 'Monasticism and the Hindu Temple', surveys and emphasizes the relation between temples and monastic traditions. She has noted inscriptional and archaeological evidence which establishes the relationship between temples and ascetic/monastic traditions; a few of them will be discussed below.[17]

The Gadhwa inscriptions, when seen together with the Bilsad and Podagarh inscriptions, show that temples were attached to institutions known as *sattra*s, which acted as community kitchens to feed 'wandering ascetics' along with others. Similarly, a sixth-century inscription of the Chālukya king Mangaleśa refers to the king making a grant for the maintenance of wandering ascetics; this grant was made at the time of the installation of an image of Viṣṇu in a cave temple. Even in visual depictions, we find ascetics associated with temples; for instance, in the seventh-century relief of Arjuna's penance at Mahābalipuram, we find ascetics depicted around a shrine of Viṣṇu.[18]

This visual representation of ascetics in connection with temples continues to exist even the medieval period. J.P. Losty has compiled various Mughal paintings depicting Hindu ascetics, some of which will be discussed below.[19] A painting in the manuscript of the *Bāburnāmā* commissioned by Akbar depicts the encounter of Bābur with Nātha ascetics at the shrine of Gur Khattri, outside Peshawar. Gur Khattri emerged as an important pilgrimage site for Hindus of the region, and the painting shows ascetics surrounded by individual temples.[20] The relation between ascetics and temples becomes even starker as we move away from paintings depicting imperial encounters to simple paintings of ascetics.

A painting by Dhanarāj, which can be dated to CE 1595, depicts an ascetic sitting with a temple shrine in the background.[21] A painting belonging to the early eighteenth century depicts Nātha ascetics gathered around a Śiva temple.[22] In a painting from Awadh from the 1760s, the courtyard of a Hindu noblewoman is shown housing a small temple with ascetics around it.[23]

The depiction of ascetics in colonial-era paintings becomes highly individualized, thus alienating them from their surroundings, so it becomes hard to trace background information. However, some paintings do give some visual clues about the background of these ascetics. A company painting catalogued by Mildred Archer, by an artist Bani Lal of Patna and belonging to CE 1880, depicts a Hindu 'faqir' with arm raised, and in his background stands a temple.[24] Clues about such interactions are not limited to visual sources alone, but even in literary sources such as Sufi hagiographies or colonial ethnographies we find ascetics associated with temples. The above discussion should suffice to point out the linkages between temples and Hindu ascetic traditions.

One reason behind this arduous task of tracing the historical linkages between the ascetic traditions and temples from the early historical to the early-modern period, before discussing our case studies which are situated in early-modern to modern period, is to avoid the mistake of attributing everything to the processes engendered by the onset of British colonialism in the subcontinent, as is often done by scholars who study colonial societies, since it is very much possible for a tradition or a phenomenon which is manifested in modern period to have deep historical roots in periods long before the colonial period. This is not to deny the significant and obvious impact of colonialism on various traditions of the subcontinent, religious and otherwise, including ascetic traditions.

The excellent work of William Pinch, *Peasants and Monks in British India,* is of great significance for our purpose, since the case studies which will be discussed in the next section fit well into the overall understanding which he propounded.[25] According to Pinch, Indian peasants and monks during the colonial period did not lived in isolation from each other; rather, their lives intersected. While monks' dependence on the peasantry was more material, concerned with patronage, sustenance and recruitment, the peasants depended on monks for various spiritual or religious concerns; this interdependence affected the way these groups reacted to questions of religious identity and status.[26] Bringing peasants into the picture automatically suggests the importance of local small village shrines, and the possible role they played in facilitating ascetic interaction with the larger society. It is important to note that Pinch does not simply attribute this phenomenon exclusively to the colonial period, but rather accepts the long history of the interactions between peasantry and ascetics who resided at various places, including small village temples or shrines.

The larger concern of this article is not to locate the ways through which the linkages between monks and peasant groups during the colonial period manifested itself in the arena of politics and ideology, something which the work of Pinch deals with, but rather to explore temples as spaces for such interactions, and the possible socio-cultural manifestations of such interactions.

## Case Studies

We will discuss three temples situated in the various localities of Delhi and belonging to the late-medieval to colonial period of Indian history. These temples are the Guru Gorakhanātha Rāma Tālāba Mandir in Katwaria Sarai area, the Laṭuriyā Bābā Mandir in the Kishangarh village of Vasant Kunj, and Bābā Ganganātha Mandir in Munirka. In all these temples we find a similar pattern, where initially a small temple becomes the refuge of a wandering ascetic, only to emerge as a cult centre facilitating community formation. However, if we are to map the actual processes through which these varied cults emerge, we can broadly divide the above-mentioned temples into two categories: temples with an active ascetic lineage, and temples which have no active ascetic lineage but have gone through a process of Brahmanization. While the temple at Katwaria Sarai represents the first category, the temples of both Kishangarh and Munirka are examples of the second category. This is important to highlight, as we shall see in the course of our discussion, the ways through which these cults emerged and how they projected themselves vary greatly. While a temple with an active ascetic lineage tends to emphasize the ascetic traditions more than the figure of any individual ascetic, one which has gone through active Brahmanization, though emphasizing the role of the ascetic figure, does so by subsuming it within the larger Brahmanical pantheon. These case studies will not only show that temples acted as social spaces facilitating the interaction of ascetic traditions with the larger society, but also show how Hindu temples were rooted within the larger ambit of local social and cultural politics.

### *Guru Gorakhanātha Rāma Tālāba Mandir*

The Guru Gorakhanātha Rāma Tālāba Mandir is possibly one of the oldest temples of Delhi (Fig. 6.1). The antiquity of the place, independent of the legends attached to it, can be observed from some material findings as well as its larger surroundings. Two images of Hindu deities have been unearthed from this place which date back to the early medieval period, attesting to the antiquity of the site.[27] However, most of the structure, including the temple, is of late medieval to modern period. According to local legends, in the *satyuga,* this place along with the adjacent Sanjay Van was the place where Guru Gorakhanātha performed austerities. However, after the demise of king Pṛthvīrāja Chauhān, this place, not unlike other Hindu religious centres, was destroyed by the invading Muslim armies.[28]

Fig. 6.1: Guru Gorakhanātha Rāma Tālāba Temple.
(*Source:* Photograph by the author)

It was only in the nineteenth century that worship was rekindled by the effort of Harsukh Sādh, whose father was Bābā Nainu. Harsukh Sādh is considered as belonging to the Sansanwal Jāṭa community. According to legend, Harsukh once took his cows to the forest for grazing, where they wandered away. Frustrated, Harsukh was helped by Guru Gorakhanātha, who reunited him with his cows. He then instructed Harsukh to dig a pond where he was to find ancient sculptures and then to establish a temple to enshrine them, along with other such instructions. However, at first the villagers of Katwaria did not believe Harsukh and ridiculed him, but later Gorakhanātha himself gave *darśana* to some villagers and reminded them of his instructions, and also asked them to perform the life-cycle rituals of their community at this temple itself, rather than going to the temple of Bābā Haridāsa at Jharoda Kalan.[29] Hence, a pond was dug which yielded a few ancient images, and was named Rāma Tālāba, linking it with the *satyuga*, and a temple was also constructed to enshrine the images (Fig. 6.2). After the death of

Fig. 6.2: Gorakhmedhi (*Source:* Photograph by the author)

Harsukh Sādh in 1876, the temple was handed over to wandering Nātha ascetics, in whose hands the temple complex still exists, with Munśīnātha as the first *mahant* who established the *dhūni* (the sacred fire) here (Fig. 6.3).

Fig. 6.3: Rāma Tālāba (Pond) (*Source:* Photograph by the author)

Currently, the temple complex can be said to be divided into three zones: the old and the new temple structures, and the pond situated between them. The original temple is known today as Gorakhanātha kī Meḍhī and is looked after by Aughara Nātha ascetics, while the new temple complex is maintained by the ordained Nātha *mahanta*, who is also the head of all the affairs of the temple complex, including those of the temple complex housing the *Augharas*.[30]

It appears that the story, much like the temple itself, is a later appropriation by Nātha ascetics. Among other reasons, the character of Harsukh is attached to the Nātha Sampradāya only through the episode of the *darśana* of Gorakhanātha; he is not initiated as a Nātha Yogī, which is usually the case with Nātha legends. Moreover, from the legend itself, it is clear that the place was appropriated by Nātha ascetics only after death of Harsukh. The decision to abandon the tradition of going to the shrine of Bābā Haridāsa at Jharoda Kalan for the performance of life-cycle rituals also appears to be part of sectarian competition for patronage. Whatever be the case, what matters for our purpose is the role of the temple along with Nātha ascetics in forging and perpetuating a sense of community.

Today, Gorakhanātha acts as a patron deity of various villages around the temple, particularly those belonging to the Jāṭa caste The legends attached to the temple constantly emphasize the linkages of the temple with the village of Katwaria Sarai along with its resident communities. The temple has emerged as an important centre for the performance of life-cycle rituals by the villagers, such as *muṇḍana* of children.[31] The surroundings of the temple are dotted with small hollow cubicles or pyramid-like structures, known as *sthān, thān* or *bhuiyān* (Fig. 6.4), which are said to signify places meant for Jāṭa ancestors; the presence of these structures shows the role played by the temple in facilitating socio-cultural amalgamation and forging a unified identity. Apart from its ritual and religious significance, the temple appears to be an active social space; it is not uncommon to find Nātha ascetics sharing the same *hookah* (a tobacco pipe) with Jāṭa elders of the locality in the temple premises.

Fig. 6.4: *Thāns* surrounding the temple. (*Source:* Photograph by the author)

This identity is further invigorated periodically, by organization of *bhanḍārās*, performance of *tapas* rituals by the residing *mahanta*, through visit of members of the Nātha *jamāt*[32] and through bi-annual *melās*. After every six-month on Navarātri,[33] a *melā* is organized by the temple with the help of the villagers. This *melā* involves the participation of twelve villages, and Nātha ascetics from across north India also visit the temple.

During a visit of the members of the Nātha *jamāt*, the *mahant* of the temple organizes a feast. It was observed that a considerable

Fig. 6.5: Plaques depicting the legends.
(*Source:* Photograph by the author)

amount of cash is transferred to individual Nātha ascetics of the *jamāt*. This possibly serves as a mechanism to enforce authority, as the *jamāt* plays an important role in the selection of the *mahanta*. The temple appears to hold considerable wealth, which is largely through the offerings by the surrounding communities. These events become ways through which the legitimacy of the temple is maintained, and community identity is reinforced.

As already mentioned, the individual figure of neither Harsukh nor any ascetic of the lineage is emphasized beyond a certain point; rather, the temple projects itself as deriving authority directly from the larger Nātha tradition by making Gorakhanātha its central figure. This is understandable, as the temple continues to operate within the ambit of the institutionalized Nātha Sampradāya with an active ascetic lineage. In our next case study we will see an example of a temple which has a defunct ascetic lineage, and has undergone full-scale brahmanization.

### *Laṭuriyā Bābā Mandir*

The Laṭuriyā Bābā Mandir is situated in Kishangarh, a predominantly Jāṭa locality (Fig. 6.6); the temple apparently derives its name from the big *laṭa*s (matted hair) of the ascetic it is dedicated to. Though the current structure is undoubtedly of the late colonial period, possibly the original temple which once existed goes further back in time, as reflected by the big dried-up pond around which the current temple is located (Fig. 6.7). We were informed that the Shiva shrine situated within the temple complex dates back to CE 1756, though we have no means of confirming such a date.

The legend attached to this temple is that long ago the place had a *Śivālayā*, and that a wandering ascetic known as Mangal Singh from the Motihari area of Bihar came to settle here in 1913; soon he became extremely popular among the villagers for his miracles, and came to be known as Laṭuriyā Bābā.

Laṭuriyā Bābā died in 1945, and his *samādhi* was established here. On enquiry from the current *mahaṃta* of the shrine, who

Fig. 6.6: Shrine of Laṭuriyā Bābā.
(*Source:* Photograph by the author)

Fig. 6.7: The dried-up pond. (*Source:* Photograph by the author)

introduced himself as Sūrdāsa Bābā, he said that Laṭuriyā Bābā was possibly an *Udāsī Santa.*

The theology of the end of the *kaliyuga* and the coming of the Kalki *avatāra* is prominent in the cult of Laṭuriyā Bābā, as is evident from various mentions of Kalki in the *chālisā*, *āratī*, and *mahimā gāna*s composed for Laṭuriyā Bābā and displayed prominently across the temple complex. Today, Laṭuriyā Bābā is the patron deity of various villages of the Kishangarh-Mehrauli area, and particularly of the Jāṭas of the area; this engagement is evident particularly through the presence of *thān/sthān/bhuiyān* structures within the temple complex. Moreover, the *āratī* and *chālisā* dedicated to Bābā Laṭuriyā constantly emphasize his association with the Mehrauli area of which Kishangarh was a part.

The temple has become an important part of the ritual life of the villagers; however, the biggest event which provides legitimacy to the Laṭuriyā Bābā cult and reinforces a unified sense of community built around the temple is the annual *melā* on the death anniversary of Laṭuriyā Bābā. The importance of the *melā* for the cult can be gauged from the fact that it comes very prominently in any discussion about the temple; moreover, both the *chālisā* and *āratī* dedicated to Laṭuriyā Bābā emphasize the occurrence of the annual *melā*.

The *melā* sees the participation of many villages, and along with the villagers many ascetics are invited to the *bhanḍārā* held at the *melā.* The other activities in the *melā* are a procession to the temple, performance of *havan*, *dhvajārohan,* etc. The *melā* is organized by the temple management committee, which derives its members from the local community.

Here, we see that the figure of the individual ascetic is very prominent; however, this figure is absorbed within the larger Brahmanical pantheon, to the extent that Laṭuriyā Bābā is identified with the Kalki *avatāra* of Viṣṇu. Moreover, we also find creation of *āratī*s and *chālisā*s for Laṭuriyā Bābā, something which is very prominent in Brahmanical temples. We encounter this in our next case study, which is of the Bābā Ganganātha Temple located in Munirka.

*Bābā Ganganātha Temple*

The historical foundations of the village of Munirka can be traced back to the fifteenth century CE, and is attributed to Raudh Singh, the ancestor of the Tokasa Jāṭas of Munirka, according to an article in the *Jāṭa Samāja Patrikā*, which bases its claims on *Bhaṭṭa Granthas*.[34] According to the legends reflected in the article, Munirka in ancient times was the place where Bābā Ganganātha, a Nātha ascetic, performed austerities. Today, a relatively large temple complex stands at the same place (Fig. 6.8), next to a dried-up pond (Fig. 6.9); the temple was renovated in 1986-8.[35] The cult associated with Ganganātha is

Fig. 6.8: Ganganātha Temple. (*Source:* Photograph by the author)

Fig. 6.9: The dried-up pond adjacent to the Ganganātha Temple. (*Source:* Photograph by the author)

very popular in the region of Western Nepal and Uttarakhand, and it is interesting to see percolation of this cult figure here in Delhi. The legends associated with Bābā Ganganātha in Munirka are rather faint; apart from the linkages with the Nātha Sampradāya, people are not much aware of him. This is possibly because of a break in the ascetic lineage. we were informed that a small Śiva shrine lying next to the pond was occupied by Nātha ascetics; however, for some unknown reason, this temple was deserted by Nātha ascetics and it was only in late 1980s that it was expanded into a larger complex and a Brāhmaṇa priest was appointed to take care of it. Today the temple houses the *samādhi* and an idol of Bābā Ganganātha, along with that of other Nātha *mahantas,* namely, Bābā Abhanñanātha and Suśīlanātha. Possibly, the earlier temple site was initially occupied by these Nātha ascetics, who later introduced the cult of Ganganātha at this site.

Though there is an apparent break in the ascetic lineage, nevertheless the figure of Ganganātha is still central to the identity of the temple, and of Munirka village and its residents. Today in the narrow lanes of Munirka village, there is hardly a house without a plaque which hails Ganganātha. The association of Ganganātha with the village is evident from the legend which tells that whenever there was a possibility of a drought in the village, a *bhanḍārā* in the name of Ganganātha was organized next to the pond, and this resulted in rains.[36] Similarly, the *āratī* dedicated to Ganganātha emphasizes his connection with the village of Munirka.

Today, unlike the earlier two case studies, no exclusive *melā* dedicated to the temple or the cult figure is organized, but we were informed that on the festival of Janmāṣṭamī, a wrestling competition is organized within the temple complex, with the help of the temple trust which is made up of village members.

In all the three case studies which we have discussed so far, what is common is that all are located in localities dominated by Jāṭas, and the interaction of non-Brahmanical ascetic traditions with these communities cannot be overlooked. Since Jāṭas have been looked as Śūdras in the view of earlier Brahmanical orthodoxy, it appears that by patronising non-Brahmanical ascetic traditions, the Jāṭas as a community were catering to their spiritual and socio-cultural aspirations. This is best reflected in a *chaupāla*-like place situated just next to the Katwaria Sarai bus stop, which houses pictures of both Guru Gorakhanātha and the Jāṭa ruler Sūrajmala (Fig. 6.10). While Sūrajmala represents the political ascendency of Jāṭas, Gorakhanātha appears to provide a spiritual legitimacy to the community. The incorporation of Jāṭas within the mainstream Hindu fold,

Fig. 6.10: The Chaupāl next to Katwaria Sarai bus stop.
(*Source:* Photograph by the author)

and the possible role of ascetic traditions like the Nātha Sampradāya in facilitating this process, is something which needs further research.

## Conclusion

The above brief discussion of the three case studies shows the importance of temples in facilitating interactions between ascetic traditions and the larger society. In the first section, we have tried to argue for a new understanding of Hindu temples, which is not limited to the mere material structure of the temple and the role of the royalty-Brāhmaṇa duo in establishing and maintaining it. Rather, we have argued for an understanding which re-imagines Hindu temples as social institutions which were in dynamic interaction with other such institutions, and as having a wide social base. This understanding includes village and local temples within its purview. In the second section dealing with Hindu ascetic traditions, we have tried to show the possible linkages between ascetic traditions and temples. Finally, in the third section dealing with case studies, we have tried to under-stand, through ethnographic studies, the phenomenon of temple asceticism and the possible socio-cultural impact of this phenomenon, which our studies show to include community formation.

Though all the temples which have been discussed by us are apparently of early-modern to modern period, the socio-cultural possibilities which they present can easily be extrapolated to the pre-modern period, as we have rigorously traced the ascetic interaction with temples in history. The aim of the case studies thus is to offer an interpretation of historical processes which are more vertical in nature rather than horizontal. This is in the sense that the case studies basically extend and build further on what we have been arguing, that's locating and understanding temples as spaces which facilitated interaction of Hindu ascetic traditions and the larger society. Through the case studies we have tried to explore the possibilities such interactions could lead to.

## NOTES

1. Salila Kulshreshtha, 'Introduction to Temple and Royalty', in H.P. Ray, Salia Kulashrestha and Uthara Suvrathan (eds.), *The Routledge Handbook of Hindu Temples: Materiality, Social History and Practice*, London and New York: Taylor & Francis, 2023, pp. 9-20. For an earlier critique of the approach of perceiving the Hindu temples as institutions created and maintained for the legitimation of political powers only, see Birendra Nath Prasad, 'Introduction', in idem (ed.), *Monasteries, Shrines and Society: Buddhist and Brahmanical Religious Institutions in India in their Socio-Economic Context*, Delhi: Manak Publications, 2011, pp. 1-15.
2. Kulshreshtha, *Introduction to Temple and Royalty,* 2023, p. 9.
3. Ibid., p. 14.
4. Ram Sharan Sharma, *Indian Feudalism c. 300–1200*, Calcutta: Calcutta University, 1965.
5. Burton Stein, *Peasant State and Society in Medieval South India*, Delhi-Oxford-New York: Oxford University Press, 1980.
6. B.D. Chattopadhyaya, *The Making of Early Medieval India*, New Delhi: Oxford University Press, 1994; Hermann Kulke, *Kings and Cults: State Formation and Legitimation in India and Southeast Asia,*

New Delhi: Manohar, 1993; Bhairabi Prasad Sahu, 'Sectional President's Address: Legitimation, Ideology and State in Early India', *Proceedings of the Indian History Congress,* 64 (2003): 44–76. http://www.jstor.org/stable/44145446.

7. B.D. Chattopadhyaya, 'Reappearance of the Goddess or the Brahmanical Mode of Appropriation: Some Early Epigraphic Evidence Bearing on the Goddess Cult', in B.D. Chattopadhyaya, *Studying Early India: Archaeology, Text and Historical Issues*, pp. 172-90, New Delhi: Permanent Black.
8. Prasad, 'Introduction', *Monasteries, Shrines and Society*, 2011.
9. Romila Thapar, 'Renunciation: The Making of a Counter-culture ?', in *Ancient Indian Social History: Some interpretations*, Hyderabad: Orient BlackSwan, 1978, pp. 63-4.
10. Louis Dumont, *Homo Hierarchicus: The Caste System and Its Implications*, Chicago and London: University of Chicago Press, 1980.
11. Richard Burghart, 'Renunciation in the Religious Traditions of South Asia', *Man* 18, no. 4 (1983): 635–53.
12. Patrick Olivelle, *The Āśrama System: The History and Hermeneutics of a Religious Institution*, New York: Oxford University Press, 1993.
13. Sondra L Hausner, *Wandering with Sadhus: Ascetics in the Hindu Himalayas,* Bloomington and Indianapolis: Indiana University Press, 2007.
14. Thomas Watters, *On Yuan Chwang's Travels in India, 629-645* AD, vol. 1, London: Royal Asiatic Society, 1904, p. 202.
15. Govind Sadashiv Ghurye, *Indian sadhus*, 1953, p. 6.; Thapar, 'Renunciation: The Making of a Counter-culture?', 1978, pp. 73-4.
16. Tara Sheemar Malhan, 'Amour and Upahāra in the Garbhagṛha: The Temple as Social Space in the Kathāsaritsāgara', in *The Routledge Handbook of Hindu Temples*, London and New York: Routledge India, 2023, pp. 218-38.
17. Himanshu Prabha, Ray, 'Monasticism and the Hindu temple', in *The Routledge Handbook of Hindu Temples*, London and New York: Routledge India, 2023, pp. 361-5.
18. Ibid., p. 360.
19. J.P. Losty, *Ascetics and Yogis in Indian Painting: the Mughal and Deccani Tradition* (accessed on 20 July 2023). https://www.

academia.edu/27189427/ASCETICS_AND_YOGIS_IN_INDIAN_PAINTING_THE_MUGHAL_AND_DECCANI_TRADITION

20. Ibid., p. 1.
21. Ibid., p. 9.
22. Ibid., p. 25.
23. Ibid., p. 31.
24. Mildred Archer, *Company Paintings: Indian Paintings of the British Period*, London: Victoria and Albert Museum & Mapin Publishing, 1992, pp. 93-4.
25. William R. Pinch, *Peasants and Monks in British India*, California: University of California Press, 1996.
26. Ibid., p. 2.
27. Mihir Keshari, 'The Yogini of the Yoginipura: A Note About Two Unreported Early-Medieval Sculptures from Delhi', *The Quarterly Journal of the Mythic Society*, 2023, pp. 53-6.
28. The discussed legend is primarily based on the story mentioned on various tiles within the temple complex. This apparently is the official canonical version of the story. Most of the residents of the village today appear to parrot the same version of the story.
29. This is a shrine dedicated to a medieval Vaiṣṇava saint.
30. This division interestingly appears to be on the pattern of division observed at Asthal Bohar Maṭh by Veronique Bouillier. See, Véronique Bouillier, 'Asthal Bohar, a New Synthesis', in *Monastic Wanderers: Nāth Yogī Ascetics in Modern South Asia,* Delhi: Manohar, 2016.
31. While scriptural sanction might limit the performance of *muṇḍaṇa* ceremony for only boys, these days *muṇḍaṇa* is also performed for a girl child. This appears to be increasingly becoming a common practice.
32. A Nātha *jamāt* is a group of about hundred itinerant Nātha ascetics, whose function is to wander across India, in a bid to re-inforce a collective Nātha identity through participation in important Nātha functions and festivities. See, James Mallinson, 'Nath Sampradaya', *Brill Encyclopedia of Hinduism* 3, 2011, pp. 407-28.
33. Navarātri occurs twice a year, in the months of *Caitra* and *Asvina*, though the latter is more widely celebrated and better-known.
34. Raj Kumar Tokas, *Munīrkā Jāṭa Samāja Patrikā*, Agra, October-November 2001, pp. 9-17.
35. Ibid.
36. Ibid.

## REFERENCES

Archer, Mildred. 1992. *Company Paintings: Indian Paintings of the British Period*. London: Victoria and Albert Museum and Mapin Publishing.

Burghart, Richard. 1983. 'Renunciation in the Religious Traditions of South Asia'. *Man* 18 (4) : 635–53. https://doi.org/10.2307/2801900.

Bouillier, Veronique. 2017. *Monastic Wanderers: Nāth Yogī Ascetics in Modern South Asia*. New Delhi: Manohar.

Chattopadhyaya, B. D. 1994. *The Making of Early Medieval India*. New Delhi: Oxford University Press.

_____. 2004. 'Reappearance of the Goddess or the Brahmanical Mode of Appropriation: Some Early Epigraphic Evidence Bearing on the Goddess Cult', in B.D. Chattopadhyaya, *Studying Early India: Archaeology, Text and Historical Issues*: 172-90. New Delhi: Permanent Black.

Dumont, Louis. 1980. *Homo Hierarchicus: The Caste System and Its Implications*. Chicafo: The University of Chicago Press.

Ghurye, Govind Sadashiv. 1953. *Indian Sadhus*. Bombay: Popular Book Depot.

Hausner, Sondra L. 2007. *Wandering with Sadhus: Ascetics in the Hindu Himalayas*. Bloomington: Indiana University Press.

Kulke, Hermann. 1993. *Kings and Cults: State Formation and Legitimation in India and Southeast Asia*. New Delhi: Manohar.

Keshari, Mihir. 2023. 'The Yogini of the Yoginipura: A Note About Two Unreported Early-Medieval Sculptures from Delhi'. *The Quarterly Journal of the Mythic Society* 114 (1): 53-6.

Kulshreshtha, Salila. 2023. 'Introduction to Temple and Royalty', in H.P. Ray, S. Kulshreshtha, and Uthara Suvrathan (eds.), *The Routledge Handbook of Hindu Temples*. London and New York: Taylor & Francis.

Losty, J.P. 2016. 'Ascetics and Yogis in Indian Painting: the Mughal and Deccani Tradition' (accessed on 20 July 2023). https://www.academia.edu/27189427/ASCETICS_AND_YOGIS_IN_INDIAN_PAINTING_THE_MUGHAL_AND_DECCANI_TRADITION

Mallinson, James. 2011. 'Nātha Sampradaya', *Brill Encyclopedia of Hinduism* 3: 407-28.

Malhan, Tara Sheemar. 2023. 'Amour and Upahāra in the Garbhagṛha: The Temple as a Social Space in the Kathāsaritsāgara', in H.P.

Ray, S. Kulshreshtha and Uthara Suvrathan (eds.), *The Routledge Handbook of Hindu Temples*: 218-38. London and New York: Routledge.

Olivelle, Patrick. 1993. *The Āśrama System: The History and Hermeneutics of A Religious Institution*. Oxford: Oxford University Press.

Pinch, William R. 1996. *Peasants and Monks in British India*. Berkeley: University of California Press.

Prasad, Birendra Nath (ed.). 2011. *Monasteries, Shrines and Society: Buddhist and Brahmanical Religious Institutions in India in their Socio-Economic Context*. New Delhi: Manak Publications.

Ray, Himanshu Prabha, Salila Kulshreshtha and Uthara Suvrathan, eds. 2023. *The Routledge Handbook of Hindu Temples: Materiality, Social History and Practice*. London and New York: Routledge.

_____. 2023. 'Monasticism and the Hindu Temple', in *The Routledge Handbook of Hindu Temples*: 360-74. London and New York: Routledge.

Sahu, Bhairabi Prasad. 2003. 'Sectional President's Address: Legitimation, Ideology and State in Early India'. *Proceedings of the Indian History Congress* 64: 44-76. http://www.jstor.org/stable/44145446.

Sharma, Ram Sharan. 1965. *Indian Feudalism c. 300–1200*. Calcutta: Univeristy of Calcutta Press.

Stein, Burton. 1980. *Peasant State and Society in Medieval South India*. New Delhi: Oxford University Press.

Thapar, Romila. 1978. *Ancient Indian Social History: Some Interpretations*. Hyderabad: Orient Blackswan.

Tokas, Raj Kumar. 2001. *Munīrkā Jāṭa Samāja Patrikā*, 9-17.

Watters, Thomas. 1904. *On Yuan Chwang's Travels in India, 629-645 AD*, vol. 1. London: Royal Asiatic Society.

CHAPTER 7

# The Nātha Sampradāya in Maharashtra

## An Ethnographic Exploration of a Living Tradition

VIJAY SARDE

The Nātha Sampradāya, with its roots steeped in spiritual practices like haṭha yoga, alchemy, and tantra, has undergone significant transformations across centuries. During the reign of the Bahāmaṇis and later Islamic rulers in Deccan, the Sampradāya also left a considerable impact on Muslims and Sūfis, evidenced by the worship of Nātha gurūs in the form of *turbat*s (sarcophagus) and *dargāha*s, and the prefixing of '*pīr*' to the names of Nātha yogīs. A rich exchange between the Nāthas and the Muslim community also characterized this period. Prominent Nātha yogīs such as Jālandharnātha, Kāniphanātha, Matsyendranātha, and Gahiṇīnātha were also known as Jānpīr, Śāh Ramajān, Baḍe Bābā and Gaibī Pīr, respectively, in some shrines in present-day Maharashtra. Jālandharnāth is described as Jānpīr and Gahiṇīnāth as Gaibī Pīr in CE 1819 (*Śaka* era 1741) text *Navanātha Bhaktisāra* by Malu Narhari.[1] Even today, in Yeola (Garbhagiri), Madhi, Chincholi, etc., in Maharashtra, there are *turbat*s in the main shrines, and Hindus and Muslims worship them regularly. Some *dargah*s still exist today under the Muslim name of particular Nāthas.

The Sampradāya saw further evolution in the Vijayanagara period, particularly in southern Deccan. Temples from this era feature thousands of carvings of Matsyendranātha and other Nātha yogīs, signifying their prominence at the time.

However, the eighteenth century marked a key point, with a noticeable decline in traditional practices and a shift in the Sampradāya's outward expressions. The worship patterns shifted more towards deities like Kṛṣṇa, Rāma, Gaṇeśa, Hanumāna, Bhairavanātha, and goddesses. This change in cultic focus was accompanied by structural transformations within the Sampradāya, including establishing twelve sub-branches under the unified banner of the pan-Indian Nātha Yogī Association (Akhil Bhāratvarṣīya Avadhūta Bheṣ Bārah Pantha Yogī Mahāsabhā).

The Nātha Sampradāya is a vibrant spiritual tradition with a rich tapestry of sacred sites and *maṭhas* across Maharashtra. To gain a deeper understanding, one must delve into the current state of Nātha *maṭhas*, shrines, household practices, festivals, rituals, and the unique identities of the Nāthas in this region. Despite the Sampradāya's pan-Indian presence, local practices and sites along the *Navanātha Jhuṇḍī Yātrā*, dotted with old and ethnographically significant Nātha shrines, are crucial for a comprehensive ethnographic study.

## Earlier Works

Prior researches like Veronique Bouillier's *Monastic Wanderers: Nātha Yogī Ascetics in Modern South Asia*[2] and George Briggs *Gorakhanāth and the Kānaphaṭā Yogīs*[3] provide extensive insights into the Nātha tradition, mainly focusing on regions in north India, Nepal, and Kadri (Karnataka). However, to grasp the full spectrum of the Nātha Sampradāya's current state, especially in Maharashtra, one must investigate the localized practices, sacred sites, and the daily lives of both monastic and householder Nāthas within this diverse cultural landscape. Let us delve into some of the prominent centres and temples in Maharashtra.

## Prominent Centres in Present-day Maharashtra

Maharashtra has several sacred sites and shrines important to the Nātha yogīs and their followers. In the border area of Ahilyanagar (Ahmednagar), Beed and Dharashiv (Osmanabad) districts, several shrines, including Savargaon, Sonari, Yeola, Chikhalinath and Dongargan are famous as shrines for Nātha Sampradāya. Madhi is known for its annual *jatrā* of Kāniphanātha; it is a focal point for thousands of devotees, highlighting the enduring legacy of the Nātha tradition. Vriddheshvar and Savargaon near Ghatshiras are other sacred shrines for the Nātha followers. Vriddheshvar is celebrated as a place of Ādinātha, while Savargaon is famous for the tomb of Matsyendranātha.

Alandi is a well-known site for Vārakaris and Nātha yogīs alike. It is home to three *maṭhas* and several tombs of Nātha yogīs, including the esteemed Jñāneśvara. Alandi remains a significant site where the traditional *Jhuṇḍī* procession passes, marking its spiritual importance. Anjaneri and Trimbakeshvar are noted for the Gorakṣanātha *maṭha*, Nātha caves, and the tomb of Nivṛttinātha; these shrines are central to the Nātha yogīs, with the *Jhuṇḍī yātrā* originating from Trimbakeshvar.

In addition to these sites, Nagnath-Vadval, Pai-Dhuni, Kendur, Kaniphanathgad at Bopgaon, Macchhindragad, Battis Shirala, Redi, Pavas, Parunde, etc., are also famous shrines in the Nātha Sampradāya in the present time.

## Nātha *Maṭhas*

Nātha *maṭha*s are distributed throughout Maharashtra, with some dating back several centuries. *Maṭha*s at Toranmal, Sonari, Rashin, and Trimbakeshvar have long traditions steeped in history, reflecting the region's deep roots of the Nātha teachings. The records from Toranmal mention 115 sub-*maṭha*s, tying the region to notable names such as Matsyendranātha and Gorakṣanātha, Bhartṛhari, and several late Nātha yogīs which can be traced back to the early fourteenth century CE.[4]

The Akhil Bhāratvarṣīya Avadhūt Bheṣ Bārah Pantha Yogī Mahāsabhā is a body that lists and organizes the Nātha *maṭhas* in Maharashtra (Table 7.1).[5]

TABLE 7.1: LIST OF PRESENT NĀTHA *MAṬHAS* IN MAHARASHTRA

| *Sr. No.* | *Name of the* maṭha/*temples* | *District* | *Present Head of the* maṭha *(2016)* |
|---|---|---|---|
| 1. | Śiva Gorakṣa Yogāśrama, Amaravati | Amaravati | Kaśinātha |
| 2. | Śiva temple, Manchar *Tekadi* | Pune | Ravinātha |
| 3. | Brahmanātha Bābā *Maṭha*, Parunde | Pune | Aśvanīnātha |
| 4. | Kāniphanātha *Maṭha*, Dhavashi, near Otur | Pune | Gaṇeśanātha |
| 5. | Bhairavanātha *Maṭha*, Tambe | Pune | Ravindranātha |
| 6. | Gorakṣa Temple, Bhimashankar | Pune | Gaṇeśanātha |
| 7. | Gorakṣanātha Temple, Bhivde, near Narayangaon | Pune | Tejanātha |
| 8. | Gorakṣanātha Temple, Parvati | Pune | Gaṇeśanātha |
| 9. | Nāthajī kī Kuṭiyā, Alandi | Pune | Tejanātha |
| 10. | Dattātreya Temple, Kusur, Junnar | Pune | Kailaśanātha |
| 11. | Nāthajī kā Mandir, Dudulgaon | Pune | Adbaṅganātha |
| 12. | Nāthajī kā *Sthāna*, Bhimashankar | Pune | Trayanātha |
| 13. | Gorakṣanātha Temple, Subhash Nagar, Old Dhule | Dhule | Badrīnātha |
| 14. | Gorakṣanātha Temple, above the hill, Lendane ?, Sindkhed tahsil | Dhule | Maṅgalanātha |

| | | | |
|---|---|---|---|
| 15. | Gorakṣanātha Temple, Kalambhir | Dhule | Gahinīnātha |
| 16. | Gambhiranātha *Maṭha*, Chochi | Raigad | Govindanātha |
| 17. | Gorakṣanātha *Maṭha,* Juna Vashi Naka, Rankala *Talav*, Kolhapur | Kolhapur | Dharmanātha |
| 18. | Nāthajī kī Bagīcī, Gondiya | Gondiya | Somavāranātha |
| 19. | Nāthajī kā *Derā*, Gondiya | Gondiya | Ghanaśyāmanātha |
| 20. | Gorakṣanātha *Maṭha*, Kangar | Ahilyanagar | Sūrajanātha |
| 21. | Madhameśvara Śiva Temple, Nevasa | Ahilyanagar | Manoharanātha |
| 22. | Devendranātha *Maṭha*, Madki tahsil Nevasa | Ahilyanagar | Devendranātha |
| 23. | Nāthajī kī *Koṭhī*, Dhumaval, tahsil Chopda | Jalgaon | Rāmanātha |
| 24. | Gorakṣanātha Temple, Upkhede | Jalgaon | Bhūtanātha and Maṅgalanātha |
| 25. | Śiva Temple, near Taskhede | Jalgaon | Maṅgalanātha |
| 26. | Śiva Temple, main Lendane | Nashik | Hirānātha and Maṅgalanātha |
| 27. | Nāthajī kā *Derā*, Sakpada, Ambaner | Nashik | Raṅganātha |
| 28. | Śānti Guphā, Saptshringi | Nashik | Prītamanātha |
| 29. | Gorakṣanāthaji Temple, Vadgaon | Nashik | Muktinātha |
| 30. | Gorakṣanātha *Maṭha,* Narmada Kui, Musalgaon, | Nashik | Bhairavanātha |
| 31. | Nāthajī kā *Derā*, Munjvad | Nashik | Rameśanātha |
| 32. | Gorakṣanātha Temple/*Maṭha*, Trimbakeshvar | Nashik | Sundaranātha |

| | | | |
|---|---|---|---|
| 33. | Gorakṣanātha Temple, Panchvati | Nashik | Ratananātha |
| 34. | Kāla Bhairava Temple, Chatori, | Nashik | Amaranātha |
| 35. | Aghorī Devī, Yogamāyā Mandir, Saykheda | Nashik | Bṛhaspatinātha |
| 36. | Sri Gorakṣanātha Śiva Pañcāyatana Temple, Galne, Ganeshpur | Nashik | Ānandanātha |
| 37. | Kāla Bhairava Temple, Pay Dhuni | Mumbai | Dhīrajanātha |
| 38. | Mahādeva Kālī Kamalīvālā *sthāna*, National Park | Mumbai | Manoharanātha |
| 39. | Hanumāna Durgā Temple, Vardha | Vardha | Tulasīnātha |
| 40. | Sonarī Bhairava, Sonari | Dharashiv | Badrīnātha |
| 41. | Sunaharī Bhairava, Bada Paranda | Dharashiv | Janārdhananātha |
| 42. | Sunaharī Bhairava, Vashi? | Dharashiv | Badrīnātha |
| 43. | Gorakṣanātha Temple, Kanhe/Kavhe? | Solapur | Naumīnātha |
| 44. | Nāthajī kā *Dhūnā*, Pandharpur | Solapur | Śāntinātha |
| 45. | Dhakaneśvara Temple, Dhakna | Thane | Bṛhaspatinātha |
| 46. | Tākeśvara *Maṭha*, Takeshvar | Thane | Avinātha and Phūlanātha |
| 47. | Saṅgameśvara *Maṭha*, Kinhavali | Thane | Rāmanātha |
| 48. | Kapileśvara *Maṭha*, Lavale | Thane | Viśvanātha |
| 49. | Gurū Ānandanāthajī kī *Samādhi*, *Maṭha*, Chervali | Thane | Baikunṭhanātha |

| | | | |
|---|---|---|---|
| 50. | Tākeśvara *Maṭha*, Khadir? | Thane | Rāmanātha |
| 51. | Dvarikānāthajī kī *Maṇḍī*/ Durgāmātā Temple, Ulhasnagar | Thane | Janakanaṭha |
| 52. | Siddheśvara *Maṭha*, Sakharvadi/Sarkalvadi? | Satara | Sāīnātha |
| 53. | Gorakṣanātha Temple, 32 Shirala | Sangli | Śivanātha |
| 54. | Macchindranātha Temple, Mitmita | Chhatrapati Sambhaji Nagar | Maṅgalanātha |
| 55. | Adinātha-Gorakṣanātha Temple, Ramtek | Nagpur | Śivanātha |
| 56. | Tapasthalī Āśrama, Mohgaon | Bhandara | Lakṣmaṇanātha |

*Source:* Table prepared by the author.

The Akhil Bhāratvarṣīya Avadhūt Bheṣ Bārah Pantha Yogī Mahāsabhā has unified numerous Nātha *maṭhas*; however, a few remain autonomous. Specifically, the Garibanātha *maṭha* in Tuljapur, the Gorakṣa *maṭha* in Rashin, the Śivadinanātha *maṭha* in Paithan, the Nātha *maṭha* in Deulgon Raja are not part of this federation. Notably, no *maṭhas* in the Marathvada region are affiliated with the Mahāsabhā. This omission may stem from the region's political status in CE 1904, under Nizam's rule at the time of the Yogī Mahāsabhā's foundation, potentially explaining their exclusion.

The pie chart indicates that the *maṭha* of the Nātha Sampradāya is most prevalent in the Nashik and Pune districts, as the *Jhuṇḍī* also traverses these areas (Fig. 7.1). Adjacent to these districts lies Thane, which serves as a hub for Nātha activities. Remains from the c.eleventh[6] to the fifteenth century in these districts point to the Nātha Sampradāya's significant influence in the region. Beyond these areas, a few *maṭhas* of the Nāthas are also found in Marathvada.

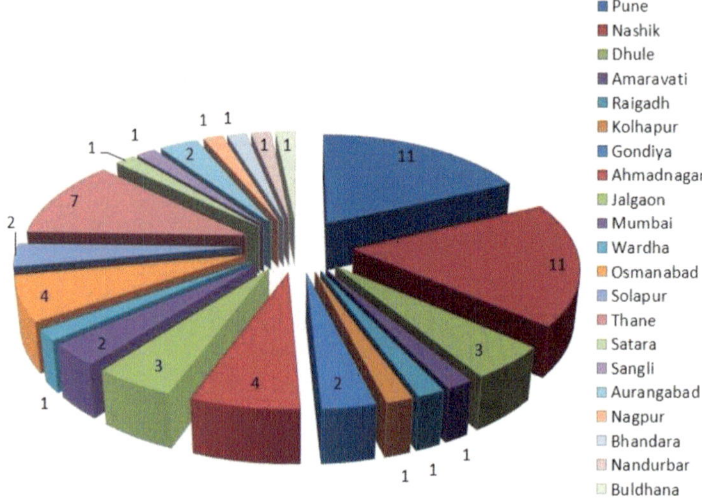


Fig. 7.1: A pie chart showing the numbers of *maṭha*s in various districts of Maharashtra. *Source:* Pie chart made by the author.

## The Sonari *Maṭha*

Bhairavanāth at Sonari is revered as the family deity by many locals. Near Bhairavanāth Temple is the Nātha *maṭha*. Every 12 years, coinciding with the Nashik-Trimbak Kumbha, a *Mahant* is appointed to lead the *maṭha*. The *maṭha's* surroundings are adorned with several *samādhi*s of Nātha yogīs and the land granted to them. K. N. Chitnis (2002) holds a CE 1794 manuscript bequeathed by Mahadaji Shinde concerning the Sonari *maṭha*.[7] Historical disputes dating back to CE 1475, such as the one between Malik Jogī and Davarī Kānaphaṭā regarding *maṭha* rituals, are documented in this manuscript. This dispute originated between Avadhūtanātha and Nimbanātha of the Rāval branch—evidence from CE 1475 to 1779 has been preserved to assert the *maṭha's* authority. The manuscript also details *Pātara Pūjā* (the worship of *Pātradevatā*), suggesting that the *Jhuṇḍī* practice in the Nātha Sampradāya began prior to the fourteenth century CE. During the *Jhuṇḍī*, Nātha yogīs still visit to select the *maṭha's* head.

## Trimbakeshvar Maṭha

The Trimbakeshvar *maṭha* is the culmination point of the *Jhuṇḍī* after the *Kumbha melā*. It draws hundreds of Nātha yogīs to the Gorakṣanātha *maṭha* at Trimbakeshvar, where they participate in the *Jhuṇḍī Yātrā*. Here, the *Rājā Yogī* (King Yogī) for the Kadri seat is chosen, and a new *mahanta* is appointed for the Trimbakeshvar *maṭha*. Recently, a grand temple dedicated to Gorakṣanātha has been constructed at the *maṭha*. Many yogīs reside within the *maṭha*, which houses both ancient and modern *samādhis* of Nātha yogīs.

## The Monastic Structure

Modernization has reshaped the monastic life in most *maṭhas*. Compound walls now enclose them and host small temples for deities like Gaṇeśa, Bhairava, and other goddesses. Some *maṭhas* also feature temples dedicated to Gorakṣanātha. Daily rituals include morning and evening *ārati*. Additionally, the yogīs can access well-furnished living quarters and cultivate crops on *maṭha*-owned land, utilizing local labour. Annual festivals and *jatrās* add to the vibrant cultural life within these *maṭhas*.

## Householder Yogīs in Maharashtra

The Nātha Sampradāya enjoys a robust presence in Maharashtra, with householder yogīs from various nomadic castes and communities residing throughout the state. These groups include the Davarī-Gosāvī, Rāval Yogī, Masan Jogī, and Bharāḍis, who are interconnected with the Nātha tradition. Castes like Sapernātha, Faqirs, Macchendra (Bhoī), Gaḍī Vadār, Dombāris, Mākaḍawāle, Gāruḍī, Kolhāṭī, Beladār are also influenced by the Nātha Sampradāya. Bharāḍī caste has some sub-castes like Bāl-Santośī, Kingarīvāle, Nāthabābā, Nātha Jogī. They continue to practice their spiritual traditions, worshipping deities such as *pīr*, Nāthabābā, Sailānī Bābā, Kāniphanātha, Sitalā Devī, Mankeshvar Saṭavāī, Bhairava, Canḍakī Mātā, Mahābhairava, and Cāmuṇḍā. Davarī Gosāvis sings songs of Nātha yogīs. Kañjar Darveśī, Madārī, and Beldār, Gaḍī Vaḍār, Kolhaṭī, Mendhagī also worship Kāniphanātha or Kānhobā. The Davarī Gosāvīs are particularly noted for their devotional songs dedicated to Nātha yogīs. Traditionally, the Davarī Gosāvīs solicited alms (*bhikṣā*) for their livelihood. While many have transitioned to other employment forms, they honour their rituals symbolically, such as ear-cutting and *bhikṣā*.

The Nātha Sampradāya tradition is still actively practiced by householders in the village of Tala in the Raigad district of the Konkan region, where there is a temple dedicated to Kāniphanātha. In Panderi, the Nātha Yogī community lives in large numbers, and nearby rock-cut caves are believed to be their ancient abode. The Nātha caves in Panhale Kaji, close to Panderi, are also significant to this tradition.

Madhi, Sonari and Beed are traditional venues for the *Jāta Pañcāyata* of the Davarī Gosāvīs. The *Kānhobācī Jatrā* festival is a prominent celebration among the followers of the Nātha Sampradāya.

## *Kumbha Melā* and the Related Activities

The *Kumbha melā* in Nashik is a pivotal event for the Nātha Sampradāya, during which thousands of Nātha yogīs congregate at Trimbakeshvar to partake in a sacred bath in the Godavari River and engage in various *pūjas*. One of the most significant events for Nātha yogīs is the *Jhuṇḍī Yātrā*, starting from the Gorakṣanātha *maṭha* at Trimbakeshvar and culminating at the Kadri *maṭha*.

## Navanātha *Jhuṇḍī Yātrā* and its Traditional Routes

The *Navanātha Jhuṇḍī Yātrā*, organized after the *Kumbha melā*—which occurs once every twelve years—sees yogīs journeying on foot to Kadri with the *Pātradevatā*, carrying objects of the Nātha yogīs in a vessel known as *Pātra*, which represents Gorakṣanātha. This pilgrimage concludes on Mahāśivarātrī when they reach Kadri, where the appointment of a new King yogī takes place. The route of the *Jhuṇḍī* passes through historical sites associated with the Nātha Sampradāya and the legend of Paraśurāma, traversing Nashik, Ahilyanagar, Pune, Satara, Sangli, and Kolhapur districts in Maharashtra before reaching Karnataka (Fig. 7.2). Table 7.2 below shows the various stops of the *Jhuṇḍī* route between Trimbakeshvar and Kadri.

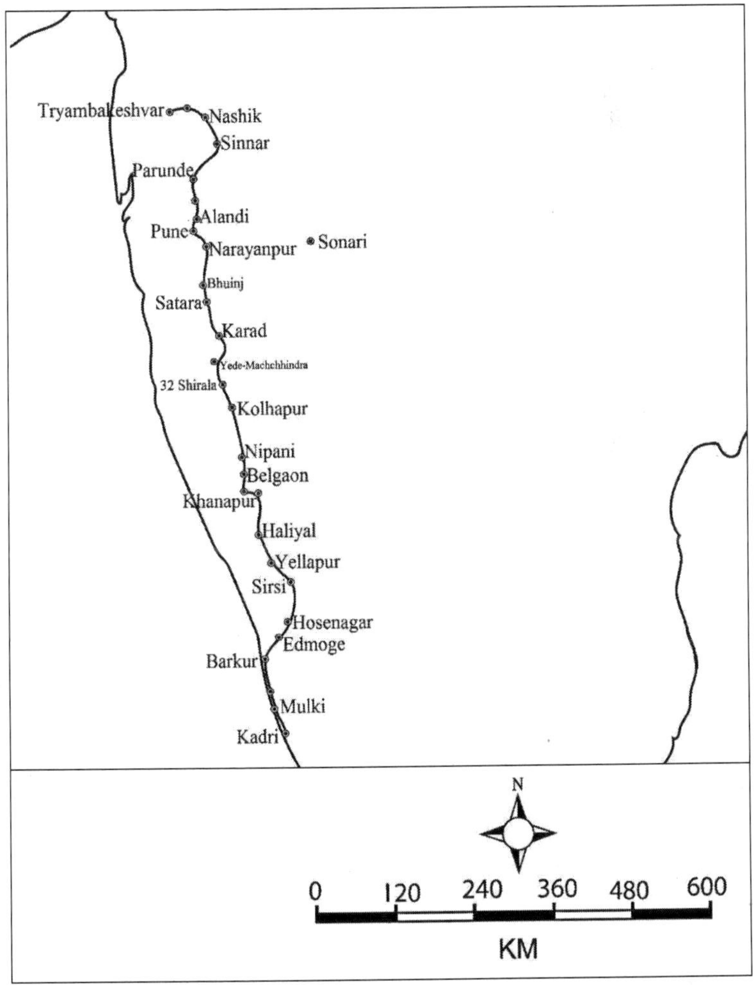


Fig. 7.2: Navanātha Jhuṇḍī Route. *Source:* Map made by the author.

TABLE 7.2: VARIOUS STOPS OF THE *JHUṆḌĪ* ROUTE BETWEEN TRIMBAKESHVAR TO KADRI

| *S.No.* | *District* | *Stops* |
|---|---|---|
| 1. | Nashik | 1. Trimbakeshvar 2. Nashik 3. Saykheda 4. Sinnar 5. Dodi BK |
| 2. | Ahilyanagar | 6. Sangamner 7. Dolasne 8. Ghargaon |
| 3. | Pune | 9. Ale Phata 10. Pimpalvandi 11. Arvi 12. Gunjalvadi 13. Savargaon 14. Parunde 15. Chincholi 16. Khilarvadi 17. Mahalunge 18. Vadgaon 19. Manchar 20. Goraksha tekadi 21. Avasari Khurd 22. Khed (Rajgurunagar) 23. Chakan 24. Alandi 25. Moshi 26. Bhosari 27. Someśvara temple (Pune city) 28. Pimpaleśvara temple (Pune city) 29. Aranyeshvar (Pune city) 30. Kondhava 31. Bhairav Nala 32. Hadapsar 33. Fursungi-Bhekarai Nagar 34. Sasvad 35. Bhivadi 36. Kikvi |
| 4. | Satara | 37. Shirval 38. Bhuinj 39. Satara 40. Koregaon 41. Kumthe 42. Rahimatpur 43. Padali 44. Masur 45. Karad 46. Vadgaon-Haveli 47. Phulegaon |
| 5. | Sangli | 48. Matsyendragad 49. Islampur 50. Rethare Dharan 51. Battis Shirala 52. Mangale 53. Mohare |
| 6. | Kolhapur | 54. Kolhapur 55. Gandhinagar (Kolhapur) 56. Gokul Shirgaon 57. Kagal |
| 7. | Belgaon (Belgavi) | 58. Nipani 59. Sankeshvar 60. Narsinghpur 61. Belgaon 62. Jati *maṭha* 63. Belgaon city, Bālājī temple, Kapileshvar 64. Khanapur 65. Dādā kā *maṭha* 66. Kiravale *maṭha* 67. Balavadi/Balakvadi 68. Londa Junction 69. Handi Bhadang 70. Nagargali 71. Godageri |
| 8. | Uttar Kannada | 72. Mangalvada 73. Haliyal 74. Karalkatte 75. Karal Katta (Ravinātha) 76. Sambrani 77. Yellapur 78. Manchkeri 79. Sirsi |
| 9. | Bagalkot | 80. Bhagvati gaon |

| | | |
|---|---|---|
| 10. | Shimoga | 81. Chandragutti 82. Soraba 83. Sagar 84. Not known 85. Hosnagar 86. Halenagar |
| 11. | Udupi | 87. Halvari Jogi *maṭha* at Yedamogge/Edmoge 88. Halady 89. Barkur 90. Udupi |
| 12. | Dakshina Kannada | 91. Mulki 92. Panambur |
| 13. | Mangalore | 93. Kadali *maṭha* (on the eve of Mahāśivarātrī) |

*Source:* Table prepared by the author.

A troupe of Nātha yogīs began their journey on Nāgapañcamī, the nineteenth of August 2015, for the *Navanātha Jhuṇḍī Yātrā* from Trimbakeshvar and reached Kadri on Mahāśivarātrī, the 7th of March 2016. The *Jhuṇḍī* comprised approximately 500 Nātha yogīs from all over India and Nepal. At the outset, Nirmalnātha was selected as the next *mahanta* and *Rājā Yogī* at Trimbakeshvar for the Kadri *maṭha*. He is to serve as the chief *mahanta* of Kadri for twelve years until CE 2028 (Fig. 7.3).

Fig. 7.3: Nirmalnātha—New *mahanta* of Kadari *maṭha*.
*Source:* Photograph by the author.

The *Jhuṇḍī* is revered as the 84th *Navanātha Jhuṇḍī Yātrā* by some *maṭha* traditions, a practice that began nearly a thousand years ago and includes 91 stoppages en route to Kadri, with 57 of these in Maharashtra. At Sinnar in the Nashik district, the *Jhuṇḍī* splits, with a branch heading towards Sonari in the Dharashiv district of Marathvada, for the appointment of a new *mahanta*. Additionally, 17 other *mahanta*s are appointed at various *maṭha*s during the *Jhuṇḍī* for the next twelve years, with provisions for reappointment. When a new head is appointed for the Yogeśvara maṭha at Kadri, celebrations such as the *King Paṭṭābhiṣeka*, *Gurūvandanā,* and *Gurūbhojana* are organized by the respective trust or locals. Nātha yogīs take a rest at these places during the *Jhuṇḍī*.

## Appearances of Yogīs in the *Jhuṇḍī*

The *Jhuṇḍī* showcases a diverse array of ascetics. For instance, devotees of Kālī Mātā dressed in black, carrying offerings in a *kapāla*, are likely descendants of the Kāpālika and adorn themselves with *hāra, keyūra*, and *valaya* featuring skull-shaped beads.[8] Some yogīs maintain a vow of silence. In contrast, others remain seated in a single posture continuously. A few have vowed to stand on one leg only, and others are engaged in crafting thread, *yajñopavita*, and *yogapaṭṭas* (Fig. 7.4). Some apply ashes on their bodies, with certain yogīs sporting *jaṭā* that reach down to their knees and others having shaved heads (Fig. 7.5).

Variations are also noted in their turbans; some are round, while others cover their heads with cloth. Yogīs without *karṇakuṇḍala* are termed *Aughaḍ* and assist the *Darśanī yogīs*, who are characterized by their *karṇakuṇḍala*. Some yogīs carry a *daṇḍa* and *yogapaṭṭa*, signifying the ongoing practice of haṭha yoga within the Nātha Sampradāya, although this tradition seems to be waning in contemporary times.

No female Yogīnis are seen in the *Jhuṇḍī*. However, they are present in *maṭhas* like the one at Gorakṣa Tekadi in the Pune district (Fig. 7.6). An exceptional case was observed in a *maṭha* at Tuljapur, where a Nātha yogīnī, who lived for hundred and

Fig. 7.4: Nātha Yogīs engaged in crafting thread, *yajñopavita*, and *yogapaṭṭas*. *Source:* Photograph by the author.

Fig. 7.5: Yogīs sporting *jaṭā*. *Source:* Photograph by the author.

Fig. 7.6: Female yogīni at Gorakṣa hill, near Manchar, Pune district. *Source:* Photograph by the author.

Fig. 7.7: Young Nātha Yogīs at Navanātha *jhuṇḍī*, 2016. *Source:* Photograph by the author.

fifty years, served as the head of the *maṭha*. Participants in the *Jhuṇḍī* range across all ages, from teenagers to the elderly (Fig. 7.7).

## Exploration of the Olden Remains/ Sites of the Nāthas on the Route

The *Navanātha Jhuṇḍī* is a prominent pilgrimage that spans over 1,750 km across Maharashtra and Karnataka, traversing districts such as Nashik, Ahilyanagar, Pune, Satara, Sangli, Kolhapur, Belgaon, Bagalkot, Uttara Kannada, Shimoga, Dakshin Kannada, Udupi and Mangalore. This six-month pilgrimage is characterized by morning and evening *āratī* rituals, local fairs, and the fervent participation of thousands of devotees. Integral to the Nātha tradition, the route features temples and *maṭhas*, many of which are historical sites with land donations, with some dating back to the twelfth or thirteenth centuries CE.

The pilgrims' journey is demanding, cutting through the Western *ghāts* and dense forests and overcoming natural adversities to remain on schedule. Some sites on the route, such as 32 Shirala, Vadapuri, Kadri, and Hadi Bhadangnath, are connected to the legend of the Nātha yogīs.

## The *Jhuṇḍī* tradition in Nāthas and Antiquity

Key landmarks along the path include Gorakṣa cave, Gorakṣa *maṭha*, Nivṛttinātha *samādhi*, and Sita cave in the Trimbakeshvar region. These sites are rich with historical and mythological significance; for instance, the Gorakṣanātha cave holds an image of Gorakṣanātha from the eighteenth century CE, and below it lies the *Anupam (Anupan) śilā*, where Nātha yogis congregate during the *Kumbha melā*. The *samādhi* of Saint Nivṛttinātha, a thirteenth-century saint, rests at the base of Brahmagiri hill. According to legend, he encountered Gahiṇīnātha in one of the caves during his circumambulation of Gangadvar hill. Nashik is already a well-known pilgrimage centre for all Hindus, and today, one of the *maṭha* of the Nātha Sampradāya is located in Nashik.

The *Jhuṇḍī* route includes significant Nātha sites such as caves and *maṭhas*, all deeply rooted in the region's spiritual heritage. Temples and *maṭhas* dedicated to various deities and chief Nātha yogis, like Bhairavanātha, Reṇukā, and Mahākāleśvara, are also situated along the route from Trimbakeshvar to Kadri.

The following old temples and cave sites are near the *Jhuṇḍī* route: The Goṇḍeśvara temple at Sinnar (Nashik district), the Bhavānī temple at Tahakari, the Siddheśvara temple at Akole, the Amṛteśvara temple at Amritvadi, Harishchandragad caves (Ahilyanagar district), the Bhimāśaṅkara temple, the Siddheśvara temple at Rajgurunagar, Bhāmcandra caves near Chakan, the Bhuleśvara temple at Malshiras, the Nārāyaṇeśvara temple at Narayangaon (Pune district), the Bhairavanātha temple at Kikli near Bhuinj, Pāṭeśvara temple/caves (Satara district) and the Mahālakṣmī temple at Kolhapur.

Inscriptions from the thirteenth century featuring names of Nātha yogis, including Jñāneśvara and Nāmadeva, were found at Harishchandragad, indicating the long-standing reverence of this spiritual path. The Reḍā *samādhi* associated with Jñāneśvara in Ale Phata near Junnar and an ancient temple of Siddheśvara in Alandi are among such venerable sites. Saint Nāmadeva's fourteenth-century *abhaṅgas* reference Alandi as a convocation site for Siddhas, who is venerated in the Nātha Sampradāya.[9]

Siddhas were highly regarded in the Nātha Sampradāya. Images of Siddhas from the twelfth-thirteenth century have been noticed in Bhuleśvara temple. Pimpri-Dumala, close to Alandi, has fourteenth-century images of Matsyendranātha and Gorakṣanātha. All this evidence indicates the *Jhuṇḍī* tradition and this region's association with the Nātha Sampradāya. It is highly probable that after being inspired by the *Navanātha Jhuṇḍī*, *vārakaris* also started their *vārī/yātrā* from Alandi to Pandharpur.

Several temples of Bhairavanātha and Kāniphanātha are noticed in the villages around this region. The Kendur village and various temples in the surrounding regions attest to the prominence of Bhairavanātha and Kāniphanātha worship. Evidence of haṭha yoga prevailing in the Nātha Sampradāya is carved on the pilgrim route on the Brahmanātha temple at Parunde, the Someśvara temple at Pimpri-Dumala, and the Bhuleśvara temple near Malshiras. There is a temple of Cāṅgā Vaṭeśvara near Sasvad, which is on the *Jhuṇḍī* route. Graffiti of Nātha yogīs Acyantadhaja and Cāṅgā Vaṭeśvara have been inscribed on the Nārāyaṇeśvar temple at Pur, which also has an inscription of CE 1285. The ancient Bhairavanātha temple at Kikli and the Pāṭeśvara caves, dating back to the fourteenth-fifteenth centuries, are also situated close to the *Jhuṇḍī* route, highlighting the area's historical significance to the Nātha community.

A few images of Matsyendranātha and other Śaiva/Śākta images at Pateshvar indicate the influence of the Nātha Sampradāya. Probably, these caves were used by the Nātha followers for their tantric practices. It seems that Pateshvar was one of the prominent centers of the Nātha Sampradāya.

Sites such as Yede Machchhindra and Machindragad in the Sangli district further enrich the tapestry of Nātha's spiritual geography. It is believed that there is a *samādhi* temple of Matsyendranātha on Matsyendragad. There is also a temple of Gorakṣanātha on the fort. The hill of Kāniphanātha and Kundal caves are located on the fort's north and east. Several Nātha householders are living in the region. It is believed that Matsyendranātha's *samādhi* temple is on Machindragad, which also features a temple of Gorakṣanātha.[10] The fort's name, included in Shivaji Maharaj's records in the seventeenth century, suggests the pre-existing veneration of Matsyendranātha in the region. There is also an image of Matsyendranātha of the late period in the Reṇukā Mātā temple at Aundh near Karad. All these sites are located near the *Jhuṇḍī* route.

Historical accounts by travellers like Pietro Della Valle and Marco Polo provide external validation of the *Jhuṇḍī*'s antiquity and the region's yogic traditions. A Portuguese traveller named Pietro Della Valle visited Kadri *maṭha* in CE 1624 and mentioned King Yogī in his travelogue. In this coastal region, Marco Polo saw the alchemy practices of yogīs in the western coastal region of India in CE 1295.[11] All this evidence indicates the antiquity of the *Jhuṇḍī*. According to records of several *maṭhas* in Karnataka, the *Jhuṇḍī* tradition goes back about one thousand years. Several images of Matsyendranātha and other yogīs are also noticed on the *Jhuṇḍī* route and elsewhere in Karnataka. All this evidence underscores the profound historical roots of the Nātha Sampradāya and its *Jhuṇḍī* tradition.

## Evidence of the *Jhuṇḍī Yātrā* Elsewhere in the Country

The tradition of *Jhuṇḍī*, a collective of Nātha yogīs, has been prevalent in north India, at Hiṅgalujā Mātā in Baluchistan, and in Nepal.[12] The *Līḷācaritra,* the extensive reach of this tradition, notes that Kāniphanātha had 1,400 disciples and Makaradhwaja Jogī had 700. This indicates a deep-rooted and widespread practice of *Jhuṇḍī* and pilgrimage among the Nāthas.

## Worshipping Deities

In contemporary worship within important sectarian Nātha *maṭhas* and *jamāt* groups, the *Pātradevatā*—a divine vessel—takes centre stage (Fig. 7.8). This vessel is a small clay pot holding sacred items such as the *śṛṅgī* (horn), *pavitrī, karṇakuṇḍalas, sumiranī*, and *cillam* (a clay pipe used for smoking cannabis). Gorakṣanātha is revered as a divine embodiment within this context.[13]

In present-day Maharashtra, devotion to the Nātha Sampradāya encompasses deities like Bhairavanātha, Jogeśvarī Mātā, Mahiṣāsuramardinī, Dattātreya, Gorakṣanātha, and others. *Maṭhas* here typically enshrine images of Bhairavanātha, Jogeśvarī, and Gorakṣanātha, with Dattātreya also receiving veneration in several places. The worship of Kāniphanātha is particularly prominent in Pune and Ahilyanagar districts.

Fig. 7.8: Nātha yogīs involved in evening *āratī*.
*Source:* Photograph by the author.

## Discussion

The Nātha Sampradāya's rich heritage in Maharashtra embodies a unique synthesis of spiritual, cultural, and historical elements woven into the region's diverse religious landscape. Over the centuries, this tradition has not only adapted to changing socio-religious contexts but has also influenced and been influenced by them, creating a multifaceted spiritual lineage. The enduring presence of the Sampradāya, as seen in the revered *maṭha*s, the devotion of householders, and the grandeur of the *Jhuṇḍī Yātrā* underscores the living nature of this tradition. It continues to flourish, drawing together people across various communities, sustaining its practices, and contributing to the shared spiritual heritage of Maharashtra. As such, the Nātha Sampradāya remains a vital thread in the tapestry of Indian spirituality, exemplifying resilience and the dynamic continuity of religious traditions.

The reverence for the Navanāthas is also deeply embedded in today's Maharashtra cultural fabric, transcending caste and community lines. Stories and songs about the Nāthas are widespread, and the sacred text *Navanātha Bhaktisār* is an integral part of spiritual readings or *pārāyaṇa*. Many individuals in Maharashtra are named after these yogīs, and the Nātha Sampradāya maintains a robust presence, including among householders. The Ḍavarī Gosāvis and Jogīs, along with several nomadic tribes, have embraced the Nātha tradition. Celebrations like *Urs* and fairs linked to the Nātha yogīs are commonplace across the villages of Maharashtra.

## NOTES

1. *Navanātha Bhaktisāra*, Jangamvadi Maṭha Collection, vol. 40, pp. 95-6.
2. V. Bouillier, 2017. *Monastic Wanderers: Nāth Yogī Ascetics in Modern South Asia*. New Delhi: Manohar.
3. G.W. Briggs, 2007. *Gorakhnāth and the Kānphaṭā Yogīs*. New Delhi: Motilal Banarsidass.
4. A. Nevasakar, 1976. Samsthān Toranmal-Nathpanthī Maṭha-sambandhicā ek Aitihāsik Abhilekh (in Marathi). *Alakh Niranjan*, Dipavali, 57-69.
5. Source: https://gorakhdham.blogspot.com/2011/
6. Ambarnath Temple in Thane district has the earliest material evidence related to the Natha Sampradaya in Maharashtra.
7. K.N. Chitnis, 2002. *Socio-Economic History of Medieval India*. New Delhi: Atlantic Publishers and Distributors.
8. Nātha-Yogīs: Personal Communication, 2016.
9. *Śrī Nāmadeva Gāthā* (in Marathi). Published by Maharashtra Rājya Sāhitya āṇi Sanskruti Maṇḍaḷ, Mumbai, 2008.
10. *Maharashtra State Gazetteers*. 1969. Sangali District. Bombay: Directorate of Government Printing, Stationary and Publications, Maharashtra State, p. 700.
11. D.G. White, 1996. *The Alchemical Body: Siddha Traditions in Medieval India*. Chicago and London: The University of Chicago Press, pp. 94-5.
12. Nātha yogīs provided this information during the *Jhuṇḍī Yātrā*.
13. Bouillier, 2017: 31.

## REFERENCES

Bouillier, V. 2017. *Monastic Wanderers: Nāth Yogī Ascetics in Modern South Asia*. New Delhi: Manohar.

Briggs, G.W. 2007. *Gorakhnāth and the Kānphaṭā* Yogīs. New Delhi: Motilal Banarsidass.

Chitnis, K.N. 2002. *Socio-Economic History of Medieval India*. New Delhi: Atlantic Publishers and Distributors.

*Maharashtra State Gazetteers*. 1969. Sangali District. Bombay: Directorate of Government Printing, Stationary and Publications, Maharashtra State.

*Navanatha Bhaktisara*, Jangamvadi Math Collection, 40, pp. 95-6.

Nevasakar, A. 1976. Samsthān Toranmal-Nathpanthī Maṭhasambandhicā ek Aitihāsik Abhilekh (in Marathi). *Alakh Niranjan*, Dipavali, pp. 57-69.

*Śrī Nāmadev Gāthā* (in Marathi). Published by Maharashtra Rājya Sāhitya āṇi Sanskruti Maṇḍaḷ: Mumbai. 2008.

White, D.G. 1996. *The Alchemical Body: Siddha Traditions in Medieval India*. Chicago and London: The University of Chicago Press.

# Contributors

AHMAD SOHAIB earned his MA, MPhil and PhD degrees in History from Jawaharlal Nehru University, New Delhi. His PhD thesis explored the theme of the process of Buddhist identity formation in the Middle and Upper Ganga Valley during the early historic period. At present, he is an Assistant Professor at the Centre for the Study of Comparative Religions and Civilizations, Jamia Millia Islamia (A Central University), New Delhi.

BIRENDRA NATH PRASAD earned his MA, MPhil and PhD degrees in History from Jawaharlal Nehru University, New Delhi. His PhD thesis explored the theme of archaeology of religion in early medieval Bihar and Bengal. At present, he is an Assistant Professor at the Centre for Historical Studies, Jawaharlal Nehru University, New Delhi. His recent publications include *Archaeology of Religion in South Asia: Buddhist, Brahmanical and Jaina Religious Centres in Bihar and Bengal, c. AD 600–1200* (Delhi, London and New York, 2021); *Rethinking Bihar and Bengal: History, Culture and Religion* (Delhi, London and New York, 2021); *Religion in Society: Social Dimensions of Buddhism, Hinduism and Jainism in India* (Delhi, 2023); *Maritime Southeast Asia: History, Culture and Religion, c. First Century CE—Fifteenth Century CE* (edited, Delhi, 2023); and *History, Economy and Religion: Mainland Southeast Asia, c. First Century CE—Fourteenth Century CE* (edited, Delhi, 2024).

JAY VARDHAN SINGH is a PhD scholar at the Centre for Historical Studies, Jawaharlal Nehru University, New Delhi.

MAHESH SHARMA is a Professor in Dept. of History, Punjab University, Chandigarh. He was also India Chair Professor,

Department of East Asian Studies, Tel Aviv University (2014-15: Fall Semester); and Visiting Faculty, University of North Florida (2006-7). His publications include The *Realm of Faith: Subversion, Appropriation and Dominance in the Western Himalaya* (Shimla, 2001); and *Western Himalayan Temple Records: State, Pilgrimage, Ritual and Legality in Chambā* (Leiden and Boston, 2009).

Mihir Keshari is a PhD scholar at the Centre for Historical Studies, Jawaharlal Nehru University, New Delhi.

Umakanta Mishra earned his MPhil and PhD degrees in History from Jawaharlal Nehru University, New Delhi. His PhD thesis explored the theme of social history of Vajrayāna Buddhism in early medieval Odisha. At present, he is an Assistant Professor at the Dept. of History, Ravenshaw University, Cuttack, Odisha. His recent publications include *Vajrayāna Buddhism: A Social Iconography* (Delhi, 2009) and *From Villages to Palaces: An Archaeological History of Early Farming and Early Historical Cultures of Odisha* (Delhi, 2023).

Vijay Sarde earned his MA and PhD in Archaeology from Deccan College, Pune. At present, he is an Assistant Professor in Dept. of History and Archaeology, Central University of Karnataka. His recent publications include *The Archaeology of the Natha Sampradaya in Western India, 12th to 15th Century* (London and New York, 2023).

# Index